THE ART OF MEMES IN FEMINIST DIGITAL CULTURE

DIGITAL MEDIA, FEMINIST RESISTANCE
Shana MacDonald and Brianna I. Wiens, Series Editors

THE ART OF MEMES IN FEMINIST DIGITAL CULTURE

Shana MacDonald

THE OHIO STATE UNIVERSITY PRESS

COLUMBUS

Library of Congress Cataloging-in-Publication Data
Names: MacDonald, Shana, author.
Title: The art of memes in feminist digital culture / Shana MacDonald.
Other titles: Digital media, feminist resistance.
Description: Columbus : The Ohio State University Press, [2025] | Series: Digital media,
    feminist resistance | Includes bibliographical references and index. | Summary:
    "Examines activist memes as a form of digital resistance, demonstrating that
    countercultural meme makers, like practitioners of earlier countercultural art
    movements, intervene in the status quo and offer cultural critiques with potentially
    broad circulation"—Provided by publisher.
Identifiers: LCCN 2025017299 | ISBN 9780814214954 (hardback) | ISBN 0814214959
    (hardback) | ISBN 9780814284315 (ebook) | ISBN 0814284310 (ebook)
Subjects: LCSH: Memes—Social aspects. | Memes—Political aspects. | Digital media—Social
    aspects. | Digital media—Political aspects. | Feminism. | Social media. | Internet and
    activism.
Classification: LCC HM626 .M325 2025 | DDC 302.23/1—dc23/eng/20250510
LC record available at https://lccn.loc.gov/2025017299

Other identifiers: ISBN 9780814259566 (paper) | ISBN 0814259561 (paperback)

Cover design by Susan Zucker
Text design by Juliet Williams
Type set in Adobe Minion Pro

CONTENTS

ILLUSTRATIONS

PREFACE

I find myself completing the final draft of this book in the weeks following the 2024 US presidential election. The task of writing on the countercultural value of memes and digital activism seems heavy in ways that are markedly different than they have been at all previous points of this writing journey. I have, for the last decade, held steadfast in my belief that digital media offer important and necessary opportunities for activist and critical interventions into our precariously perched and deeply stretched world. I have written about and championed feminist, queer, antiracist, decolonial uses of digital media to expand and advance conversations around equity and social justice to a broad public. I have suggested that hopefully these media are pushing the needle in the direction it needs to go. The day after this recent election, in a fit of mourning and rage (to borrow from an important Suzanne Lacy performance of the same name from 1973), I deleted all my social media apps off my phone and wrote in bold letters in my notebook, "SOCIAL MEDIA WILL NOT SAVE US." I was exhausted, terrified, and nauseated at the prospect that we now need to fight longer, better, and more precisely against a swell of rising hate and cruelty leveled at those most vulnerable to the existing structures that constrain us.

To put it bluntly, in that early aftermath, I felt that all the efforts and labor of those using digital media to circulate calls for change were for naught. I wondered how I could stand by the faith I held when I argued for the value of activist memes in these pages that await you. However, in a moment of weakness and a search for a dopamine hit, I opened my go-to social media app on my browser. I was met with a wave of very important reminders on the purpose and continued need for activist practices, from some of my favorite accounts. This ended up grounding me and offering some much-needed balm for my frazzled soul. The account of activist adrienne maree brown (@adriennemareebrown) provided a slide deck with a quote from Rosa Luxemburg that reads, "The most revolutionary thing one can do is always proclaim loudly what is happening" ("empires fall"). In a slide deck of wisdom from Black Liturgies (@blackliturgies), I saw the mantra "INHALE / I'm not foolish for hoping / EXHALE I won't rush from this grief." A story posted by Bluegrass musician Clover-Lynn, known on social media as Hillbilly Gothic (@hillbillygothicc), included block text in front of a leafy fall landscape that reads, "Hey yall just a reminder that the people around you likely don't hate you. Use this moment to be the person to take the first step. Get to know your neighbours even when you don't understand them and especially if they don't understand you. And in moments of darkness is when we tend to hold each other the tightest" ("Hey yall"). A post from the parody account Reductress (@reductress) included the headline "Nation Rejects Far-Left Position of 'Woman.'" Many accounts reposted a message from Rebecca Solnit's Facebook account that read, "They want you to feel powerless and surrender and let them trample everything and you are not going to let them. You are not giving up and neither am I. The fact that we cannot save everything does not mean we cannot save anything and everything we can save is worth saving." I spent time sitting with this communal outpouring of wisdom and reminded myself that for better or for worse the internet is one of the key places we gather and seek meaning in culture. While this can be weaponized through disinformation and the specious spread of online hate, it also where we can build relationships, solidarity, and coalitions. So please take this book as an offering and an account of some of the ways feminist and queer activists have used the tools at hand to bring forward critical perspectives, build communities of support, and articulate truths that are too often overshadowed. It is also an account of the ways in which activism can engage in irreverence, humor, and joy to stand against the waves of hate directed at those of us that heteropatriarchal, white supremacist, capitalist systems seek to control and silence. It is not enough; no one element of our tool kit is. However, making and sharing activist memes gives us the chance to creatively speak new possibilities into being, to imagine together what our resistance can look like and what it can offer for those who want to join in along the way. In this way, feminist and queer memes, like the media histories I consider that came before them, are a siren call. They call us to assemble and use our wit—our keen sense of seeing the world starkly for what it is—and to use our love for the earth and each other to articulate how we can do this differently.

Countercultural Aesthetics and Medium Specificity in the Digital Era

In early spring 2023, the catchphrase "the horrors persist but so do I" was popularized through a meme where the phrase was placed over an image of a "guinea pig with pink sunglasses driving a pink toy car" (Hamilton). The meme image centers the small white guinea pig in the frame. The toy car emanates a pinkish hue, and the background grass is awash with a sparkly glittering filter that makes it look golden and full of miniature sunbursts (see fig. 0.1). The text over the top includes a comma after "the horrors persist," to give readers a pause to contemplate "the horrors" being alluded to. The follow-up "but so do I" is a rallying cry to keep on persevering "in the face of it all." Matched with the delightful and ridiculous image of a small creature in a tiny car, the meme evokes a sense of the absurd and an irreverence that indexes one of the reasons why many of us find internet memes so compelling and so central in our everyday lives.

Interestingly, the earliest recorded version of "the horrors" phrase found in meme form is from a cross-stitch that was uploaded to Tumblr by Secrets From Whole Cloth (@secretsfromwholecloth). This suggests that the meme's origins emerge partially within the context of craftivist content circulating online. The popular guinea-pig-in-toy-car version, however, garnered a great deal of popularity, and it is the form that gets most specifically remixed and reimagined to this day. The meme collection surrounding "the horrors" text now includes an almost endless set of stickers, T-shirts, mugs, posters, vintage

FIGURE 0.1. "The Horrors Persist." Unpublished, used with permission
from Feminist Think Tank (@aesthetic.resistance).

prints, memes, and illustrations. In many of the iterations, some kind of small
animal, aesthetic cuteness, and the central catchphrase are put in combination with one another. In the feminist activist spaces I study, you will find
many cross-stitch iterations, alongside nostalgic neon graphics, gothic witchy
remixes, cartoon dogs, and neon skulls with slushies. In my personal favorite,
the phrase has been extended to an illustration of a possum in a jaunty green
hat and cape, with red flowers growing all around the frame. The illustration

was made by illustrator S Wild and is circulated frequently on their Instagram account, @ruminationsofthewild.[1] It is part of a collection of compelling illustrations featuring outcast figures of femme swamp monsters, walking root vegetables, and flowers with an eye at their center, accompanied by activists' mottoes around love, resistance, community, healing, and the power of everyday actions. This merging of art, feminist activism, and meme culture is a constellation I return to frequently throughout this book, as it points out for me the most interesting merging of artistic and popular culture in the present moment.

The collection of remixes of the "Horrors Persist" meme reflects hallmark elements of early 2000s internet vernacular from which memes emerged on more niche spaces like 4chan and Reddit (Phillips). These include a never-ending remix of sometimes odd and oddly misplaced images paired with absurdist humor, wordplay, and irony. As Whitney Phillips notes of this earlier moment, "the act of trolling and the act of making memes were so interconnected during the subcultural origin period that the existence of memes on a given page or forum almost guaranteed that trolling was or had been afoot" (137). Twenty years later, trolling and memes have evolved beyond these original niche spaces to become forms of communication with both broad application and even broader public appeal. Even within this more generalized landscape, memes maintain their use of humor, irony, and sarcasm to draw audiences and achieve circulation.

Memes as a Countercultural Practice

In this book, I look specifically at memes circulating in activist spaces; namely those advancing a queer, feminist, and anticapitalist focus. What I have found is that the earlier connection between memes and trolling vernaculars has been appropriated and transformed by more current meme cultures, making

---

1. Best practices for citing online content are somewhat fluid. Because most of the social media sources I cite do not contain page numbers, parenthetical citations are rarely helpful, assuming the name of the creator (and work, when necessary) has already been provided in the main text. In the works cited, I list social media creators under the account name, with the handle appearing in brackets afterward. When an account name matches the real name of known artist, scholar, or journalist, the source is alphabetized under the last name (e.g., Solnit); other account names are alphabetized under their first word, ignoring any initial articles (e.g., S Wild is under *S*; A Soft Wrongness is under *Soft*). General accounts are not listed in the works cited, as the handle and platform mentioned in the text should provide enough information to locate the source, but specific posts are included, provided the URL was active at the time of publication. Descriptive titles for these posts contain text from either the image/meme or comment/caption under discussion.

it possible for them to engage in and disseminate forms of cultural and political critique. The feminist uses of the Horrors Persist meme genre are a clear example of this. It is often contextualized by feminist meme makers as a critique of heteropatriarchal capitalist culture that is found in the memes themselves, their remixes, and in the paratextual commentary surrounding them. Acknowledging that horrors abound is a political sentiment; it is a naming of that which constrains us, outlining the patterns of power that require us to address them (Lorde; hooks; Solnit). The meme and its comments speak directly to this, pointing out all the possible ways to demarcate the consequences of power but also, through humor, how we resist, and as the meme goes, persevere. Importantly, this larger critique does not occur via established legacy venues like news media, investigative journalism, or a policy brief, but through a humor-laden internet meme and its comments. This is indicative of how meaningful critical political discourse is increasingly found in memetic gags directed at subgroups of social media users who are both in on the joke and more than willing to recirculate the joke's critiques.

The meme thus reflects this book's examination of internet memes as being particularly well equipped to advance countercultural discourses within digital space. The "Horrors Persist" meme indexes some of the more recognizable aspects of internet meme practices, including parody, narrative reenactment, and absurdist humor (Glitsos and Hall; Sparby). In its feminist form, I argue, it also reflects a much longer history of countercultural media found in previous eras of art, film, and performance art. Countercultural media circulates via "sub-cultures that intentionally oppose mainstream norms and values" and "acts as an organizing principle" that connects such communities together over space and time (Lingel 6). This book demonstrates how internet meme practices draw together earlier avant-garde tactics of collage, reenactment, and montage, merging them into a highly remixable contemporary aesthetic that responds to the demands and the possibilities of digital culture in the twenty-first century. This is evident in the 2017 exhibition *By Any Memes Necessary,* curated by meme artist ka5sh (@ka5sh), which moved feminist memes from online enclaves into the offline spaces of the fine art gallery (Johnson). The exhibition, held in Los Angeles, established meme makers such as Jo (@tequilafunrise), binny debbie (@scariest_bug_ever), Jack Wagner @versace_tamagotchi, and gothshakira (@gothshakira) as "not only internet masters, but also artists" (Johnson). I agree with the curator's assertion that memes are a new art movement that is responsive to the demands but also the possibilities of the digital present. As such, this book takes time to carefully place current feminist memes into dialogue with their feminist cultural pasts.

Countercultural Legacies of Memes

I am expanding here on the work of other scholars who have previously made this connection between memes and historical art movements. For instance, Bradley Wiggins describes memes as "a new form of artistic expression . . . that conceptually traces back to Dadaism, Surrealism, and related forms of art" (xvi). For Marijn Bril, meme culture's absurdist and nihilistic tendencies dissipate "the boundaries between high and low culture," which pushes them firmly "within the tradition of postmodernist art" (181). As Bril notes, this also makes memes more akin to "performances rather than merely visual objects" (181). Alice Bucknell argues similarly that "the artistic lineage of memes is spun out of some of 20th-century art's most revolutionary ideas." These references to Dadaism, surrealism, postmodern art, and performance art, among others, suggest that memes recall larger historical lineages of resistant art and, as such, are arguably well equipped to act as revolutionary agents of and in digital culture. These impulses apparent in memes' form and content are what make them so compelling for contemporary scholars of media and culture.

Drawing on Raymond Williams, my use of the term *culture* in this book includes the ways in which we collectively cultivate and tend to the belief systems we inhabit in dialogue with others (90). It is a process, an ethos, and the outcome of putting that ethos into material, textual, visual, and conceptual form (90–91). My use of *culture* equally considers how power exists in both hegemonic and counterhegemonic ways and explores the consequences of this in different moments in time (Bates; Durham and Kellner). Here, hegemony is understood as "how dominance is sustained in advanced capitalist societies" (Hebdige 15), or the ways in which dominant structures present their own interests as "natural" and of interest to all (Hartley 99). This is done through representation and cultural practices, that act to contain subordinate groups via ideological coercion not at the level of overt violence but via signification masked as common sense (Hebdige; Althusser). However, as Dick Hebdige notes, "the symbiosis in which ideology and social order, production and reproduction are linked is neither fixed nor guaranteed," as it can be "fractured, challenged, overruled" via counterhegemonic, or subcultural, resistance (16). I use Hebdige's definition of subculture in this book to outline the "expressive forms and rituals of subordinate groups" (2) whose challenge to hegemony is "expressed obliquely, in style" at "the level of signs" (17–18) and is often located in "mundane objects," which often "hold double meaning" (2). These objects and style gesture toward the subversive and in doing so both repel the dominant sensibilities of the status quo and become a signal of identity for those hailed by the subculture (Hebdige 3).

Memes, I argue, emerge as counterhegemonic practices that operate, following Williams, emergent technology's ability to enable social changes and new forms of interaction through situating "people, places and events, that are distant" as "dispersed communities of interest, affiliation, and feeling" (Barnett 62–63). This "more or less coherent and concrete assemblage" of cultural practices is both "everyday" and "ideological" at once (de Certeau 9). The function of culture, then, is to translate the "fragments of" cultural technologies "into social visibility" (de Certeau 9). Further, memes circulate within, and themselves make up, subcultural spaces by formally creating sometimes subversive content via mundane and everyday digital objects. As per Hebdige, they produce and maintain a particular style of digital communication. Memes are subcultural insofar as they tend to repel dominant sensibilities and become a very clear maker of subcultural identity for those who consume and circulate them. As Hebdige notes, "all aspects of culture possess a semiotic value" that holds an "ideological dimension" that is infused with coded meanings (18). This is what makes the study of memes so significant and necessary. As cultural artifacts that uphold subcultural communities, memes hold valuable meanings that contain ideologies within them. They also expertly operate through the formal spaces of coded and double meanings. This is part of what makes their style of communication so effective: they speak to those who are "in the know," giving them cultural cachet and an entry point into groups of like-minded media users. These affiliations and in-group conversations shape the digital cultural landscape we move within.

Memes are no exception. As digital artifacts, they are an important form of culture tied to new technologies of the digital era. Memes, emerging from digital technology, connect people and events across space, allowing for the formation of memetic communities based on shared interests, identities, or affect. As such, they are a clear example of digital remix culture and its explicit merging of different historical eras and aesthetic styles, different national cultures into a global vernacular, and communication practices with computational tools (Manovich 2003). Memes are a medium made up entirely of remix practices, and what is most interesting for the study presented here is how they use these tools of cultural remix to advance in-group camaraderie and differing forms of countercultural expression.

This book maps explicitly how memetic countercultural practices are tied into longer histories of countercultural media. Memes are of course distinct from earlier resistant media counterparts because of the expansive and rapidly shifting landscape of digital culture within which they are embedded. As such they need to be both treated for their overlaps with previous media practices but also considered for their specificity in the present. What this book pays attention to is how these longer histories are taken up in unique ways by internet memes and how this linkage or dialogue to the past informs their "political power as a networked" form of "critical resistance" (Bucknell). In the chapters that follow, I look in detail at three different tactics used by memes to evoke critical resistance to earlier countercultural aesthetic movements: collage, reenactment, and montage. In doing so, I make links between contemporary memes and some of the most influential artistic movements of the twentieth century, namely, in the areas of visual art, performance art, photography, and cinema. These connections help me to situate more clearly how memes hold great cultural import and consequence in the present.

The Cultural Significance of Internet Memes

The already extensive literature on internet memes defines them as digital content that can be rapidly remixed and circulated across online platforms in ways that impact our social frameworks and communication behaviors (Shifman; Milner, *World Made Meme* and "Pop Polyvocality"; Sparby). Memes are an "ideological practice" that provides "some form or degree of critique" on culture (Wiggins xv). A meme is also "a piece, series, or recognizable use of media" that is readily "shared, transformed, or performed" in online spaces by communities of users (Parry 137). Usefully, memes are both singular artifacts and "groups of items or actions" that can exist in multiple ways (Parry 137). Important for the purpose of this book is the understanding of memes as both a "genre of online communication" and "artifacts . . . of digital culture" (Wiggins xvi). Memes are also one of the more direct ways to announce one's identity or positionality to a vast audience. As the authors of *Meme Wars* argue, memes, "even when they are popular and accessible . . . contain a point of view and announce the position of the sharer" (Donovan et al. 2). Often this announcement of an identity or position is used to specific cultural ends. This duality of memes as both a genre of expression and cultural artifact also suggests the need to study them for their formal properties as well as for how they operate as a communicative agent. This delineation of both practice and cultural object, tied to an identity position, can help scholars clearly establish how memes hold the potential to compel audiences and intervene into social and discursive online spaces. The examples analyzed in this book map a way to address both the form and discursive power held within countercultural memes, to understand the impact they have for activist purposes online.

The most discussed form of meme is the image macro meme, which describes any digital artifact that includes an image framed with text overlaid on top of it. However, in this book, I use a more expansive definition that also includes hashtags, short videos, reels, stories, stitches and duets, infographics, and carousel slide decks. I argue each of these meme iterations produce semantic forms of digital culture that are highly remixable and circulatable. Most importantly, in all these forms, memes make discursive impacts that can both reify and intervene in culture. Internet memes are a thing (i.e., artifact, object of meaning and consumption) and a thing done (i.e., ideological practice, or tactic). This expanded definition helps get at both the mass appeal and the social impact of memes. The interplay between practice and meaningful outcome is central to this book, as it brings up a set of questions around form and content that link them to larger histories of resistant art. Perhaps most important, they support the central claim of this book, that we need to read memes as a medium with their own formal specificity.

The Medium of Memes

My use of the term *medium* refers to the specific qualities and characteristics "of the raw material being used as a mode of artistic expression," which includes both the "operation and effect" of these specific materials (Bernstein). The concepts of operation and effect highlight a dynamic between the practice of making a text and the meaning making that results from its reception. It also speaks to how both operation and effect emerge from the medium's specific materials. With memes, the raw materials of the medium are digital images, sound clips, performing bodies, text overlays, and editing tools. These are used by meme makers to establish some kind of effect on those that view and circulate their memes. The claim of memes as a medium is seemingly contradictory as they are not a singular art form per se but a mixing of many art forms, devices, technologies, and communication styles. The combined use of various media and visual-textual repertoires in memes evokes what I define as a bricolage aesthetic. Bricolage, as I detail below, is defined as a form of craftsmanship that works with the materials at hand, constructing new tools and objects from one's everyday surroundings. I wish to suggest that this bricolage aesthetic is what ultimately defines the medium of memes.

My central claim in this book is that memes are an aesthetic and communicative medium that relies on specific formal practices to convey meaning. To demonstrate this claim fully requires the scope of my analysis to go beyond popular understandings of what constitutes memes. My analysis ventures into areas of digital art that are informed by the medium of memes even if they are not memes per se. This broader view opens scholarship up to the interrelationship between previous modes of resistant or countercultural art and the memetic forms they take in the present. I offer in this book an invitation to explore the dialogue between memes and much longer histories of visual art. The boundaries represented by memes and visual art, or those of popular culture and high art, are not discrete in digital culture, nor in the aesthetic movements that precede it. This book is about how memes and art share spaces of overlap and how this overlap reveals the emergence of memes as a new aesthetic form. In the chapters that follow, my analysis shuttles between internet memes and historical art movements that I see them in dialogue with. In this trajectory, a greater understanding of how internet memes operate as a significant part of our current cultural zeitgeist emerges.

My focus on memes as a medium thus offers a more fulsome inclusion of what can be considered an internet meme. By reading memes as a medium, we are better able to situate memes in their position both within and against the capitalist excesses of digital platform culture. What needs to be more clearly assessed are the power relations at play within meme practices. This can get at how internet memes provide communicative and aesthetic tools that extend power and agency to everyday digital media users. Likewise, this focus highlights how constellations of techno-capitalism, in all their benign and startlingly violent forms, can be transgressed and resisted by memes. Part of what this book seeks to uncover is how memes engage aesthetically and performatively with dominant discourse to index and upend these power relations.

Memes as a Medium of Participatory Counterculture(s)

The cultural context that memes exist within includes the rise of spreadable digital media which "are reshaping the media landscape" into one that centers participatory forms of culture above the pipeline hierarchy of legacy media (Jenkins et al. 2; Lievrouw). The internet and its resulting social media platforms that emerged within Web 2.0 brought forward forms of participatory culture (Jenkins, *Convergence Culture*), remixability (Manovich), remediation (Bolter and Grusin), and shareability (cf. Milner, *World Made Meme*; Wiggins) that ensured internet memes as a medium could fully emerge as a communicative practice. Participatory culture indexes how "user-generated content exists both within and outside commercial contexts and supports as well as subverts corporate control" (Jenkins and Deuze 7). Web 2.0 technologies, such as social media platforms, facilitated this shareability of content that includes memes. In doing so, they produced the conditions for memes to become a highly visible and popular mode for participatory communication that shaped not only the media landscape but also how we communicate our desires, identities, emotions, and politics.

It is important to point out that our current era of participatory culture is not the utopia it was intended to be. Earlier optimistic visions of an open, connected, information-sharing internet (Berners-Lee; Chander and Sunder) did not come to pass. Instead, large corporate platforms have become de facto spaces for online public gathering, and these come with constraints and a social cost. Most pernicious is how the social media sites used as part of our everyday communication landscape circulate toxic, divisive, and at times false content that has weakened our social fabric and democratic institutions and contributed to a troubling rise in online hate, the demonization of targeted communities, and the rampant spread of disinformation currently impacting the work of public institutions and political campaigns (Benjamin, *Race*; Noble; dos Santos et al.; Anable; Copland; Bucher and Helmond; Chun, *Discriminating Data*; Phillips and Milner; Murthy). Two decades into the twenty-first century, we must constantly negotiate the relentless spread of platform capitalism to every corner of our existence (Srnicek; Gibbings et al.; Ferrari and Graham; Wood).

It is easy to dismiss memes as an overabundant pop culture presence in our digital landscape, one that is at times benign and other times spurious in its shaping of public knowledge (Alhassen and Ali). Yet, like previous sites of media interventions, memes utilize easily accessible forms of creative expression to further necessary critical conversations. Memes, like other media, are dependent on the apparatus they emerge from. For internet memes, this includes the platforms they are produced on, circulate within, and gain virality through. The "socio-technical milieu" of memes importantly "become[s] woven into our communicative repertoires" (Arkenbout et al., "Introduction" 16). And yet for some this integration into our "communication repertoires" is where memes lose their "claim . . . as a unique cultural or digital object" (Arkenbout et al., "Introduction" 16). I would argue that how memes operationalize the social-technical milieus they exist within, as well as the communicative repertoires they produce, precisely demonstrates what makes them worth further consideration as a medium. The notion of communicative meme repertoires is of interest to me as it gestures toward the world-building and ideological aspect of meme practices. It is useful to pay attention to how power dynamics and social relationality are informed by and caught up in the prevailing media of memes in significant ways.

What meme making offers is "a personal tool to deal with the daily horrors of late-stage capitalism" (Arkenbout 26). As one of the most popular forms of participatory, spreadable media, memes significantly articulate cultural touchstones and relatable aspects of everyday life that reinforce group bonds. Within this context, the mutually shaping role of memes and spreadable and participatory culture technologies are clear to see. Memes constitute forms of "participatory culture in which people jointly produce, combine, and circulate content and make connections among dispersed pieces of media content" (Schmidt and Kloet 3). Memes explore the audio, visual, and textual errata available at a given time and space of the internet to aid in the effectiveness of cultural expression and circulation. From within the media ecology of participation, particular forms of remixing, remediation, and sharing have emerged. I am interested in mapping out across the following chapters specific examples of memetic form. These include first the use of collage and juxtaposition in image macro memes to defamiliarize viewers into new forms of critical engagement. I am also interested in the use of narrative and short-form scripted vignettes as a type of reenactment of everyday social and fantasized encounters. I also explore the memetic use of montage, drawing on experimental cinema, to create contiguous representational arguments across a variety of memes and memetic frames within a single social media post. My mapping of these practices suggests how widely varied and innovative meme cultures are now and the important critical uses of these innovations.

Historical Countercultural Practices

The memetic tactics I explore as part of this emergent digital participatory culture hold a longer history than the dominant narrative suggests. As Henry Jenkins rightfully points out, "participatory culture is something we have struggled toward over the past 100 plus years; we've gained ground and lost ground in and around each new technology" (Jenkins and Carpentier 266). The history of the twentieth century includes a long-standing use of different mass media technologies by activists and artists in ways that were not intended by dominant culture, as an important means of advancing critique and resistance (Barlow; Berger; Goldberg; Iles; Jones). This is especially the case for women, queer, and racialized artists whose work exemplifies tactics of building politicized communities of makers to operationalize mass media forms for critical and activist ends (Lippard; Chadwick; N. King; McMillan; Pena; Robinson).

This picks up on something outlined by Umberto Eco decades ago in his consideration of texts that become cult objects. For Eco, a shift to cult—or perhaps, in today's terms, viral—status requires a rupture or dislocation of the text "so that one can remember only parts of it, irrespective of their original relationship with the whole" (Eco 198). Cult, and now viral, objects develop an independence of their authorial confines and thus gain a capacity to speak with other texts fully outside original intentions (Eco 198). This linking of textual objects with a viral or cult status suggests that for memes there is always the possibility of a contextual rupture. For Eco, such texts hold instead what he calls a "living textuality," which is what gives them that power to interact and dialogue with and in other cultural texts and moments, or what I would argue are usefully called by Carrie Rentschler and Samantha Thrift "media events."

To fully grasp the relationship between past and present forms of cultural resistance in earlier art movements and memes requires outlining the forms of participatory media that any given techno-cultural context allows for. It also means identifying what forms of participatory culture remain from previous historical contexts and older media spaces and mapping how they are reanimated in the present to resistant ends. Part of understanding these earlier media histories is to map out how they reoccur and are employed and referenced in the present. Taking up an historical view with an eye to specificities of different media and their contexts of emergence can help scholars get at how power operates within meme cultures in the present. The aim, then, is to better articulate "how specific participatory practices are characterized by specific power balances and struggles at different levels, moments, and locations" (Jenkins and Carpentier 267). To that end, this book explores how memes operationalize mass media for critical and activist ends especially when employed by feminist and queer communities of makers. The memes I am interested in exploring in this book are significant for the ways they hold the seeds of resistance and refusal in their content and form. They do so by making use of a set of digital tools that make them highly relatable, endlessly remixable, and easily disseminated. This is what makes memes valuable as an object of study—they offer insight into emergent forms of countercultural pushback in the contemporary digital landscape. The analysis of specific memetic tactics in the chapters that follow considers what this looks like in terms of form and content, and how such media experimentations in memetic form intervene in cultural discourses and to what ends.

The Cultural Logics of Memes

The medium specificity of memes informs current notions of politics, power, social life, cultural meaning making, and personal identity. Memes contain a set of medium-specific logics (Sharma) that can either assert or run counter to dominant culture. The countercultural media tactics found in memes reveal how one-way participatory culture disseminates political critique in the digital era. Memes, regardless of their political positionality, are countercultural and build upon different forms of resistant aesthetic tactics that echo previous activist media histories. This work is especially vital for communities that are not well served in dominant cultural and media spaces. What memes offer to those communities that are "structurally disadvantaged and discriminated against" is a sense of shared purpose and understanding (Neghabat 140). Memes that reflect shared in-group lived experiences usefully construct "alternative discourse—beyond the one-dimensional, often harmful depictions and narratives pushed by conventional media and public discourse" (Neghabat 140). Like important feminist archival accounts of these former media activisms have done (Eichhorn; Darms; Groeneveld; McKinney; Duncombe; Atoe), it is crucial we apply a thoughtful analysis to activist memes in the current moment, as they are, I would argue, the heir apparent of not only zines but activist media interventions by racialized, queer, and feminist makers.

As addressed above, memes are embedded in intimate, community-driven forms of activism that occur daily, and, on the ground, memes offer ideological affinities with earlier media activisms. This is especially so as the content they replicate resonates powerfully with various aspects of our everyday life. Such resonance across users "signif[ies] membership in an in-group" that directly "announce[s] the position of the sharer" and, by consequence, the audience (Donovan et al. 2). These in-groups largely split on cultural and political lines and contribute to the identification by online users to one side or the other within the contemporary iteration of the "culture wars" (Nagle; Tuters). Much has been written, for example, on the great meme wars of 2016 and how alt-right media encouraged voters to elect Donald Trump as president via meme tactics (Miller; Nagle; Woods and Hahner; Pollard; Moody-Ramierz and Church; Haddow; Zuckerberg). Ryan M. Milner argues image-based memes "are a populist means to express public perspectives, even when those perspectives are diverse" ("Pop Polyvocality" 2360). What I wish to pay attention to in this book is how the impact of politicized content is equally present in activist meme subcultures on the left as it is in alt-right ones, by looking at feminist, queer, and anticapitalist memes. What subcultures on the left and right share is a tactical interest in using memes to disseminate perspectives, ethos, identity, or cultural critique.

This book's focus on leftist and activist memes considers how they employ potentially "democratic . . . powers of virality" to "help establish new trends within public discourse" (Denisova 2). The stakes for such analysis have never been clearer. We currently face continued swells of fascist and alt-right media organizing that successfully turns misinformation and white nationalist, anti-queer, transphobic, and misogynist rhetoric into a viral experience of fear-mongering and othering. In this way, it is often hard to see how virality and the platform affordances that encourage it have any ties to the democratic exchange of ideas. Yet, these spaces do exist and deserve critical attention, documentation, and amplification. They reveal subcultural resistance dispersed in and among these other seemingly more prevalent spaces of social media. This reflects how in previous decades the Birmingham school readily associated bricolage tactics with "the aesthetic practices of working-class subcultures of the 1960s and 1970s" that tackle cultural bourgeois hegemonies "'obliquely' through style" (Markham 44). The activist memes considered in this book also rely heavily on style to make their critical interventions. This emphasis on stylistic and aestheticized content in meme cultures is what contributes to their popularity and value as shareable forms of media. The more attractive and innovative the meme, whether it brings in new aesthetic tropes or remixes classic meme templates, the more it is celebrated as desirable content to consume and share. One of the most significant aspects of meme aesthetics is how it elicits affective responses.

The use by memes of affective appeals can sometimes turn a select meme into a viral event or longer-term meme genre that gets widely adopted and reinterpreted by a range of users. This is one of the more potent ways memes contribute to an ongoing shifting and expanding of critical discourse within activist and leftist meme cultures. These affective appeals largely center around humor (Miltner; Highfield and Leaver; Mortensen and Neumayer) and rage (Griffin; Kuo; Guadagno et al.), but also relatability (Kanai; Ask and Abidin). These are readily employed by many meme makers to engage audiences and gain a loyal following. The more resonant a meme, the more likely it is to be shared and engaged with by others. What I wish to suggest throughout this book is that the resonance held by memes has a large part in how they operationalize their medium-specific qualities to persuasive, remixable, and shareable ends. They use such resonances in formally complex ways that have yet to be fully accounted for. To address this, I suggest there is a need to address memes as a medium with specific formal practices that are uniquely suited to the aims of the medium and to its import in our cultural moment.

The Medium Specificity of Memes

My understanding of medium specificity draws on the idea that any form of art "has its own domain of expression," which is "determined by the nature of the medium" itself (Carroll 6). Memes are an art form whose domain of expression includes sometimes critical or humorous takes on the vicissitudes of contemporary culture. These are expressed through a rapidly evolving online vernacular that is part of what forms their ephemeral and remixable nature. This is why I position internet memes as a medium well-suited to advance current countercultural discourses in both niche and broader public spaces. While I do not believe, as early medium-specificity theorists do, that memes, as a medium, should "pursue those effects" that they alone can "can achieve" (Carroll 6), I do think it is useful to question what it is about memes that makes them relatable, shareable, and conducive to uniquely advancing political positionalities and critical discourse. In this way, I am embracing a committedly "pluralist" understanding (Parry 138) of memes in trying to understand how they operate as aesthetic media.

This book thus takes up longer-standing questions of medium specificity within the context of internet memes to position them as a prevalent and structuring form of contemporary digital culture. Scott Wark argues that digital platforms have produced a "new 'situation'" of "concrete mediatic conditions" (170), which usefully supports my interest here in understanding how memes, as tied into these new mediatic conditions, impact the shape and flow of contemporary culture. Internet memes' operations and effects are tied to the technological and social context within which they are produced. This includes the cultural histories and media ecologies they emerge from as well as the conditions of late-stage capitalism they circulate within. For me, what sets memes as a medium apart from other media are the unique tactics they employ, which, while they may not seem terribly serious, are well suited to advance critical discourse. These tactics include, as noted above, forms of collage or visual and textual juxtaposition, reenactment or reperformance of a script, and aesthetic experiments with montage. I explore these tactics throughout the book to demonstrate the political potential for resistance memes can open. Even when a meme is being shared for the lulz, it indexes elements of cultural life that open audiences up to critical questions and the possibility for collective dissent in the form of both discursive and practical actions.

Memes' Medium-Specific Foundations: Bricolage

The medium specificity of internet memes centers on the fact that what they express is never fully unique. Memes are built from existing genres, scripts, formats, references, and other media. In drawing on these visual cultural histories, viral templates, and genres, internet memes are decidedly intertextual. The memetic text contains layers of referentiality. I would argue they are also intermedial, as they integrate various media within their frame. This presence of intermediality and intertextuality illustrates how memes are a medium of bricolage. By this I mean memes employ bricolage tactics of using whatever tools and materials are at hand (Lévi-Strauss; Markham; Weick; Rogers) and in doing so take up the tools of interplay between long histories of cultural texts and a range of media to make their own unique forms.

I draw here explicitly on Annette Markham's definition of bricolage as the practice of using "any available means or whatever is at hand" to produce "structures, in the form of its artifacts, by means of contingent events" (43–44). Her definition retains Claude Lévi-Strauss's interest in bricolage as meaning-making made possible through the creative use of leftover cultural ephemera, extending it to the space of digital artifacts. Digital bricolage is "the highly personalized, continuous, and more or less autonomous assembly, disassembly, and reassembly of mediated reality" found in "the ways in which we click, publish, and link" through our online worlds (Deuze 66–70). Through our participation in and remediation of our digital realities, we "reflexively assemble" these realities in our communicative practices (Deuze 66). This suggests our entire experience of being online is one long practice of bricolage, with us as the bricoleurs. Bricolage isn't just "a principal component of digital culture" but also "an accelerating agent of it" (Deuze 71). Conversely, what accelerates digital uses of bricolage is the sheer number of tools and visual and textual repertoires at hand for internet users to employ. Bricolage plays an outsized role in how memes and our engagement with them shape and inform our digital lives. Reading internet memes as bricolage opens an understanding of how they offer "an approach . . . well-suited . . . for political resistance," including a long history as a "cultural counter-practice" (Markham 43–48). In arguing memes are a medium of bricolage, I aim to get at the ways at how they can expand countercultural practices in both conceptual and creative ways and help us to understand what is at stake when "the tools at hand" for meme making are largely tied to the domain of capitalist platforms.

Memetic Tactics: Making Do

My use of the term *tactics* here highlights the countercultural impulse of memetic practices that work in opposition to the normative strategies of dominant institutions (de Certeau). Tactics in this sense emerge from everyday spaces of struggle against any number of constraints but also in sites of pleasure (de Certeau). Tactics, as practices of the ordinary and the everyday, subvert dominant structures of power by their ability to "use, manipulate, and divert" the status quo and provide "their audience [with] a repertory of tactics for future use" (de Certeau 23–28). Within the context of digital culture, tactics allow us to "maintain a sense of self in the midst of larger cultural institutions" and "make everyday life easier or more joyous" (Lingel 10). The memetic tactics I explore in this book are of both the digital moment and more extended histories of experimentation and disruption.

In the following chapter, I look at how collage is used as a site of nonsensical interjection into the horrors of capitalist logic. In the chapter following that, I consider how the different ways we reperform existing cultural scripts allow for critical mimesis that, like Brechtian alienation, gives us necessary distance from dominant ideologies of gender to circumvent and imagine the image of women differently. In another chapter, I look to memes' tactical uses of montage, or the bringing together of disparate images to create new meanings. This is particularly useful for understanding how meme makers are working with different platform affordances, drilling into the technical possibilities of reels, stories, and other design features to expand what memes can do. The result is a spectacular rendering of images, video, audio, text, and animation to advance ideas and forms of political resistance. In the concluding chapter, I consider intentional infusion of joyful content into our social media timelines by activists and content creators invested in pleasure and delight as part of our digital experience. This tactic may be the most radical of all, as it refuses to play by the rules of both legacy and platform capitalist media that amplify fear, anger, and hate for the purpose of optimizing traffic and attention to their own sites and networks. This perhaps shows an alternative way of being with and in media that is sorely needed at present.

Memetic tactics live in the everyday both in terms of their outsized presence in our daily consumption of digital media as well as in their frequent commentary on quotidian absurdities. They have also historically been in the domain of nondominant forms of cultural expression. Memes question different forms of power largely through appealing to pleasurable forms of communication, including humor and in-group resonances. There are some formal tactics that can be found as a common denominator across the medium of memes despite the array of meme content, meme genres, and meme templates that we encounter in our digital lives. These inform both the recognizability of the medium but also support it in its constantly emerging trends, styles, and uses of platform affordances.

On the broadest level of analysis, these tactics index elements that, I argue, make up memetic specificity overall. Beyond the general use of bricolage as a conceptual and practical aim, these include tactical appeals to affect and remix. If earlier theories of medium specificity argue that "each art form has its own domain of expression and exploration" (Carroll 6), I am interested in how fundamental affect is to the specificity of memes as a medium. Affect is crucial to how memes act as a connecting medium that gathers like-minded social media users together in forms of community and counterpublics (Ringrose and Lawrence; Rentschler and Thrift). Memes leave "an affective impression" and, in doing so, make possible forms of "belonging and political subjectivity that exceeds the capture, extraction, and frozen identities of platform capitalism" (Burton 18). This affective excess holds great value for resistance in late-stage capitalism, offering a unique set of appeals for audiences situated in a very specific (and at times incredibly bleak) historical moment. In this way, how memes take up the vicissitudes of our time echoes the efforts of avant-garde and counterculture art practices during earlier iterations of capitalist ruin and bleak geopolitical landscapes in the previous century.

Memes employ humor and other affective responses to "incite a collective reaction to everyday life" using "a format no less playful than it is political, decoding the murky structural screw-ups, paradoxes, and hypocrisies of our current political climate" (Bucknell). Humor is a particularly popular way memes produce forms of digital intimacy and a calling-in to community, often via affect. Such intimacies create conditions for meaningful relations via the immediacy of digital technologies employed to share them (Rambukkana and Wang). Internet memes largely employ "satirical humor for public commentary" to provide "a populist means to express public perspectives" (Milner, "Pop Polyvocality" 2359–60; Lievrouw; Mina). Memes often leave "an affective impression that exceeds their circulation" (Burton 18). This affective impression sets the conditions for new forms of "belonging and political subjectivity" beyond what capitalist platforms intend (Burton 18). Alongside humor, memes also use states of affect such as anger, outrage, concern, and care to produce resonance and recognition that fosters in-group conversations on a range of contemporary concerns. I am most interested in mapping in this book how different affective states enable collective conversations around misogyny, racism, queer- and transphobia, techno-fascism, and capitalism in memetic form and what medium-specific formal tactics they draw on to advance these conversations.

Alongside affect, another area of meme aesthetics to consider is their use of remix practices, which ties to broader questions of their use of intertextuality and intermediality. Memes' circulation as a digital lingua franca creates new understandings of intertextuality and intermediality within the context of digital remixing. It is within this constellation of remix and widespread circulation that the specificity of meme as a medium emerges. The central element of remix in meme culture suggests that the medium of memes is at its core a medium of bricolage. This can be seen by how memes merge together different media forms, visual and cultural lexicons, and contexts into a new text. Importantly, as "a participatory practice that produces texts" (Huntington 79), what memes express, and how this is received, is contextually dependent on the cultural milieu they circulate in and the social, political, and media events of a given moment. As rhetorical texts situated in concrete contexts, memes express ideological flows that help those who create and share them make sense of the world. Internet memes are thus a medium as well as a system of affectively charged, remixable communication tied to a moment in time and a cultural context.

Intertextual Remix:
The Memetic Repurposing of Digital Debris

Memes are a medium that employs bricolage and uses the ubiquity of digital media as its resource. They work with the "debris" of digital cultural landscapes and, in this way, make the most out of digital "pervasiveness" as well as the "constant obsolescence" and, I would argue, reconfigurations of its content (Wark 172). This is readily seen in the use of obsolete media texts in new meme forms many decades after they are popular. Memes' use of older content purposefully as niche content makes it easier for memes to infuse it with "a wide range of content" (Dango). What memes do well is operationalize "these conditions" of ubiquity and ruin "as they are iterated and are reiterated; or . . . as they circulate, in excess" (Wark 172). In the context of twenty-first-century digital culture, excess and debris then become the tools or, as I am suggesting, part of a bricolage-centered approach. Meme creators make do with what is available and through this a new medium emerges that collages together the debris of mass culture. Memes thus "manifest . . . a condition of being overwhelmed by media—and being forced to think within this condition whilst also, and necessarily, thinking this condition" (Wark 172).

Internet memes thus employ a bricolage aesthetic that is attendant to their techno-social reality. This relies, as noted previously, on two interrelated elements within the aesthetic that contribute to the medium specificity of memes: intertextuality and intermediality. Together they index concretely how memes employ bricolage so artfully and effectively. Through intermediality and intertextuality, memes bring together texts and media into a layered whole that matches the complexity of the media ecologies that the memes themselves reside and circulate within. The aesthetic center of the meme medium is these bricolage practices of intermediality and intertextuality. Within this operational logic, memes use certain tactics to further their countercultural messaging and critique.

Intertextuality is defined as how "images, sounds and spatial delineations are read on to and through one another" (Rogoff 24). The term outlines the relations "between and among texts" (D'Angelo 33) and more specifically "a layering of referentiality" within a text (Hale 510). These relations between texts are created via the use of "citations, quotations, allusions, borrowings, adaptations, appropriations, parody, pastiche, imitation," that produce "a dialogical relationship with other texts" (D'Angelo 33). Intertextuality is a useful concept for discussing memes because the entire practice of meme making is predicated on forms of citation and borrowing that produce meaning via allusions, adaptations, and imitations. These meanings are often imbued with parody and pastiche. In this way, the presence of past texts within memes both references those original texts while also producing "*new* experiences . . . [and] texts" through the act of "*re-contextualization*" (Hale 510; emphasis in original). Intertextuality is found, then, in how memes borrow and repeat past visual and textual histories to create new cultural meaning. The newly recontextualized content of memes draws from the previously discussed repertoire of cultural debris to create "an unlimited set of *meme*-like reincarnations" (Hale 523).

Intertextuality is seen clearly in the popular practice of remixing older visual ephemera into new meme content and "recasting them . . . into a new form" (D'Angelo 34–41). This recasting of old texts into new forms also recasts the histories of visual culture and their long-standing meanings in a new light. For instance, in the chapters that follow, I discuss in detail how intertextual juxtapositions and performative reenactments of iconic images of women reveal forms of memetic temporality that critically queer, or make strange, dominant gender narratives for countercultural ends. Establishing intertextuality in memes suggests they are not tied to one genre or period of representational forms. Equally, memes as a medium are not reliant on one specific type of apparatus to deliver their content, which makes them also intermedial. I suggest this because memes tend to produce pairings of audio, visual, and graphic text with a photographic image or moving image in one memetic frame. If intertextual elements of memes point to the cultural logics of the digital era, their use of intermediality indexes some of the techno-logics of the moment in equally compelling ways.

Intermedial Interplay: Mimetic Cross-Media Mash-Ups

The concept of intermedia was first employed by Dick Higgins in 1963 to describe "a conceptual fusion" within some art, where it is not possible to "separate out the different media in an integral way" (24). This is different from multimedia work, which places various media alongside one another without any sense of integration. Not quite illustration, photography, cinema, collage, performance, or literature, but a space between these, memes are structured as a remix of many different media at once. Memes' continuous exploration and remediation of formal boundaries between different media shifts how we experience digital media across various platforms and has precipitated the development of certain affordances that better showcase meme content on these platforms.

Take, for example, the practice of curated slide decks, which first appeared on Instagram, as one example of this conceptual fusion of memetic media into an intermedial whole. I have written elsewhere about the specific platform affordance of carousel decks on Instagram, which give users the ability to combine up to twenty images or video clips in a single post on their account. This usually takes the form of an intentionally curated slide deck tied together by a shared theme (Wiens and MacDonald, "Dwelling"). This is a popularly used option on the platform because it ensures viewers will have a longer engagement with a post given the time it takes to scroll multiple slides of images instead of one. The more time users spend with a given account determines the account's access to a greater pool of users, as the greater engagement elevates the account to the top of feeds and algorithmic searches. While I will speak to this as a tactic widely used by activists in chapter 3 and the conclusion, for the meantime, I wish to point here to how the carousel deck itself is an example of intermediality within meme culture.

For instance, in a carousel deck from the environmental activist account For The Wild (@for.the.wild), which I have previously written about (Wiens and MacDonald, "Dwelling"), a variety of different media are employed across the curated set of ten slides. These include images from nature photography, ink drawings, a collage with a quote from Bertolt Brecht, a video of a live volcano, a still image from a film with subtitles, and a painting with added text. This mash-up of distinct media contained within a memetic context is a widespread aspect of how carousel slide decks are being used presently. The integrated media work together in the service of extending the possibilities of the meme medium. They set together visual, textual, or audio markers into larger assemblages of meaning. This is especially true of carousel decks that curate a connected set of memes to evoke a sense for users of walking through a digital microgallery. The boundaries between media are not only dissolved but wholly subsumed by the demands of the meme context.

This intersecting relationship between bricolage, intermediality, and intertextuality reflects a shared set of tactics that I believe run common across internet memes and are central to their specificity as a medium. As outlined briefly above, the tactics I consider in detail across the following three chapters focus on the elements of collage, reenactment, and montage found in contemporary meme practices. When studying tactics within media, it is crucial we consider what they "reveal about the strategies in which they operate" (Lingel 11). What these three elements of collage, reenactment, and montage reveal are a memetic medium specificity around time, space, and cultural assemblage. For me, the most compelling aspect of this in-depth analysis of space, time, and cultural movements and connections is that the formal properties of the memes studied ultimately mirror the kinds of spatial, temporal, and cultural collapses and connections that we are experiencing in our everyday lives in significant and instructive ways. Being able to link more fully the world of memes and the world of everyday life through the frames of collage, reenactment, and assemblage helps establish memes as contemporary cultural and aesthetic objects worthy of scholarly attention.

Dwelling with Memes

My approach to studying memes as a specific aesthetic medium stems from digital research methods I have codeveloped previously in collaboration with Dr. Brianna Wiens. Elsewhere Dr. Wiens and I have advocated for a practice of small-data curation which requires collaborative, intentional, and reflexive dwelling in digital spaces. This small-data approach draws on Wiens's foundational work on the concept of digital dwelling (Wiens, "Virtual Dwelling"; Wiens, "Creative and Embodied Digital Methods"). The "dwelling as method" framework includes collecting and sitting with digital cultural content over time to produce close textual readings of the content from an embedded and engaged perspective (MacDonald, "City (as) Place"; MacDonald and Wiens, "Multi-Mangle"; Wiens and MacDonald, "Dwelling"). What this looks like in practice is a research team of five to ten scholars of different positionalities using both personal social media accounts as well as generated research accounts to collect digital ephemera from social media platforms. We do this daily and code it continuously through a shared repository of screenshots and links that includes all necessary related metadata. These collections are reviewed periodically to develop a sense of content themes and formal approaches so that we may build theoretical frameworks for closer analysis. We have developed in collaboration with digital archivist Nick Ruest a visual archive to hold the collection, which holds a continuously growing set of thousands of memes.

The intimate and up-close nature of this approach helps us trace the ebbs and flows of meaning that circulate in our complex digital network constellations. It is from sitting with the data together that we can generate observations around patterns, trends, and emerging uses of platform affordances. Often, dwelling with a particular profile sets off a "deep dive" into related content or similar accounts that themselves make up smaller subcultural networks within these larger media platforms. The interrelationship between accounts in these subnetworks are equally valuable for understanding the way memes operate as discursive data. Equally important is the self-reflexive awareness we bring to the task of dwelling, wherein our own positionality is indexed in collective conversations, coding, and analysis.

This approach takes standpoint theory as a core orientation. It understands that data, as a form of knowledge, needs to be "always socially situated" (Harding 4). As such, standpoint theory is careful to register and integrate our positionality as researchers so that we ensure our "particular, historically specific" and socially located perspectives are foregrounded when undertaking analysis (Harding 6). The method of digital dwelling I outline in the above paragraph expands upon standpoint theory's key contributions to feminist praxis and places them in the context of studying new and emerging media ecologies and their dominant texts, including memes. This method aims to extend Harding's insights that there exist in any given moment both "explicit and implicit" histories that are made up of both "intellectual" and "folk" frameworks (Harding 3). These folk histories are of particular interest to the study of memes. For Harding, folk perspectives emerge as an "apparently spontaneous appeal to groups" who are "seeking to understand themselves and the world around them in ways blocked by [dominant] conceptual frameworks" (Harding 3).

This seems an apt description of the why and how of meme usage in contemporary culture. Memes and viral meme events do operate through apparently spontaneous appeals by subsets of a society and are significant vehicles for articulating identity positions and particular understandings of the world. Collective sensemaking via memes is often done in some form of critical or oppositional stance to dominant culture. In this way, memes need to be read for their specificity, their locatedness in group settings, and for what their "folk" history reveals about a given moment. From a feminist perspective I would add, we as scholars analyzing memes need to always index how our own positionality within different social locations absolutely determines the sensemaking we bring to the project of analysis; there may be areas of the meme-osphere that are not and cannot be known to us. This recognition of limitations and the need for broader sets of diverse analytic voices usefully emerges in the active dialogues that occur through digital dwelling.

Small-Data Analysis of Memes

In addition to dwelling, the use of small data in this collaborative method of digital analysis explicitly offers an alternative to prevailing big-data analysis of social media. While useful in some key contexts, big data cannot always get at the specific nuances of networked social movements and their cultural impact on flows of information to the same degree as sitting with the artifacts over time can (boyd and Crawford). Further, as the well-established research within data feminism has proven, computational and data science approaches to the collection and organization of knowledge largely upholds sexist, racist, and highly normative perspectives that underserve, erase, and at times do violence to gendered, racialized, and otherwise marginalized communities (Noble; Benjamin *Race*; Chun; Nakamura; D'Ignazio and Klein). As such, the method developed by Dr. Wiens and me considers the socio-technological power dynamics of a digital text. This is an analytic approach that works well with smaller sets of data so that they may be contextualized and explored through more carefully engaged and relational forms of analysis.

We center a relational approach in small-data methods because we also recognize how limited social media research is by the algorithms of any given platform and what we can access. This has long been an issue with platforms like Facebook and Instagram where big data pulls are difficult if not impossible to obtain for researchers. Twitter (X), which for a long time offered some forms of data access to researchers by way of APIs (application programming interfaces), has more recently become an unstable and less reliable site of research for a variety of reasons since Elon Musk took over the platform in late 2022. The lack of algorithmic transparency by large platform corporations leaves large gaps in what we can and cannot do as social media researchers, especially when seeking big data sets and the kinds of insights they may offer. Instead of fighting to find tech-specific work-arounds, a small-data method uses this reality as part of how it structures research practices, what questions are asked, what data is sought, and how to approach the analysis of the materials that are ultimately collected.

What this book offers then is a humanities-based, close reading approach to social media, situating the memes analyzed here as part of an open collection housed through the Digital Feminist Network (www.digfemnet.org) that I codirect with Dr. Wiens. The collection of memes drawn on in this book is only a tiny part of a much broader pool of digital artifacts contained within this collection and thus offers a fairly contained perspective and reach. To better connect these memes to the larger networked movements and communication ecosystems they work within, I employ a three-part approach to meme analysis that considers the cultural, aesthetic, and semantic contexts of the memes.

The book thus analyzes memes as texts. It considers such memetic texts within their larger cultural contexts, as well as the paratextual responses they inspire. *Text* here refers to the semantic meme artifact, including its form and content. *Context* includes both the technological and sociocultural spaces the memes exist and circulate in. Finally, paratexts are the discursive responses and remixes of these memes by audiences and users. Taken together this allows us to frame memes as artifacts situated in specific techno-logics that are never neutral but rather do things in the world (Conley 27). As such, this method builds explicitly on Tara Conley's imperative that we look at the interrelationship between digital discourse, the embodied practices that circulate it, and the ideologies it contains (21).

The method I employ in this book also holds much in common with practices of feminist media archaeology (Skågeby and Rahm; Chun et al.; Thompson and Wood) that bring attention to how "power differentials . . . [are] inscribed in both bodies, artifacts, and emotions" (Skågeby and Rahm 2). Or put more simply, I am interested in how "power, affects and practices are entangled with media materialities" (Skågeby and Rahm 2). Like Conley's framework outlined above, my analysis combines an understanding that memes as artifacts exist in relationship to not only the technologies that support them and the ideologies that flow *from* them but the bodies and emotions that surround, interpret, and remix them. It is in these constellations of interrelationship that power dynamics as well as forms of resistance can be most clearly seen.

A Feminist Media Archaeology of Memes

Feminist media archaeology is especially well suited for considering the medium specificity of memes because it questions how "media technologies have certain material facilities and specific operations that produce a certain way of knowing" and keep at the fore how the "mutual transformation" of technologies and their outcomes "jointly (re-)produce power asymmetries" (Skågeby and Rahm 6). This framework ensures that the outcomes of media and their specificities are always located in their cultural, historical, technological contexts and produce knowledge and power formations that are equally necessary to attend to in our research. I have spent a great deal of attention in this introduction to laying out the cultural, historical, technological context of internet memes and the power formations they exist within.

What I have also tried to suggest thus far is that these histories are in direct dialogue with earlier aesthetic histories that had their own cultural and technological contexts. The overlapping interest between these different eras is how artists, activists, and countercultural actors employed tactical uses of dominant technologies of their time to intervene in cultural discussions. Here my focus on countercultural meme practices is well aligned with earlier eras of Dadaism, surrealism, and postwar avant-garde movements from the 1960s and beyond. Like these earlier moments, meme makers "seem to be fighting capitalism from within the system" (Arkenbout 25). What this book ultimately considers is what the discursive effect of memes as an activist practice is in the present moment.

This points to a necessary reckoning around why we should study memes and what value they offer for broader conversations around digital culture. Memes, quite simply, are, as many have pointed out, a lingua franca among groups of largely younger internet users (Milner, "Pop Polyvocality" and *World Made Meme*; Mielczarek and Hopkins; Zhang and Kang). In exploring the meme characteristics outlined by Richard Dawkins, Wiggins notes that while the concept of longevity makes sense when applied to internet memes, the concept of fecundity is not as useful (14). Wiggins argues that an "internet meme . . . is not particularly fecund, in the biological sense of being bountiful, fertile, productive, prolific, etc.," and instead we should attend to the "social semiotics" of memes, which gets at their "mass appeal and virality" (14). While I agree with Wiggins that the social semiotics of memes is crucial, I believe resistance in countercultural memes occurs as a form of productive, prolific, and bountiful discourse. The examples I explore throughout this book reflect a sense of the prolific and fecund.

As a media scholar steeped in the Frankfurt and Birmingham schools, I would argue it is vital to read memes for what they can tell us about the cultural temperature of a given moment. Memes offer us insights into the desires, anxieties, and tensions of our times. Beyond this, memes, and their "ways of operating" (de Certeau) within specific techno-cultural contexts, offer us insight into discursive flows online. In the case of countercultural memes, this includes how resistant culture is undertaken by specific aesthetic forms that use power-laden platforms and technologies while also challenging them. It demonstrates where meme-based resistance does its greatest damage, and the semiotic effects of this. Memes, especially the kinds of nihilistic, absurdist, intertextual, irreverent multilayered memes within counterculture, function as cultural excesses that destabilize the structure of capitalist platforms by circulating critical discourse in their operations via a deeply popular form of media. As de Certeau points out, it is in such unimaginative and constraining structures that countercultures emerge. This is a hopeful intervention, then, into the prevailing and somewhat crushing reality of our dystopian moment of unfettered and unregulated abuse of online platforms by obscenely wealthy tech billionaires, as well as into the climate crisis and the nonstop repeals on human rights across nation-states globally. Countercultural memes help us to understand how structures of power in mass media operate, while equally showing how we can set up the conditions for resistance within their affordances and how we can retool media for activist ends (Gajjala et al.).

Tactics Uncovered:
Collage, Reenactment, and Assemblage

Throughout this book, I argue that memes are an aesthetic medium tied to larger countercultural trajectories that hold significant critical influence in the present. To do so, I pay attention in the following chapters to three tactics employed by memes that exemplify their aesthetic specificity as a medium of bricolage with innovative uses of both intertextuality and intermediality. Each chapter explores a specific tactic in depth, including collage, reenactment, and montage, respectively. Each chapter defines how memes employ one of these tactics and outlines its relationship with past uses of the tactic in a variety of earlier art movements and media. Once the tactic is defined in its longer countercultural histories, each chapter explores specific uses in contemporary activist memes and the significance of the critical interventions they produce. The concluding sections of the different chapters expand further on the value and significance of memetic tactics by considering how they disrupt our experiences of time, space, and discursive movement in our digital cultural landscapes.

The chapter "Collage, Juxtaposition, and Spatial Collapse" looks at different forms of collage from feminist and queer meme culture and places them in dialogue with the use of collage in earlier art movements. These examples employ starkly different visual repertoires, and yet between them they produce a clear calling for better collective futures from a variety of positionalities. This chapter explores in detail the relationship between memes, collage tactics, and how they complicate our definitions of space. To do so, I look at how memes take up the tactical use of collage in a variety of textual and visual ways. I explore memes that employ juxtaposition within their collage aesthetics to produce forms of defamiliarization in viewers. These juxtapositions produce disparate and sometimes competing spatial indexes into the singular site of a meme. In the later part of the chapter, I argue memetic collages operate as forms of heterotopic space (Foucault, "Of Other Spaces"). What I am most interested in is how such tactics of collage and spatial juxtapositions produce forms of spatial collapse that create effective, critically resistant activist memes.

In "Reenactment, Nostalgia, and Performative Ruptures," I look at the tactical use of performative reenactment in memes. I outline how this appears in two different ways: first, through the textual reenactment of narrative scripts; and second, through the performance of iconic images, people, or events. This includes scripted dialogues staged within the meme frame and the remixing of historical photos that displaces the image out of its original time and place to stand in for contemporary critical interventions into a variety of issues. The chapter argues that reenactment in memes produces a very specific sense of memetic time that is dependent on a nostalgic sense of the past made critically anew. The set of case studies in this chapter reveals forms of temporality that both refracts and collapses discrete temporalities from various eras into a richly complex temporality specific to the meme being considered. Through the temporal richness of these examples, a set of sophisticated interventions into issues of gender, sexuality, subjectivity, and agency emerge that I argue are worth contemplating further.

The chapter looks at Barbie memes that utilize tactics of reenactment to (re)perform cultural scripts of gender ideals, both narratively and visually. These reenactments can alienate viewers (in a Brechtian sense), critically distancing them from harmful cultural values, stereotypes, and ideologies around idealized femininity. The chapter brings feminist readings of mimesis from performance scholar Elin Diamond (*Unmasking Mimesis*) into dialogue with contemporary feminist meme cultures to outline what is at stake in the political performances of reenactment in meme culture. The reperforming of our cultural scripts offers agency to the viewer of the meme in continuing the critical dialogue of the meme, even outside their reception of it, through sharing it within their intimate networks. The second half of the chapter considers a different site of reenactment seen via the reperformance of images from the past, remixed into new contexts with textual references that alter the original images beyond their previous uses and reception in feminist meme accounts, including notthirsttraps (@notthirsttraps). Looking specifically at images of women celebrities, including models, early 2000s influencers, musicians, film characters, and Barbie, the chapter considers how past images of womanhood and femininity are reimagined through critical textual framings to produce reckonings with the legacy of these images. By taking them out of context and into often absurd recontextualization, much is done to undermine the stranglehold of popular, neoliberal white femininity in our present moment.

The chapter "Montage and the Memetic Assemblage of Attractions" extends Kyle Parry's recent exploration of memes as assemblage, where he notes that aesthetic assemblies are collaborative, thematic, and expansive (12). Here, I expand on the previous chapter's inquiries into mimetic space and time to consider the tactical uses of montage prevalent in the emergent meme practices of carousel slide decks, CapCut superimpositions, video reels, and stitches. As noted above, carousels combine slides of still or moving images in one post, usually structured around a particular theme. CapCut and other editing software superimpose a cut-out, usually moving image on top of a background scene. In a video stitch, a user incorporates other videos into their own post and reacts to it or performs alongside it. This is usually done to extend a viral trend into their own page and content so they may reperform it or comment on it. These are ways of assembling two discrete forms of moving image content together into a dialectical relationship to create a new, third form of moving image content. I read all these tactics as extensions of the practice of montage, as they splice different audio and visual content together to produce new meanings. What my close reading of carousels, superimpositions, and stitches suggests is that meme engagements with various forms of montage and assemblage produce communities of action as well as rhetorical connection, offering us "an active tool for unifying different communities" on the left into shared forms of digital action (Arkenbout 21). To further ground this assertion in a historical context, I make links between memes and Riot Grrrl zine cultures of the 1990s. I look at how zines and memes both create cultural forms of assemblage through their texts, and then I consider how memes and meme culture have returned to zine making in digital form as a way of sustaining feminist and other activist communities outside of capitalist platforms.

The concluding chapter, "Embracing the Pleasure Activism of Joyscrolling," looks to the future possibilities of meme activism by considering the phenomenon of joyscrolling. Here several case studies are examined, including the "Bernie Sanders Mittens" memes from the 2021 US presidential inauguration. Using adrienne maree brown's concepts of pleasure activism and emergent strategy, this chapter suggests that an additional countercultural tactic we can employ is that of pleasure and joy. While it is easy to critique joyscrolling and pleasure-centered meme collections as shying away from real issues of inequity and violence, this chapter argues for the need to consider the role they play in setting out the seeds for future resistance. I will consider the kinds of utopic articulations contained in these joyful artifacts of digital culture and the ideological critiques of our current culture that they seek to address despite their playful facade. To that end, the chapter's different examples show us the direction some feminist and queer meme cultures are taking to encourage discursive resistance.

Collectively each chapter aims to do foundational work in defining the medium of memes while also directing the conversation toward the broader impacts of memetic specificity on our media experiences. While each chapter is focused on one tactic apiece, the argument set out in this introduction around memetic specificity is built gradually throughout. The chapters in this way engage in a dialogue with each other, and the examples considered throughout also contribute to this broader dialogue. The concluding chapter seeks to tie these threads together by considering the radical possibilities of pleasure and joy as alternative forms of media for activist ends.

Reflexivity and Scholarly Specificity in the Study of Memes

One of the things I am consciously aware of in writing this book is that digital cultural artifacts and viral media events go stale very quickly. I am writing on memes that will look dated the moment the book is published, as academic publishing timelines are at complete odds with the constant churning out of content in our digital cultural landscapes. That is why attention to form, aesthetics, and the larger communication practices memes express and engender is a useful place to do research. The examples used by Roland Barthes to explore mythologies, or Guy DeBord's cultural objects in discussing the society of the spectacle, will not hold the same impact or resonance now as they may have sixty years ago; in the case of memes, two months ago. However, the fundamental insights of theorizing on the formal and structural aspects of cultural content still hold. These frames offer ways into thinking about the operative factors of ideological exchange at any given moment in time, within the context of ever-changing technological and mediated spaces.

It is equally useful to point out that as a straight-passing, bi, white, cis femme who is a married, middle-aged mom on the cusp between Gen X and millennial, this book reflects my algorithmic and cultural perspective. The fact that I am left-leaning, explicitly feminist, and cued into queer, anticapitalist, antiracist activist spaces online and offline shapes my arguments and the examples I use in significant ways. My algorithm, which I dwell within daily and from which I pull a lot of the artifacts I study, analyze, and write on, skews in a way that reflects all these specificities. The insights, examples, and analyses I offer here are a highly idiosyncratic slice of meme culture that more than likely doesn't reflect the meme spaces of this book's various readers and audiences. This snapshot of the internet is not reflective of my students' timelines, nor that of close colleagues who may be a decade or so younger. It is useful, then, to keep constantly aware of this level of algorithmic specificity we experience as part of what makes the medium of memes truly unique. The curious thing about memes is how deeply specific they are to our algorithmic silos but also how relatable and shareable they are; they define us, and they divide us, for better and for worse.

It matters that we name these contexts of how we encounter and make sense of the memes delivered to us by untransparent algorithmic codes employed by capitalist platforms. This is part of the reflexivity needed when we study memes, as it helps us get at the performativity of memes and how that combination of algorithm and cultural performativity produces consequential ripple effects of meaning in the world. So, take the examples I offer close readings of in this book for what they are—blips of affective and persuasive culture that fall out of the zeitgeist as quickly as they enter it. They are archives of our digital cultural history of the twenty-first century. Some will remain part of a pantheon of classic meme templates and genres. This often is hard to determine in the moment they shine the brightest or circulate the most. In this I invite readers to take the ideas put forth by this book as a different kind of template, one that can be utilized in various settings, to think more clearly about memes in expansive ways in preparation for what they will become.

CHAPTER 1

Collage, Juxtaposition, and Spatial Collapse

This chapter considers the role of collage tactics within memes' larger position as a medium of remix and bricolage. As I outlined in the introduction to this book, a core imperative of medium specificity is that "each art form should pursue ends distinct from other art forms" (Carroll 7). Aesthetically, collage is hardwired into how internet memes operate; they mix disparate digital ephemera into a conceptual whole along the same lines as analogue collages have done before them. The term *collage* has been used as a popular descriptor when discussing memes (Lessig; Shin; Sederholm et al.). This largely has to do with memes' status as a medium that employs remixes. Lawrence Lessig suggests that the use of collage in digital media generally opens a range of accessible options for quick remix and circulation (70–71). Remix for Lessig "is collage" (76), and if memes are a remix medium, they are by their very nature a form of collage; they mix media and different textual, audio, and visual artifacts into a legible whole for viewers. Collage is central to the production of memes and is a part of their overall aesthetic and ethos.

It is useful to consider this relationship between memes and collage more fully, especially in terms of collage's much longer history as a countercultural art form (Merjian and Rugnetta; Wiggins; Hencz; Bucknell). Memes are part of this broader legacy, manifesting a similar countercultural impulse in the digital era. In this chapter, I am interested in defining the relationship between previous iterations of collage and how they are used in memes. To do so, I will map the variety of ways collage shows up in digital meme culture and how it indexes earlier countercultural impulses embedded within previous artists' and activists' uses of the formal tactic for resistant and critical ends. I begin the chapter with an overview of the role of collage in twentieth-century avant-garde art movements, including Dadaism. I look at feminist uses of collage from artists including Hannah Höch as well as Barbara Kruger and others. I link their aesthetic strategies with those of contemporary meme artists as a way of unpacking how collage leads to important forms of defamiliarization via formal juxtapositions. In the closing of the chapter, I consider how such juxtapositions open the possibility of spatial collapse, which suggests that memes are heterotopic spaces. It is within these potential heterotopic spaces of memes that important forms of critique can emerge.

The meme in figure 1.1, from the parody account ihatekatebush (@ ihatekatebush), was posted in January 2024. It offers a feminist take on the popular "starter pack" meme and remixes it with a second viral trend: people posting "what's in my bag." The genre of starter pack memes often gathers cut-out fragments of different pop culture ephemera and places them into a visual collage that ironically defines a "brand" or "aesthetic" through the mash-up of images. It also in some instances, through the remixing of such disparate or nonsensical objects, provides critical distance from the branded performance of the pack's object. Ironic reperformances of the starter pack meme are a way of signaling cliché cultural objects associated with different identities and cultural groups, as a means of disputing them.

This post by ihatekatebush begins with the statement "what's in my bag" at the top of the frame in large, bold, black font and then lists four things in square thumbnail images with accompanying descriptive text directly below each thumbnail. These are spread across two lines each, with two image and text combinations per line. The collage is thus comprised of four interrelated memes under a general theme, yet each image could also stand as a meme on its own. The bag items include, in the top left corner, a cutout of a Georgia O'Keeffe flower from the painting *Black Iris* (1926), with the words "the erotic, to be harnessed as power," and beside it is a hot-pink girlish diary with flower cutouts on the cover, with a notepad and pen and the text "the tools to divest phallologocentrism" underneath. On the bottom row on the left of the collage are cut-out pictures of Audre Lorde smelling a flower and Joan Didion in sunglasses and a scarf, with the caption "my girlfriends" below them. The final image, on the bottom right, is a cutout of a worn, yellowed, handwritten letter described by the text as "tear-stained letter written to father" underneath. The conceptual interplay between them becomes an equally important part of the collage process.

what's in my bag

the erotic, to be
harnessed as power

the tools to divest
phallogocentrism

my girlfriends

tear-stained letter
addressed to father

FIGURE 1.1. "what's in my bag." Used with permission
from ihatekatebush (@ihatekatebush).

The brand ironically portrayed in this collage of memes is that of a "rebellious, melancholic feminist with daddy issues." The images brought together in the stark white, somewhat clinical frame create what I would argue is an intertextual spatial collapse through the mashing-up of feminist and feminine iconic tropes in the single space of the meme. The meme creates a heterotopia where very disparate forms of intertextual cultural references merge with text snippets to evoke an almost atemporal vision of feminist resistance. It is, in short, a meme that performs itself as a mood board: an aspirational utterance of the parts needed to evoke a whole, that whole being an affective iteration of feminist identity.

The entire conceit and structure of the meme collage advances a discursive position that for some viewers may confirm their own identity markers and for others offers a template for future identity performance. However, as an ironic take on the whole starter pack genre, it is more likely that the meme reflects a tongue-in-cheek take on the identity young moody feminists are meant to enact in digital cultural space. It thus gives us the time to laugh alongside the creator of the meme as we contemplate what these collaged feminist markers or tropes reflect when grouped together. This opening example, and the other collage memes discussed throughout this chapter, exemplify the tactical use of collage aesthetics in memes and their political value for producing feminist countercultural digital content.

In this meme's form I see a direct embrace of the nonsensical and the absurd. O'Keeffe paintings, Didion texts, and Lorde's prose are all touchstones of an imagined youthful feminist identity. Merging them with early 2000s visual culture and melancholic letters from a previous century is provocative and a silly send-up of stereotypes placed on young, politicized women. As such, I situate this feminist starter pack meme in a lineage of avant-garde artists who have also embraced the nonsensical and the absurd in the face of hegemonic logic. The most immediate linkage between earlier avant-garde movements and memes is via Dadaism, an art movement deliberately named after a nonsense word and that was invested in the political potential of collage. What this chapter seeks to explore is not only how the antihegemonic logic of feminist meme cultures emerges through collage tactics but also how this logic and these tactics in meme culture put them in conversation with a long countercultural history that I believe requires greater consideration in the digital present. College, then, is an element of meme specificity that employs various forms—assemblage, photomontage, repurposing, and remixing—to advance comedic punch lines and critical interventions. Key is its use of the tactics of juxtaposition and defamiliarization, which allow for different forms of spatiality to be merged, creating new imaginary landscapes that at times offer the visual and textual seeds of new and imagined futures. These defamiliarized and layered forms of spatiality are integral to advancing the central claim of this book, that memes are an aesthetic medium.

The meme content I analyze in this chapter may not always look like a standard or recognizable form of an internet meme. Many of the memes veer into the realm of digital art, and some are sold as art prints. I maintain, however, that even the examples that shift furthest away from image macro memes retain the impulses of remix and juxtaposition that are both central to memes as a medium and built in part on practices of collage. They also represent the ways in which meme culture is directly informing how art is currently produced, circulated, and received. Memes, in my estimate, are themselves a remixing or collage of different art forms, including performance art, conceptual art, comic and graphic art, film, photography, and literature. These are all already media that often utilize some form of collage or remix aesthetics. Their presence in meme form suggests we attend to the layers of collage that are contained in one frame. Memes further this idea of collage formally in their intermedial remixing of discrete media forms. Memes transpose different media into the unique format of digital content including the image macro but also GIFs, moving video overlays such as CapCut superimpositions, carousel decks, stitches, and duets, which I take up in greater detail in further chapters. I start here by laying out how the most popular form of image macro memes brings different media, images, and concepts together via collage and the kinds of critical discourse that arise as a result.

The History of Collage Aesthetics

Collage as an aesthetic form stems from early twentieth-century experiments with Cubism. It has historically been used by artists to intervene in prevailing modes of representation and dominant perspectival structures. For many scholars, collage is "a major mode in all of the arts in the 20th century" (Raaberg 155). As a mode of expression, it formally "assemble[s] fragmented elements or portions of prior works and juxtapose[s] them in a continuous manner" (Raaberg 155). It is aligned with the emergence of avant-garde interventions in the post–World War I era as well as the rise of postmodern aesthetics in the post–World War II era and greatly impacted approaches to art throughout the twentieth century, including in painting, literature, music, pictorial, and moving image arts.

Collage's origins are found in the work of Cubists Pablo Picasso and Georges Braque, who were both interested in employing collage as an experiment for "dismantling traditional realistic representation" by "assembling fragmented" everyday found materials and objects (Raaberg 154) to make critical interventions into traditional art and dominant culture. Taking up these forms of "fragmentation and discontinuity," Dada and surrealism expanded collage into modes of "cultural critique and psychological exploration" (Raaberg 155). Dada inherited collage from Cubism as a device they employed as "the main weapon in the critical artists' armory against convention" (Harrison and Wood 223). Dadaists Duchamp and Picabia offered "cultural gestures with a broader ideological . . . impact" aimed at resisting "the order of bourgeois capitalism organized around the form of the nation state" (Harrison and Wood 223).

Dada thus produced "anti-art objects" that discredited traditional art forms in favor of an aesthetic "*gesture*" (Ades 112–13; emphasis in original) that, via collage, centered "explosive, modern forms of expression" on "the events of the day" (Makholm 19–21). The cultivation of critical gestures exploring the everyday reappears in subsequent avant-garde art movements beyond that point, including in the present. This is particularly the case in feminist art and media of the last hundred years. I am interested in how this impulse circulates across different art media to emerge, as my examples below indicate, in feminist meme culture in the last decade. In particular, the work of Dada collage artist Hannah Höch set out specific practices of feminist critique later expanded upon by feminist artists in the 1960s US American avant-garde, the "Pictures Generation" in the 1970s and 1980s, and arguably with feminist meme makers of the last decade.

Feminist Collage

Hannah Höch's collage work, emerging from Dadaism, politicized photomontage to address the explicit masculinism of Dada and shifted focus to "the everyday life of women" (Sugg 31). Höch's critical interventions make extensive use of irony and juxtaposition (Sugg 31) as well as alienation and humor (Herrmann 11) in the service of satirical visual displays. Höch described collage as an alienating process with no limits on the "materials that are available" to communicate "complicated thought processes" (Höch 16). Höch deconstructed "elements of popular culture" to "*re*present" them (Sugg 31; emphasis in original), creating critical imagery that produced a "poignancy from the very alienation" they formally "create . . . and retain" (Herrmann 12). Alienation as a driving force of the work is something I pick up again in the following chapter when I consider Brechtian uses of alienation in feminist performances of idealized femininity both in performance art of the 1960s and 1970s and in contemporary feminist memes. I wish to focus specifically on the deconstruction and juxtaposition of readily available images of women by feminist artists and meme makers that work to defamiliarize and thus throw into question the gendered assumptions that constrain women and femme-presenting communities.

Höch's early work is foundational here, as it explored the dominant image of the postwar German "New Woman," using domestic appliances and machine technology images to comment on "the ambiguities and deep conflicts that accompanied the new female presence in the public realm" (Makholm 22). This is evident in Höch's well-known collage *Cut with the Kitchen Knife Dada through the Last Weimar Beer-Belly Cultural Epoch in Germany* (1919). The collage is a riotous, cacophonous assemblage of sepia-toned black-and-white news clippings floating in a chaotic frame with typeset text including the word *dada* repeated throughout. There are machines, buildings, all out of scale. But what dominates is faces, mostly men's, including the German Reich president and the Kaiser, sometimes interrupted by other images, sometimes askew, placed in relationship to the machines and crowds of bodies. Women's bodies are much more background players in the scene, a commentary on their role in German society, no doubt. The only women-coded body to stand out is at the top left where the image is in negative with grayish-blue coloring, and the face is cut out as a black hole contrasted by a shock of white hair. This is picked up just to the left with the only other piece of blue in the frame—a strip of textured material that stands out but also anchors the entire frame. The overall effect is topsy-turvy, like we are watching a circus cascade across the page with no way to orient ourselves.

As the 1997 MoMA (Museum of Modern Art) review of Höch's work suggests, in this collage she "puts a proto-feminist spin on the image by metaphorically equating her scissors with a kitchen knife cutting through the traditionally masculine domains of politics and public life" (MoMA). Women were not immune from her exacting collage statements, and her use of imagery of Germany's New Woman pointed out "the complicated relationship between the sexes" at that moment in the country, including the "ambiguities and deep conflicts that accompanied" women's emergence into "the public realm" (MoMA). This focus on women's representation in her work, while receding to the background during the Nazi occupation of Berlin, became central once again in her later career, where she was "spurred on by the women's movement of the 1960s and anti–high art movements such as Fluxus, neo-Dada, and Pop" (Makholm 23). Here she found a like-minded community "devoted to irony and critique," where "montage and collage again [took] center stage" (Makholm 23). A very clearly like-minded approach was taken by experimental filmmakers Gunvor Nelson and Dorothy Wiley in their first film, *Schmeerguntz* (1966), which equally made use of cut-out figures of women and appliances from magazines to pair with the everyday labor of women, including morning sickness, cleaning diapers, and clearing out the "guntz" from a dirty sink. Nelson and Wiley expand Höch's collage aesthetic, layering both images and sounds to animate the cacophony of experience present in Höch's two-dimensional images in very visceral and affective ways.

The use of irony within montage and collage art was equally taken up from a feminist perspective in the decades after Fluxus via the Pictures Generation of artists including Cindy Sherman, Sherrie Levine, Barbara Kruger, and Laurie Simmons. This group of artists made a distinct mark within the 1970s by their use of the "sea of images" they were immersed in (Eklund), which they turned into collage media that explored how images shape our perceptions of ourselves and the world (Wolfe). Laurie Simmons's *Purple Woman / Kitchen / Second View* (1978) expands upon the work done by Höch, as well as Nelson and Wiley, by photographing a recreated miniature scenario of a plastic woman in a purple dress standing over a table of food in a toy kitchen. The intentional use of the vintage dollhouse commented on the "untenable illusions" and "persuasive indoctrination" (Simmons) the image of the 1950s housewife held even in the 1970s.

The women artists central to the movement were, like Höch before them, employing photography and collage to advance critiques of the position of women in social life as objects and images. Like Dadaist artists before them, artists from the Pictures Generation were "suffused with disillusionment from dashed hopes for political and social transformation" of their contemporary American milieu" and turned this into an aesthetic exploration of identity not as "organic and innate, but manufactured and learned through highly refined social constructions of gender, race, sexuality, and citizenship" (Eklund). Together, Höch's Dadaist legacy, early feminist experimental film, and the work of the Pictures Generation set out a strong lineage for feminist memes that employ collage to similar ends. Politically engaged meme makers equally grapple with the tumultuous and often dispiriting throes of social transformation, which includes new iterations of "culture wars" with gender firmly taking center stage in the divisive battle.

As Ringrose and Lawrence and others have suggested, feminist memes bring together networks of activist content producers and audiences in successfully "creating new ad hoc feminist publics and ways of knowing" (687; Rentschler and Thrift). This new way of knowing, or seeing, the gendered status quo reflects "the cultivation of new feminist lexicons and forms of visual and discursive humour" as well as other affective states that resonate across users (688). As the opening example suggests, this often successfully employs juxtaposition to evoke affective resonances for viewers that further solidify feminist positionalities, ideas, and comradery. These new ways of disseminating critical positions have energized feminist activism in the fourth wave and rely on complex visual-textual interfaces to do so. My consideration of the feminist legacies of collage pays particular attention to the fragmenting and juxtaposition of women's images in relation to text to produce critical distance from dominant understandings of gender and women's everyday life.

Feminist Collage in Memes

One clear example of this is from the collage meme account A Soft Wrongness (@asoftwrongness), which has over ninety thousand followers on Instagram. The account tagline is "Collage artist + accidental poet (garbage collector spilling my guts)," with a link in the bio to a limited set of prints from the account for purchase. The description of a garbage collector seems apt as the account's memes use bricolage tactics to collect and produce meaning from visual cultural debris of previous decades. The account's collages bring together a variety of visual images that stem from storybooks and children's media from the 1960s through the 1990s. These are artfully arranged by remixing the nostalgic ephemera with text to situate the intent or focus of each piece. The effect is a brightly colored set of images invitingly displayed on the account's grid. The overall impression is one of vibrant, nostalgic imagery that pulls on our sense of childhood wonder and at times intense experiences of yearning.

In March 2023, a slide deck of five prints was posted; each slide had a different color palette, but together they evoked the shades of a rainbow, which was reinforced by the final slide in the deck whose palate was rainbow-hued (A Soft Wrongness). The five collaged images were joined together thematically by their use of text, with a different phrase accompanying each of the images. These phrases included "One has the curious feeling of having been here before," "Exhilarated and exhausted by the everlasting process of evolving," "My thoughts are adrift in a mindless abyss," "I turn the same age every year," and "The better version of me has a habit of unravelling." The accompanying images were swirling colorful melanges of foxes, clocks, storybook characters, nature, and other cultural ephemera, each collage holding a unique visual theme in response to the text. Together these texts and image combinations comment on the repetitive yet changing nature of identity as well as the effort and perils contained within our self-growth over time. It is not an explicitly activist or political set of memes, and it does not directly address experiences of contemporary womanhood or femininity. Rather, it evokes something more contemplative about the nature of identity, while still interrogating the vision of femininity and the self that our "sea of images" from our cultural debris offers us.

The slide deck image collages rely on intertextuality insofar as popular visual touchstones are integrated into the formal whole of each collage. For instance, slide 1 includes an image of Bambi looking at a forest scene full of images from children's books, including the man in the moon looking kindly down on the scene from above, a cuckoo clock, a toad on a mushroom stool, and a fox licking its lips. Even if the actual books aren't identifiable, the iconic images point to classic fairy tales and nursery rhymes. The third image uses a more soothing pale sky-blue and bright yellow palette that again features a moon, this time as a crescent, alongside images from *Alice in Wonderland,* including Alice falling down the rabbit hole and the startled and anxious doorknob from the animated film. Alongside these are an image of the character Bubbles, from the 1990s cartoon *Powerpuff Girls,* flying in the top left corner of the frame with a frown. Bubbles is a highly emotive character on the show, prone to bouts of intense rage. These two figures are paired with an off-kilter farmhouse in the bottom left of the frame, which intertextually evokes a narrative of another unsettled young woman, Dorothy in *The Wizard of Oz.*

The push and pull of these figures creates a dynamic sense of movement within the collage. Together these images look like they are swirling in a vortex (or the inside of a tornado). This provides a visualization of the text in the third image, which reads, "My thoughts are adrift in a mindless abyss." The intertextual collapsing of Bubbles and Alice, and Dorothy by proxy, is compelling here. The swirly, ungrounded, emotionally charged abyss of the text is captured and amplified in what we know or connote from the journeys of these three young characters on the precipice of womanhood. The intertextual narratives referenced here reflect a pastiche of multiple referents and styles at once, all constellating around a psychic state of thoughts adrift in an abyss. These are tied with the visuals to a series of images of young women in a state of transition. This is further reinforced through the formal composition of a swirling set of figures and objects in motion. The merging of these three narrative figures offers a complex set of referents to help establish the kinds of abyss and unsettled thoughts that are central to the collage. They add a depth and a dynamism to the collaged meme through their intertextual interplay. These layered forms of intertextuality themselves entwine to produce a rich set of meanings within one single meme image.

Critical Juxtapositions in Feminist Collage

I wish to connect these examples of collage tactics in memes to previous eras of feminist art, where collage in both two- and three-dimensional forms has always been full of potential for feminist resistance. What makes collage such a useful tool across these eras is how it highlights "that which remains unaccounted for in conventional representation and logic" and through "radical juxtaposition" brings forward that which has been erased and held in opposition for so long (Harding 24). This use of collage is seen early in the work of Hannah Höch but appears throughout the history of feminist artists, especially since the 1960s avant-garde. Artists like Carolee Schneemann, Joyce Wieland, and Gunvor Nelson and Dorothy Wiley (discussed earlier) explore collage tactics across a variety of media, including their painting, performance, and film works. In the last four decades, this lineage of feminist collage is reflected in the work of Barbara Kruger, Jenny Holzer, and third-wave feminist Riot Grrrl zine culture, among others. Kruger's work is not only an excellent example of feminist collage tactics from the 1980s but also acts as a clear precursor to feminist zines of the 1990s, which I discuss in later chapters. Kruger's signature form of a photo collage with text is a clear prototype of the image macro meme we so frequently see today. I wish to map the linkage here more fully, between her earlier feminist collage and the present of feminist memes.

Kruger's recognizable collaging of black-and-white photos with overlaid text emerged in the late 1970s after a decade of working in painting and weaving ("Barbara Kruger"). One of her most well-known works, *Untitled (Your body is a battleground),* is a poster from 1989 with a black-and-white photo of a woman's face staring straight at the camera. The photo is black and white, and the right side of the frame shows half of the image in a photographic negative that inverts the colors of the woman's face. The contrasting positive and negative image of the woman is overlaid with white text in red rectangles that reads: "Your body" (on the top), "is a" (in the middle), and "battleground" (on the bottom of the image). The piece was "used as the rallying poster for the 1992 pro-choice march on Washington" (Reckitt and Phelan 152). Closely related is the collage *Untitled (Your gaze hits the side of my face),* an equally popular work of Kruger's from 1981, almost a decade earlier. It employs a similar use of black-and-white photos, this time a white marble bust of a woman in profile looking off to the right of the frame. This is overlaid with the words "your gaze hits the side of my face" alternating between black text in white rectangles and black text in white rectangles. The words are placed sequentially, one after the other, down the left side of the frame.

This piece stems from Kruger's interest in both poststructuralist and feminist theory (Raaberg 162) and directly references Laura Mulvey's deeply influential theory of the "male gaze" as outlined in her foundational feminist film text "Visual Pleasure and Narrative Cinema." The success of both collages is how they force an encounter with the audience through the weight of the words they are reading as they simultaneously interact with the images.

These standard images of women upholding the ideals of Western femininity resonate with what we see over and over in our daily consumption of magazines, celebrity news media, and across the history of art. Yet Kruger turns this word-and-image interplay into a conceptual conceit where viewers feel the weight of the words and their inherent critique in a more fulsome way. Kruger defamiliarizes these iconic images of women by taking them out of their original context and juxtaposing them with textual additions that represent very real threats to women viewers: reproductive autonomy, the objectifying gaze, threats of violence in public and private space.

Kruger's use of collage produces confrontational text-image compositions that "engage directly in political criticism" and "reflect the understanding that sign systems—both images and language—have the power to construct identities" (Raaberg 162). The dominant modes of collage used by Kruger include "fragmentation and discontinuity" employed to "intervene in the seamless cultural representation of gender" (Raaberg 162). Kruger's use of collage as tactic of political criticism preempts feminist image-text macro memes with the same intentions. The same principles of signification are at work in both, as they each use juxtaposition in ways that move beyond the original intentions of the images used in order to make something new via textual overlays. This new form is sometimes discomforting and at other times offers a relational set of meanings that either disrupt and displace the viewer or resonate and confirm some part of their identity for them.

Another account, @paperstackedonpaper, by artist Kaitlyn Skelly, deviates from A Soft Wrongness's adherence to nostalgic imagery, borrowing instead from a wide variety of visual ephemera, including hand-drawn lettering, printed-out copies of digital memes, and magazine lifestyle photos. The work of Skelly for @paperstackedonpaper more closely resembles earlier photomontage techniques popularized by Höch. They have a less digitally-smoothed-out look, and the textured layering of images remains visible in the final piece. Unlike Höch's work, these collages include text and merge poetic fragments with photomontage.

In one piece from November 2023, two magazine photographs are juxtaposed as the backdrop for a winding set of pink-hued images and text that meander their way from the top left corner of the image to the bottom right edge (see fig. 1.2). The backdrop on the top left is a night scene that is slightly out of focus, mostly dark, with the edges of an illuminated "don't walk" sign peeking out behind a layer of women's faces drawn in red on pale pink paper. These faces continue across the left side of the collage, interconnected by two long, thick, wavy lines in pink and red that merge as clasped hands in the middle of the image.

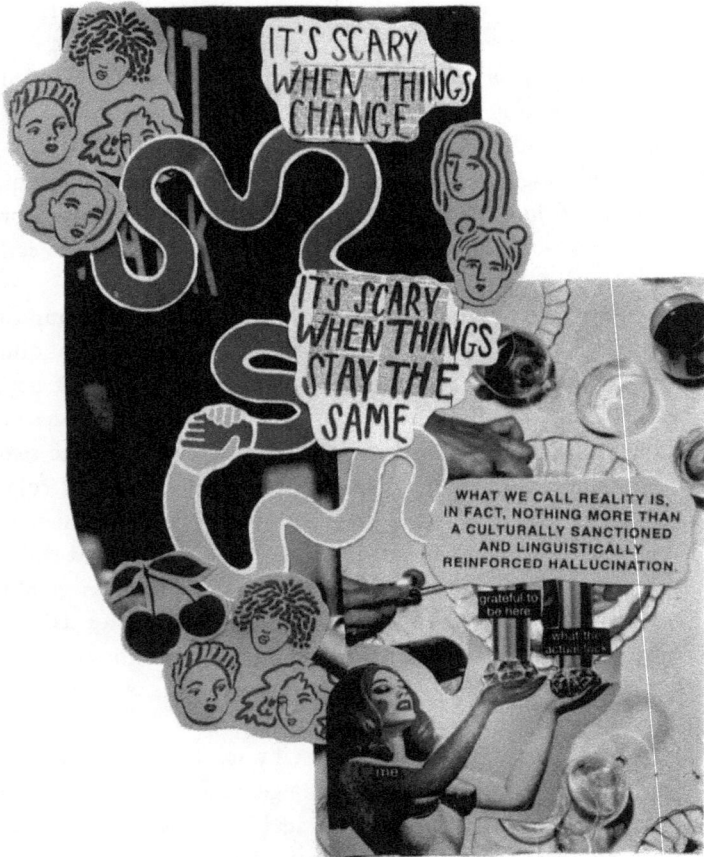

FIGURE 1.2. "It's Scary." Used with permission from
Kaitlyn Skelly for @paperstackedonpaper.

In cut-out bubbles of white paper in red hand-drawn letters, the text reads,
"It's scary when things change" and "It's scary when things stay the same."
The backdrop image juxtaposed just below these phrases is a magazine image
of a crisp white tablecloth, plates, and glasses with wine in them, shot from
overhead. In the left of the table image's frame are women's hands cutting into
food on a plate that is blocked by a set of red text on a yellow paper. The text
reads: "What we call reality is, in fact, nothing more than a culturally sanc-
tioned and linguistically reinforced hallucination." This text hovers above a
printout version of a popular meme that takes up the bottom half of the collage. The printed meme shows a vintage illustration of a woman in a strapless
golden cone bra holding up two large crystal rocks in her palms as if weighing

them against each other. The crystals beam rainbow streams of energy shooting upward. One of the rainbows has white text on a black square that reads "grateful to be here" while on the other rainbow, the same font reads "what the actual fuck"?

Aesthetically, the collage evokes the maximalism of A Soft Wrongness's collage work, but somehow this collage feels less visually oppressive and more inviting in its use of negative space. It openly invites contemplation on the intentional juxtaposition of the images and texts. The collage is not prescriptive and direct in what it offers. Instead, it asks that we meander through a variety of affective states, from gratitude to fear, to finding ourselves in scenarios and weighing life options that cause us to cry out "What the actual fuck?" in frustration. The message seems to be one of uncertainty but also a willingness to sit with that uncertainty. It also offers a sense of longing to be in community with others. The juxtaposition of central images of the "don't walk" sign, the dinner party, and the frustrated pinup girl gives an insight into the stopping and starting of one's path. The hopeful thread throughout the piece is the connected and entwined lines weaving the entire landscape together. This is not the confrontation with outdated gender paradigms of the previous meme but an articulation of relationality that invites kinship and recognition. In its intentional use of cutouts that resist blurring the collage into smooth lines, the image recalls the work of Höch and others. It also centers contemporary iterations of domestic space and women's bodies within the frame to juxtapose idealized versions of both with a more uncertain and ambiguous text. In this way the lineage of earlier feminist interventions is made apparent in more recent works.

Memetic Collage as Restorative Relationality

The tactical use of collage in postwar feminist art since the 1960s hinges on "a double-visioned cultural critique" that utilizes both "fragmentation and relational strategies" (Raaberg 157). There is a shared effort to "re-collect" existing art and culture "already fragmented and abandoned by the dominant culture" to "recuperative" and "restorative" ends (Raaberg 169; see also Lippard). This is seen in feminist collage in the 1980s, like that of Barbara Kruger or Laurie Simmons, who employed disruptive collage tactics to upend "hegemonic cultural constructions" (Raaberg 169). However, by the 1990s, this merges into a "reconstructive impulse" that "stage[s] multiple and fluid relationships" within the work of art that recognizes realities in the world beyond the collage frame (Raaberg 169). Importantly, this emergence of relationality in feminist collage art reflects the appeal of collage in meme culture later, which brings together different media, texts, and cultural ephemera to comment on what it means to be a digital subject in our unceasingly chaotic world.

I see these legacies of relationality present in the Afrofuturist account Intelligent Mischief (@intelligentmischief) and its use of photomontage to ground its meme work. The account's Instagram bio currently describes it as a "creative studio unleashing the power of Black radical imagination to shape the future." An earlier iteration of the bio also noted that the account created "propaganda for the world we desire" and that "all art is propaganda." The juxtaposition within this profile bio between the concept of propaganda, usually seen as suspect, and its potential for resistance is the first instance of a collage tactic within the account. It suggests we can utilize art as a form of propaganda to articulate and attain our desired futures. It also lays bare any pretense that art isn't propaganda and in some ways asks us to determine which forms of ideological expression we are willing to engage with.

A post from March 2024 reveals a collage that combines a photomontage aesthetic with distinctly digital elements (see fig. 1.3). Alongside cut-out vintage-looking photographic images, the collage includes highly saturated colors in the background landscape and in the futuristic font used. The center point of the frame is a group of seven sepia-toned photos of Black women all in full-length silhouette. They each wear a vintage dress, and their eyes are obscured by small rectangular cutouts that resemble 3D glasses. Collaged together in this formation, they look like a chorus, their bodies in three-quarter profile looking in the same direction of an approaching horizon. All are leaning to one side with the same leg extended slightly out, as if both resting but also at the ready.

The women are placed upon what seem like rolling pieces of concrete with hills and valleys. Each woman is on one of the peaks of the structure. Beneath that is a lush green forest of neon-colored trees that recede toward the back of the image. Above the forest is a celestial skyscape of royal blues, magenta, and purple. The text on the bottom of the collage reads, "What if we governed with wisdom, holding present and future in consideration?" The font is in all caps and is bright yellow with three-dimensional shading in deep, rich blue. It is a wavy pattern that tilts high on the left side and leans forward visually in the middle, only to rise again on the right. It is reminiscent of futuristic early video fonts, gesturing toward both a nostalgic past and the future. The caption for the collage includes several hashtags: #unleashblackimagination, #shapethefuture, and #thefutureisnow.

The visuals and text exceed the usual uses of the image macro format. The meme does not employ humor or irony, where one set of text undermines or

FIGURE 1.3. "What if we governed with wisdom?" Used with permission from Emma Asumeng for Intelligent Mischief (@intelligentmischief).

flips the script on the image or previous text. Instead, it articulates a political standpoint that holds the present together with the future. It appeals for accountability—not for immediate needs but for those we cannot anticipate but must consider, nonetheless. There is a hopefulness in the image. The chorus of women that stand as monuments to past histories of collective action are remixed with the words to suggest a need to reach back to move forward. This is encapsulated not in a place of ironic detachment or apathy but in a visual landscape of wonder and fecundity, as depicted by the cosmos and the lush greenery.

In an earlier post from the account in February 2024, the same hashtags are used for an image of a Black woman in a shiny lamé dress and matching head wrap. She is caught walking in mid-motion, striding purposefully toward the left side of the collage frame. She walks through a seemingly unending field of bright pinkish-red tulips and a blue sky with wispy clouds, and a bright yellow orb that could be the sun or a full moon. The orb takes up the top third of the image and has purplish-white cranes flying overhead in the opposite direction of the woman. The text on the bottom third of the image reads, "What if we were rooted in our own trajectory, our ethics, folktales, and our knowledge?" in the same font as figure 1.3. Both collages reflect a theme in which the start of each text asks, "What if?" and the collage image and accompanying hashtags set out seeds of possibility as the answer.

Like the previous post by Intelligent Mischief, this meme centers a woman moving toward new spaces of possibility; a fact shown by how far to one side she is situated in the frame and the direction of her gaze looking off-frame (see fig. 1.4). Equally similar is the collaging of temporalities placed in relation to one another. There is an appeal to reaching backward to the knowledge, ethics, and lore that ground and sustain our personal and collective trajectories. Within the meme form, again deviating from more widespread uses of the format for humor, the account utilizes text to offer a provocation to viewers. Like the previous meme, the use of "what if . . . ?" orients the visual content and brings viewers into a space of speculative possibility that encourages us to imagine possible futures that are grounding in our understandings of the present and the supports of the past. There is contained within the form a gesture toward relationality, an invitation to ponder together. It is paired with, or perhaps juxtaposed with, the reality that sometimes our ethics, folktales, and knowledge are silenced and erased, thus leaving us to rely on words and ideas that do not ring true. Here relationality works alongside critique, and combined together, they reveal how the tactic of collage in memes can work toward countercultural ends, raising questions that we must attend to in our search for equity and justice.

These three different examples reflect a group of artists who use collage aesthetics to reimagine the image macro meme form. Like Dada artists like Höch and later feminist work by Kruger and Simmons, digital uses of collage and photomontage techniques seen in these examples intervene into the dominance of the image macro meme as a traditional aesthetic form of the medium. A Soft Wrongness integrates the standard use of text found in image macro memes into a collaged composition, making the text part of the overall aesthetic as opposed to being in juxtaposition with the image. Skelly's @ paperstackedonpaper, while the least meme-like of the accounts, resembles older forms of collage and photomontage the most clearly. However, the account posts image-text compositions that speak to everyday struggles, while also integrating memes themselves as part of her collage image lexicon. The account in this way also extends the image macro format by having the

FIGURE 1.4. "What if we were rooted in our own trajectory?" Used with permission from Emma Asumeng for Intelligent Mischief (@intelligentmischief).

text convey the post's intentions. The text creates less pithy one-liners and more fulsome arguments and perspectives. In doing so it expands what image macro forms can achieve.

By contrast, Intelligent Mischief's compositions are the most formally like an image macro meme, but they are also the most visually defamiliarizing in terms of the collaged elements that make up their memes. Like image macro memes, the posts employ an image anchored by block text on either the top or the bottom. A dialogue is produced between the text and image that provides resonances within the frame and locates entry points for viewers into the meme's meaning. However, unlike more standard uses of image macro memes, the juxtaposition of photomontage elements overlayed on visually saturated backgrounds produces fragmented spaces of uncertainty and critical possibility open to contemplation by viewers. All three accounts are excellent examples of how memes are used for political purposes and, as such, open conversations about what protest can and does look like in the age of memes (Wiens and MacDonald).

I want to consider the lineages of these aesthetic interventions with one final example from Kruger that I believe has echoes in more recent feminist meme culture. Kruger's work *Roy Toy* (1986), I believe, directly echoes the aesthetics and ethos of meme culture today. The piece is a black-and-white photograph of a young wild cat with raw meat hanging from its mouth staring wide-eyed into the camera. The image is broken up by red lines that bisect the image into three parts and match the red framing around the photo. At the bottom of the collage in large white text embedded in red rectangles is the phrase "make my day." On the upper right side of the frame, a small cutout of Roy Cohn in blue tones floats in the image as if out of nowhere. It is easily missed due to its smaller size in the face of the larger cat staring out at the audience. Cohn, the subject of the piece's title, was a controversial figure, lawyer, and Reagan supporter who was outspokenly homophobic despite being closeted and dying from AIDS in 1986.

The "image of violent retribution for sexist chatter" that centers the piece has been described as "powerful in its directness" (McEvilley). In the image, the tiger's violent and intimidating presence overshadows and drowns out Cohn, rendering him insignificant. This juxtaposition of human and animal is matched by the juxtaposition of scale between the images. Together they encourage viewers to align with an enraged animal figure, full of affect and bite, rather than with the human figure who held the power to harm marginalized populations, in this case those facing the devastating effects of the AIDS epidemic without any form of institutional support.

Looking at the image almost forty years later, I can't help but link it to a popular meme that circulated in late October 2016 in response to the leaked audio of then presidential candidate Donald Trump bragging about grabbing women by the genitals without consequence. The meme shows a grainy black-and-white close-up photograph of an angry cat, ears back, teeth out, snarling (see fig. 1.5). The text in red and black boxes at the top of the image reads, "Nov 8," and beside it, "Pussy Grabs Back" (see Fahrenthold; Jacobs et al.; Nelson for context). The meme looks a lot like a cross between a Kruger collage and the DIY Riot Grrrl zine aesthetic from the 1990s. The meme became further remixed and circulated in feminist culture, turning into a rallying cry for voters in the 2016 election. It held within it a riotous spirit of rage and hope that this leaked audio would help swing the vote to ensure Trump was not put into office. The meme recirculated in new forms in 2024, including one of a cat peeking out through a door with a blue light

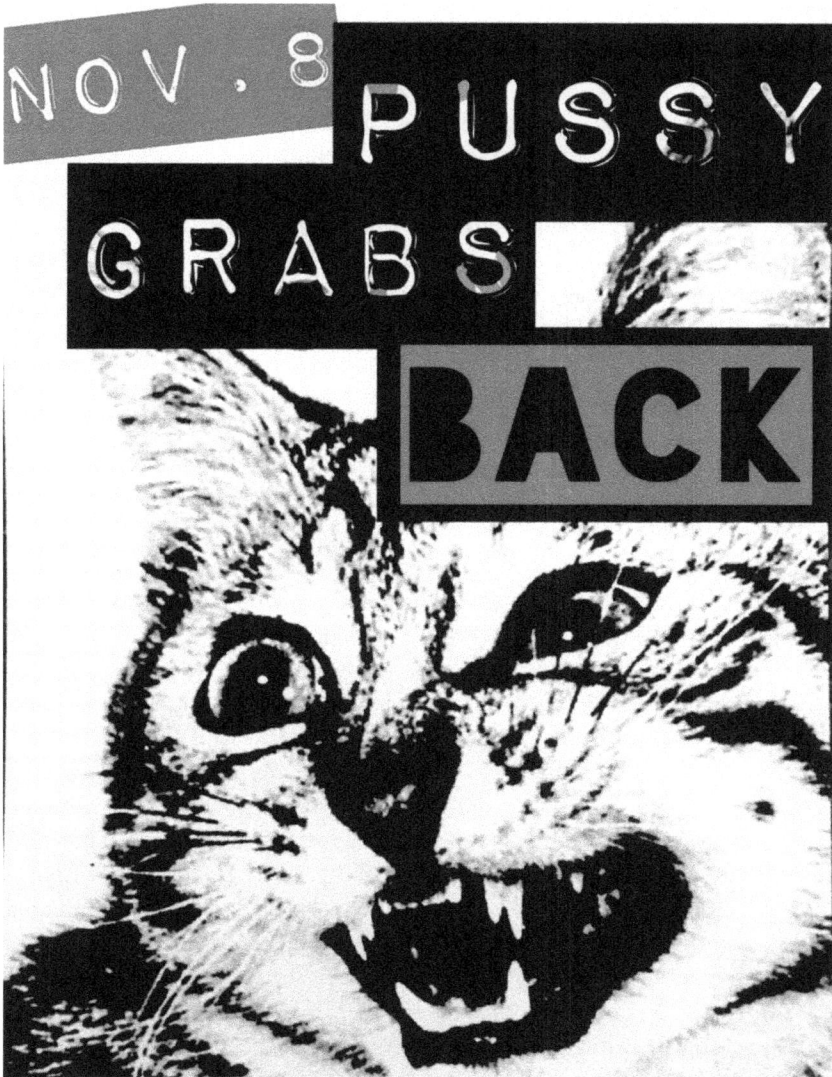

FIGURE 1.5. "Pussy Grabs Back." Used with permission from
Jessica Bennett, Amanda Duarte, and Stella Marrs.

spilling into the frame, suggesting there may be a different outcome this
time around.

The conversation I am suggesting between Kruger's germinal work and the
"Pussy Grabs Back" memes shows not only formal uses of collage in feminist
art but also the ways that different moments in feminist time become collaged

onto one another, echoing certain countercultural impulses at given points in our history. What remains thematically is the tactical use of angry animals' appeal as stand-ins for a voracious and rageful affect felt by many feminist and queer people in the face of failed election cycles or the failures of government to care for those who are most vulnerable. In both *Roy Toy* and the "Pussy Grabs Back" memes, male political figures responsible for repealing rights against women and gay communities are put on the spot as a way of focusing some of the political ire. The use of wild, angry felines is a form of defamiliarization that juxtaposes very real political causes with animalistic responses to get to the core sentiment underpinning feminist and queer political unrest. In the next section, I will spend time defining how juxtaposition is used in collage and the critically valuable forms of defamiliarization it can encourage.

Juxtaposition, Defamiliarization, and Paradox

At its core, the examples of collage in memes explored above present viewers with paradoxical scenarios where improbable pairings of images, objects, and artifacts converge and collide within a frame. As Aja Merjian and Mike Rugnetta note, memes are propelled by such forms of "displacement" that can often produce forms of "iterability" as well as "irony" (5). This is what connects memes to "an avant-garde genealogy of collage and the readymade," which centers "objects and images that are dislodged from their original context and thereby ironized" (Merjian and Rugnetta 5). The encounter between oddly placed, improbably connected objects ensures critical forms of juxtaposition can occur. These affect audiences through an aesthetics of defamiliarization, or of "making strange" the legible world. Defamiliarization emerged as a concept in early twentieth-century Russian formalist literary theory to produce visual and textual encounters that were unsettling or unusual. The unsettling was meant to jolt viewers into a form of consciousness that led to larger social-political reckonings with the status quo. In certain strands of meme practices, such as those that work with collage aesthetics, a similar use of defamiliarization is evident.

Defamiliarization moves readers away from everyday language and toward aesthetic experiences that startle us out of automation, or, our habitual ways of seeing and being in the everyday. It presents what we know in "novel" and "unexpected context[s]" (Erlich 629). Defamiliarization is appealing for those of us living in "a culture which has systematically attempted to deprive us of experience, substituting products and images and incessant tinkering with the self in its stead," as it "requires an intensity of perception" that requires us "to look again, to see, almost for the first time" (Gunn 28). Memes defamiliarize through remixing images, gestures, and sometimes moving images and sound recordings from their original everyday context into new modes and forms of signification. This collision of juxtaposing forms of visuality, aurality, textuality, and bodily gestural forms creates an experience of seeing recognizable objects anew.

In my analysis, defamiliarization, unlike Russian formalism, holds political potential, much like Bertolt Brecht's concept of the alienation effect, or how Dada uses juxtaposition to break with convention and advance an anti-bourgeois politics. In the case of memes, the juxtaposition of different image ecologies and referents can restructure ordinary perceptions of reality in both humorous and critical ways. They also produce affective resonances that address the audience as a coconspirator, standing outside the image and in dialogue with the creator. In doing so, this form of address breaks an illusion of representational realism and produces an emotional distance which allows for critical formations between meme maker and viewer. I take up the feminist uses of critical emotional distance, or alienation, in the following chapter in my exploration of the tactic of reenactment within meme culture.

Here I wish to underscore how valuable the memetic use of defamiliarization is in the current socio-technological landscape. Extending the Russian formalist distinction between the everyday and aesthetic uses of language into the present, I would argue that much in our online spaces is in the realm of prose. This is the hard currency of communication ecosystems, found across various forms of information-sharing online, from podcasts to public health infographics, listicles, and downloadable pdf courses on any conceivable topic. It is also increasingly the foundation of what large language models (LLMs) and artificial intelligence (AI) employ as part of the apps and platforms we utilize daily, often with little thought as to the actual value or veracity of the prose being generated. Memes are more closely aligned with the realm of dream logic and transgressions of linguistic codes and social mores. While memes can be prosaic sites of information sharing and brand building, they can also be spaces that explore the limits of language and upend the structures of digital culture and algorithmic platform constraints. The aesthetics of collage remixes popular culture into new forms of signification. These echo those formal interventions encouraged by earlier experiments with collage, from Cubism and Dadaism to the post–World War II avant-garde and beyond. The use of memes in this way forces us to reconsider who we are as producer-consumers of media and situate memes and media as tools of resistance, all of which speaks to different calls for revolutionary change.

FIGURE 1.6. "What if we treated our art and culture as ceremonial?" Used with permission from Emma Asumeng for Intelligent Mischief (@intelligentmischief).

In a third post by Intelligent Mischief, from April 2024, the account depicts a photomontage of two Black women dancing in Yoruban ceremonial dress in front of a vivid landscape of mountains, a celestial night sky, and lavender-hued waves (see fig. 1.6). The text asks us to reconsider what art is and can be used for. It states, "What if we treated our art and culture as ceremonial, and it supported our healing, wellness, and care for each other and the land?" with the accompanying hashtags #unleashingblackimagination, #shapethefuture, #anotherworldispossible, and #thefutureisnow in the captions. It suggests there is a way to link our creative acts not to the art market but to ritual and revolution. This offers a powerful form of defamiliarization that reminds us of the value of the poetic over the prosaic. The risk inherent in the everyday prose of the digital is that it becomes "a 'hard currency' of perception . . . an efficient but heavily deflated currency ruined by automatization"

(Kristeva, *Reader* 211). In contrast, poetic language's use of "a dream logic . . . transgresses rules of linguistic code and social morality as well" (Kristeva, *Reader* 41). These kinds of transgressions are in the realm of the carnivalesque, which "only exists and succeeds . . . because it accepts another law," one that mimics social codes to show their inconsistencies (Kristeva, *Reader* 41–42). This meme employs defamiliarization in the way it joins the image and the question posed by the text. It shows the codes of art and culture as offering more than capitalist products for consumption. It offers instead a logic, that art and culture may instead be part of our health and wellness as a society, with the invitation to honor them as sacred. The power of this post is how it shares such provocations within the context of a capitalist platform, following and yet subverting the logic of the platform structure in plain sight.

I'm interested in how each of these examples of feminist collages remixing images and text within art or memes intervenes into the seamless packing of dominant cultural representations. This, to me, is where their potential for political intervention is most clear. These collages disrupt the representational status quo by fragmenting what are, in the case of a representational painting or a clean, well-branded Instagram aesthetic, smooth forms of representation. Jump cuts and other forms of film editing in avant-garde cinema sought to actively fragment the smooth viewing experience that continuity editing brought forward and that was made popular by classical Hollywood. Similarly, memes as a form of collage often give the audience pause through the disorientation achieved in the mixing of disparate visual and textual elements. In these memes, our visual field is disrupted, and, as such, we are disoriented, as viewers. In short, memes, like experimental editing processes, produce visual forms of spatial collapse. This, for me, is one of the most potent interventions of meme form, and it is illustrated especially well by memes that explore the aesthetic potential of collage art.

Memes, Collage, and Spatial Collapse

I want to conclude this chapter by considering in more depth how memes often upend senses of spatiality via collage tactics. Memes that use collage tactics often juxtapose different spatial realities in one contained frame, which can in turn evoke forms of spatial collapse and defamiliarization and, consequently, enact cultural critique. This echoes ruptures in space within modernist art, where collage first emerges as an attack on traditional forms of spatial representation in art. The central preoccupation of the twentieth century was space. This has been characterized as an "epoch of simultaneity . . .

juxtaposition . . . near and far . . . side-by-side . . . [and] the dispersed," a world experienced and represented as "a network that connects points and intersects with its own skein" (Foucault, "Of Other Spaces" 22). This aesthetic shift in the early 1900s came about due to extenuating factors of the moment, including the proliferation of new technologies (photography, cinema, and train and air travel, to name a few) as well as geopolitical crises that forced a crisis of meaning in culture.

In this moment, "the Impressionists, Cubists and others . . . broke up" the dominance of perspectival representation, "as if an earthquake had struck" (Kern 140). This is seen in the aesthetic reckonings at this point across painting, literature, poetry, and other media. The idea emerging at that time around space as relations among sites (Foucault, "Of Other Spaces" 23) is equally a concern in the current moment as we see increased forms of relationality made available through the rapid access of all types of communication instantaneously across the globe. As such, it makes sense that digital culture would equally respond to these extenuating factors, which have created new types of crises of meaning in culture. This is part of what I believe marks the case for how memes consciously or not are using collage, defamiliarization, and juxtaposition to participate in forms of spatial collapse, and in some cases do so for political ends.

Memes as an aesthetic medium are thus a clear part of this lineage within modern art. Meme culture also arose in a moment of proliferating new technologies, including the internet, digital culture, social media platforms, and the rise of "prosumer" content creation, curation, and consumption. We are also culturally in a moment of global geopolitical crisis (alongside a climate crisis and the reverberations of a global pandemic). The tumultuous environments that inform aesthetic practices and cultural foci are a commonality across these eras. Like their Cubist predecessors, memes as collage media do not rely on a unified perspectival spatial frame; instead, they explore various points of view, moving in and out of a specific locatedness or framing of the meme's scene.

Memes in their various forms offer a multiperspectival experience of the visual. They reveal their radical and tactical potential through this expanded sense of space. There is a defamiliarizing experience within many meme collages, which throws into question the kinds of dominant aesthetics and ideological perspectives that uphold the internet as a vehicle for influencer-driven commodity distribution and promotion. This is like Höch's work insofar as meme collages also either flatten or distort the space of the picture plane, thus "creating their own type of space" (Sugg 31). With Höch's works, this results in an absence of "spatial logic," which reveals a different kind of "unified whole"

(Sugg 31). The consequence of this lineage of removing spatial logics to present a vastly different form of visual unity opens viewers up to alternative aesthetic experiences of space. In the work of Intelligent Mischeif, these new spatial unities offer vast spaces of possibility outside the constraints of dominant visual culture. In a visual lexicon of ambiguous utopia, the collages by Intelligent Mischief imagine into being spaces where humanity and nature merge, doing away with the nature/culture divide. In their collages, humans are integrated into vibrant natural spaces that evoke a sense of wonder, inspiring viewers to imagine other worlds distinct from the present one. In a very different way, the work of the account griefmother (@griefmother), which I explore below, upends our habituated sense of everyday objects and reemploys their spatial logic for aesthetic and conceptual ends that bring in a layer of nostalgia, a temporal experience, to the experience of spatial disjunction.

Memetic Spatial Collapse

In the following chapter, I explore how the memetic tactic of performative reenactment produces critical interventions into our experience of time, effectively producing multiple levels of temporality within a single memetic frame. I demonstrate how this collapsing of time is often used to critical ends by feminist activist meme makers. I wish to conclude this chapter with a similar argument outlining how the tactic of collage produces an experience of space that is destabilizing and defamiliarizing and puts into crisis our spatial certainties. Meme's use of collage to evoke spatial collapse reflects what it means to live and move within the digital sphere and is worth further exploration.

In "Of Other Spaces" (1986), Michel Foucault theorizes that spaces are discursively constructed and shift their significance and purpose over time. This framing affects how we understand the function of space; it can be seen as being shaped by the discourses of both institutions *and* lived practices. He notes that we "live in a set of relations that delineates sites which are irreducible to one another and absolutely not superimposable on one another" (Foucault, "Of Other Spaces" 23). This is not so in our online worlds. Foucault's distinction between private and public, work and leisure, and family and social spaces (23) does not fully hold in our current highly online, postpandemic world in the same way. The creep of techno-capitalist devices shaping and informing our everyday life poses new issues and relations in our understanding of the construction of space. For Foucault, the tension between the discursive constructions of space by institutions and by everyday practice is most clearly realized through the concept of heterotopic space. He contrasts heterotopias with utopias, which are "sites with no real place" that offer an image of "society itself in perfected form, or else society turned upside down"—either way, they are "fundamentally unreal spaces" (24). Heterotopic spaces are "counter-sites" where all the "real sites" of culture are "simultaneously represented, contested, and inverted" (24). Heterotopias are "outside of all places, even though it may be possible to indicate their location in reality" (24). Memes, following this formula, are heterotopic spaces. The use of collage and juxtaposition as a way of evoking visual, conceptual, and spatial collapse helps support this view of memes as heterotopic.

I wish to demonstrate three ways that spatial and conceptual collapse can occur formally in memes. These memetic formal collapses disrupt perspectival representation and discrete senses of space as well as the framing devices memes adhere to more broadly. The first occurs within the image frame and involves the collapse of traditional perspectival logic via surreal constructions of space that challenge the practical limits of our everyday world. Sara Shakeel's digital collages, which often include impossible and beautifully surreal collages of everyday objects, people, and animals in extraordinary landscapes, exemplify this. These are enhanced in their allure through Shakeel's use of a pastel color palette and digitally added layers of shimmer, glitter, and crystals reflecting light within the image. Her collages use different subjects, often animals, in vast natural landscapes that are defamiliarized by the surreal juxtaposition of what is being remixed together. For instance, a popular series by Shakeel centers on photos of half-cat and half-mermaid beings (or mer-cats) lounging and luxuriating in decadent, watery surroundings.

The first image is a peach-cream-colored, long-haired cat with fur that is slightly textured (as if the cat has beach waves), and on the bottom is a pale pink and golden-hued mermaid tail with pearlescent scales glittering in the sun (Shakeel, "It's a Fantasy"). This mer-cat is lounging on the sand and looking over its shoulder into the distance. The fantastical animal is in between a rocky boulder and a ripple of shallow waves. Sun glistens over every surface of the image. In the next slide, an orange tabby mer-cat with vibrant aquamarine crystals on its scales is curled up in a shallow beach scene, resting against some rocks, eyes half closed, as if basking in the golden hue of the image.

The series of photos continues, with each image progressively getting more surreal as the mer-cats are taken out of the beach scene and into opulent spaces where they pose, always looking slightly away from the viewer's eyeline. The mermaid scales of the mer-cats also get progressively more elaborate and ornate, like fantastical jeweled, almost armor-like constructions with gems, pearls, and filigree. They appear less like mythical creatures in their habitat and more like ornaments in a dream landscape. While these aren't memes per se, they don't include any text within the image's frame, so they function more like art images. They create forms of remix and the collapsing of unlikely images and spaces together to create a new impossible setting situated far outside the real world and in a conceptual space open to and inviting contemplation. It echoes earlier forms of collage brought into the context of AI-generated imagery and circulated or displayed on Instagram.

In a more muted series with the caption "Remind me, what is it that you are looking for?" Shakeel places pastel everyday objects in haunting, gray-toned gothic landscapes. These include a four-poster canopy bed dripping with pink gossamer fabric and pearl garland, situated in a misty pond among lily pads with a forest of green trees in the background. In the same series, there is a similarly ornate formal dinner table floating in a foggy bayou, and richly decorated vintage cars, bicycles, toilets, and claw-foot tubs emerge from similar pastoral marshy settings with lighting and color schemes that are reminiscent of rococo paintings. The series ends with an old graveyard submerged partially in water, and in the foreground is a stone coffin covered in a floral print with moss growing on the corners. The background is an out-of-focus sunset through bare trees, with vivid orange and purple streaking. The effect is haunting but beautiful and arguably reflects Shakeel's stated interest "to unveil" her vision of "a radiant existence" and reflect to her viewers "a universe suffused with the allure of the commonplace, the charm of the unnoticed" (Gordon).

The experience of Shakeel's images is one of the uncanny and the unfamiliar. And yet the defamiliarization she evokes is not an unpleasant encounter but rather the merging of objects and spaces not normally seen together, through a sheen of opulence. The images spark joy, wonder, and a sense of pleasure through her signature use of crystals to reflect light and bring beauty to the digital landscapes she constructs. Everything glows with this reflected light. The subjects also offer delight: baroque dinner tables glistening in the shallows of an ocean reef; diamond-encrusted tongues on a backdrop of smooth, pink-painted lips; horses majestic and jewel-adorned. The collages produced by Shakeel are mimetic insofar as they frame and showcase current aesthetic trends back to us in dream-like worlds for us to marvel at. The memetic quality they evoke is found in how Shakeel picks up on the aesthetic desires of the current moment with the bright pastel palette and soft, shiny sheen seen within the trend toward "coquette" chic circulating in online spaces. She juxtaposes this recognizable internet aesthetic with improbable scenarios and alluring textures. These are further made strange through the assistance of AI in generating the landscape collages. The use is intentional, as the AI image-generator she works with has its own aesthetic tendencies toward heightened color tones and a digital smoothness to images that is both present and at odds with the layer of textured jewels and props in her work.

The visual pleasure of the shimmering excess pushes us toward an uncanny sublime that, I believe, asks us to contemplate desire, beauty, and the impossible as part of our new digital worlds. They ask: What does it mean to be able to dwell as viewers in these landscapes? What concepts, insights, new imaginings can it inspire? In a moment fraught with distrust and uncertainty around the role of AI and digitally generated images, this work conceptually remixes the possible (digitally manipulated images) with the impossible (impractical placements of our everyday things in unreachable dreamscapes). In this way, Shakeel's work extends what the memetic practices of remix and collage can provide to contemporary audiences. Like some of the other memes and artists discussed in this chapter, there is here a gesture toward a future place that exists currently in the minds and visual expressions of these accounts. This is a conceptual space that, when its elements are placed together, does construct a newly imagined world, even if only online.

This world-building through visual juxtaposition and defamiliarization of the natural world is also present in the work of the artist who runs the Instagram account griefmother (@griefmother). Their posts range from traditional photomontage collages, to embroidering and imprinting on organic objects, to more standard image macro memes. The result is a truly unified whole that reveals complex and affective reverberations between the objects on display and the texts imprinted into them. This is a sculptural space rendered in the two-dimensional space of a digital art frame. In this way, the work of griefmother produces a spatial collapse between the discrete spaces of different kinds of media (photographic, sculptural) as well as the surreal spaces that are produced through these medial collapses.

In one post, a set of ripped-out photos of close-up rocks, rushing rivers, and moss are collaged together, with pressed clover leaves taped on top of the image. The cut-out black text on white paper on top of the image reads: "they are / familiar things / but I am a stranger now" (griefmother, "green green green"). The collage of nature photos defamiliarizes the landscape by arranging space differently than it appears in real life. The collage pushes this defamiliarization further by adding another layer of nature with the clover leaves, which complicate notions of scale since the clover is much bigger than the zoomed-out images of rocks in the photo. Further, the collage style used here also gets defamiliarized through the text's focus on strangeness. The wording acknowledges that "they" (the collage? the images of nature?) are familiar things, but the author is now a stranger. In the text, the author is made a stranger in their encounter with the collaged images. We cannot know what has made this strangeness occur, but we know that this is a present experience and has not always been the case. Time comes into play here, and a mystery arises that makes us question what led to the author's present experiences of strangeness. The dissonance expressed in the image between familiarity and estrangement encourages viewers to question their own relationship to seemingly familiar things and images. It is a subtle but complex set of associations held deftly within the frame.

A similar subtle address of the audience occurs in several other posts by griefmother where objects are altered in ways that "make strange" both the images and the texts. The first example is an image of a green apple cut in half, open-faced with the words "love changes you" carved out by what looks like stamp lettering into the apple flesh. The apples are photographed with high-contrast lighting on a deep black background. The top apple is fresh, but the one below it is rotting and its letters are browning. The image is defamiliarizing in its formal display of the apple's temporal dissonance between freshness and decay. The apple's trajectory gives a visual cue for the collage's conceptual theme that emotions like love change people, and with reference to the rotting fruits, perhaps not for the better. This makes strange the positive view of love changing us for the better, asking us to consider other ways it may alter us. A thematically related post has the same rich black background, with four colorful shapes molded out of clay. The top left shape is a red heart with the words "love changes you" stamped into the clay in the same lettering as the apple (griefmother, "my end of year"). The top right is a yellow-gold circle with the words "in the end." On the bottom of the image, a green triangle states, "I will not recognize," to the left of a blue square that reads, "the shape that I am." In the post, each shape has a subsequent close-up in the slides that follow this main one. Starting the phrase "love changes you" with the red heart references the more optimistic vision of the sentiment, as we tend to associate the icon with the hope and potential of love. As we progress through the phrase across different shapes, we move further and further away from the initial sentiment, ending with a square, which, alongside the wording "the shape that I am," evokes sharp edges and solid boundaries rather than the soft invitation of the heart shape.

Here, the conceptual play between word and image occurs again within the shapes changing across the images, giving us a visual enactment of how love can change the shape of a person to the point that they may become unrecognizable to themselves. There is a sense of grief and resigned sadness in this articulation of love. This is rendered all the stranger by Maria's use of primary colors and children's craft materials. It evokes a complicated kind of nostalgia and longing that equally plays into the reverberations between image and text in the piece. Maria's work on their Instagram account pushes the boundaries of the line between fine art, collage, conceptual art, and meme form. The tactility of the collages, the use of material objects, is itself a destabilizing juxtaposition that complicates our habituated relationship to the smoothness of digitally created images. It adds a visual appeal but also an evocation of physical texture that ruptures our viewing position into more visceral and sensual associations. This is a promising formal intervention into the blandness of the more corporate digital visual culture that dominates on capitalist platforms.

Spatial Collapse in Meta Meme Collages: The Case of Clusterduck

Another interesting form of spatial collapse that occurs is found in memes that stage intertextual confrontations within their frame and sometimes extend that frame beyond the bounds of everyday meme circulation on social media platforms. I am interested in these different instances, where artists and meme makers produce digital content that demonstrates the historic specificity and cultural precariousness of memes. Although far rarer than the kinds of spatiality evoked by many memes, these meta-approaches to memes can take the form of interactive meme archives and other compilations that group together memes in tenuous holdings only to reveal how saturated and disparate and fleeting memetic networks and chains of meaning are. For example, on their *Meme Manifesto* website, Clusterduck has created an interactive meme database called "The Iceberg" that takes the viewer on a journey through the history of memes.

The database is laid out as a series of memes that pop up on screen as if emerging from the depths of the watery backdrop as one explores (see fig. 1.7). The database includes a surreal, ethereal soundtrack of ambient noise, at times soothing and at other times unsettling, to accompany you on your journey. The database is described by the collective as "a voyage through the feels and the deepness" and offers viewers ten discrete yet connected meme-scape levels showing different points on the meme timeline ("Iceberg"). Together, the parts of the timeline reveal shifting formal trends over the last twenty years of meme production. You can either engage in a continuous scroll of the work, falling further and further into the meme rabbit hole the collective has created, or you can click on a diagram connecting the numbers one to ten, a clear but unacknowledged appropriation of the Kabbalah, or Jewish mysticist Tree of Life. Each number is matched with an illustration of an iconic meme image

FIGURE 1.7. Clusterduck, opening text from "The Iceberg."
From Clusterduck website, *Meme Manifesto*.

(trollface, Swole Doge, Pepe, Kermit, Clippy, Meme Man, etc.). When clicked, the icons take you to a specific point or level in the Iceberg's ten-part history.

Within each level, an opening title and distinct soundscape appears, setting the scene for the different memes collected to represent that moment of meme history. These histories are made up in part by Clusterduck's selection criteria of originality, iconicity, and usability and can be added to by anyone who visits their "Chat Archive" to submit memes for any of the levels. These are vetted by Clusterduck admin and first "passed through an antiracist, antisexist and antifascist sieve" (Clusterduck, "Chat Archive"). Part 1 includes the "rage face" illustration and the heading "The Internet Love Machine: The meme is born and Bill *Haz Cheezburger*." The memes in this section are largely the early meme genre of "demotivational" posters that replicate more standard motivational posters, using a stock nature photo framed on a black background with a phrase, word, or quote under the picture. The text is often darkly ironic and reflects the tone of early shitposting vernacular. If you click on any of the images, additional information will appear on the top left corner of the screen, including the name, year, user who made the meme, the platform it appeared on, and a live "learn more" link that brings you either to an info wiki like the *Know Your Meme* website, or a website of the content creator themselves.

The second part has Doge as the icon, and the entry text reads: "Just For Hits: The meme enters the mainstream and then dies," and as you scroll through the section, the memes begin to overlap, remix into one another, showing the conceptual collapse of certain viral memes into each other, rendered here also as a visual and spatial collapse. This is mirrored by the content and tone of the art piece. Once you get past level 6, onto "Meme Wars," things take a darker turn, until by part 9 the focus is on the dis-reality of meme logic. By level 10, it has slipped into incoherence with the title "TRIGGERED: text text text." This level includes a group of unhinged memes collapsing into themselves. It has images of SpongeBob that degrade through layers of remediation to a blurred unrecognizable visual mess. The experience of this level is an encounter with hypersaturated visuals that reflect dark despair and nihilism in both form and content, all supported by unsettling atonal sounds.

This is accompanied on the website by the "Meme Manifesto" itself as well as the "Chat Archive" and a "Detective Wall" that gathers the memes from "The Iceberg" into a more linear format of ten collections of memes laid out across the landing page. Each collage corresponds with a level from the iceberg that can be clicked to review Clusterduck's analysis of that level, or meme era. The Detective Wall offers viewers an attempt by Clusterduck to answer the pressing questions, "How to map the unmappable?" and "How to represent an object that, by its very nature, defies representation?" The chat archive is a space where audiences and users can upload memes to the ten different portals set out by Clusterduck.

The project thus exists as an art museum and archive, situating memes outside their intended infinitely remixable ephemerality. In institutionalizing them in this way, the collective creates an additional form of spatial collapse that bucks the trend of digital instability by creating a stable space to contemplate the impacts and import of meme culture. Here, there is an intentional laying-down of our everyday experiences of digital space within a meme museum; it is a new kind of memetic space to dwell in. Clusterduck, for me, stands out as a compelling example of spatial collapse, where there is a merging of meme culture with conceptual art, playing this out not within the capitalist platforms that seek to contain meme culture but through archival efforts to situate memes as a cultural force independent of those platforms. In this way, new spaces are opened for memes to be encountered that will have lasting effects that are not as easily upheld by the fleeting and precarious nature of a meme's circulation in social media contexts.

The Heterotopologies of Memetic Collage

To conclude this chapter, I want to briefly consider the political and activist possibilities of embedding forms of spatial collapse in memes and the kinds of heterotopic potential this affords us. In a post from April 2023, the Instagram account disssgrace (@disssgrace) posted a collaged photo of a gun with a large, colorful bouquet of flowers exploding out of the barrel, with bits of petals flying in all directions of the dark gray background. On the bottom, in black text on a white rectangle, is a condensed quote from Baltimore mayor Brandon Scott that reads, "When will the sanctity of American lives outweigh the sanctity of American guns?" (disssgrace, "When"). This is a straightforward collage meme speaking out against gun violence in America, posted in response to the Morgan State University shooting in Baltimore. It is, however, more than that if we consider the use of juxtaposition, defamiliarization, and spatial collapse in the meme. In this context, it is an evocative and moving image with a political purpose. A first level of defamiliarization occurs within the collage in the contrast between what we expect to emerge from a discharged gun, a bullet, and what we see, a vibrant bouquet. This is enhanced by the colors and textures of the image. Where the gun is a smooth black surface, the bouquet is a riot of color and texture that creates a visual dissonance between the two. When read alongside the quote by Mayor Scott, additional layers of resonance and defamiliarization occur.

The visual dissonance of the image is amplified through the contrast in the quote between the sanctity of life and the sanctity of firearms. In contemporary America, where firearms are widely available and mass shootings are startlingly commonplace, the protections within the law go to guns over people's safety. But in the image-text combination of the meme, it is impossible not to side with the flowers that exist in the image as a signifier of life. They are stunning, captivating, and beautiful. They are to be revered, just like, as the collage suggests, life safe from gun violence should be revered. Space is also collapsed here, as the bouquet-gun image is not possible to see or produce in our everyday spaces; it brings us to a realm outside of our lived space into a fantastical space of imagination and possibility. The disjunctive image stands in for a concept. It suggests gun violence is destructive, and a life free of gun violence should be protected. This image is trans-spatial and gives us an external site for contemplating life otherwise. This, I suggest, is where the power of defamiliarization as a critical tool can be seen in great clarity. It does, however, also exist in a variety of memes that employ collage as a tactic.

Across the examples in this chapter, memes reflect Foucauldian principles of heterotopology. Memes are "a constant" in human communication, but also they "take quite varied forms" (Foucault, "Of Other Spaces" 24). They hold "a precise and determined function in society" that can importantly be made to "function in a very different fashion" by countercultural reimagining (25). Memes as heterotopias can layer other meanings, practices, semiotic significations, and rhetorics within everyday spaces. In doing so, memes can shift society's fundamental understanding, and use, of them (25). Like other heterotopias, memes can juxtapose multiple real but incompatible spaces together (25). This is a quality that Foucault links to the cinema, and while I agree, I would argue that, as this chapter has demonstrated, it also links such spaces to visual practices of collage. However, as I will outline in a later chapter, this element of heterotopia in memes reveals how important a precursor film is to meme aesthetics in general. This is a point I will explore through my analysis of meme's tactical uses of montage.

Further, as Foucault suggests, in heterotopias we experience an "absolute break with . . . traditional time" (26). This is seen in visits to heterotopic spaces like a library or museum or when we are on vacation or at a festival (26). Memes also hold a heterotopic temporality, as our time spent consuming and sharing memes breaks us apart from traditional uses of time that are commonly segmented by labor and daily actions. In the same way that a vacation or festival operates out of time, so does our consumption of memes. Scrolling social media platforms is largely categorized as leisure or "down time." Like visiting a library or museum, the memes we consume bring us quickly into contexts, conversations, and cultural representations that are not immediately responding to our everyday environment. Memes may be topical, resonant, and quotidian in content, but our encounters with this content do not necessarily line up with the space or time we are in when consuming them. In these ways, the understandings of heterotopia outlined by Foucault help point to some of the spatial specificity of memes. I have been using the word *collapse* in this section to gesture toward the heaviness memes hold due to the many layers that make them up formally and culturally. They are, as the concepts of collage and remix suggest, media where meanings, images, ephemera, and contexts intermingle to culturally significant ends.

In his analysis of Occupy Wall Street (OWS) media outputs, Ryan Milner describes memes as "interdiscursive, intertwining multiple texts and commentaries into complex collages," noting how meme images circulated in the OWS context "would at times speak to each other" ("Pop Polyvocality" 2367). I find this useful for understanding memes as tactical collages that are located not only within their own frame of reference, which contains levels of intertextuality, but also in their relationship to the other discursive media circulating around them. Meme content is often taken out of its original time and space by the very virtue of being highly intertextual spaces of digital cultural remix. They are part of the simulacra culture that Baudrillard imagined, copies of copies with no origin. However, even more interesting is that within their intertextual milieu, there is a perhaps unanticipated outcome of dialogues running across the ruptured and dislocated images. Being outside of a grounded sense of space and time, memes float in their infinite remixing and spreadability; thus even when they are "of the moment," that specific time itself is utterly fleeting.

We are long enough into the culture of memes to be able to trace meme histories and show the various iterations of more popular memes over decades, watching them pop back up at a particular nexus where their brand of humor or cultural intervention fully encapsulates whatever is going on at a given place and time in global digital culture. In this infinite repeat, this iteration cycle, memes lack a sense of predictable coherence, as they are always already ruptured and dislocated from a firm textual foundation. Memes, in this way, are "intertextual archetypes," as they are often "cited or in some way recycled by innumerable other texts and produce in the addressee some sort of intense emotion accompanied by the vague feeling of a *deja vu* that everybody yearns to see again" (Eco 200). But the paradox here is that the moment is shifting sands, and thus there is no center, no hold to fix these meanings or access them fully once they are past. Temporality is destabilized, but so is space.

This is equally the case with memes as cross-platform phenomena that are recirculated across different media spaces, and each time, with each platform shift, another layer of the collage is added as it becomes a frame within a frame within a frame, almost unending. For instance, the cross-platform phenomena of Barbie and Barbieheimer memes in the summer of 2023, which I will take up in chapter 2, show this clearly. This is also seen within the curated carousel or slide decks on Instagram that I explore in chapter 3 and in the conclusion. There, you will find a variety of different forms of remixing, including memes reposted from other accounts, just screenshot with the original account's details included; a viral TikTok reel reshared with the app's logo at the end like a credit—these could be alongside original content made for the carousel. These are collaged together to make the carousel whole. This level of collage is what I would call more akin to assemblages. A point I ponder later in that same chapter is my thinking on the legacy and impact of memes in current discursive digital landscapes. In all these explorations of remix, collage, and intertextual merging, I aim to demonstrate that memes as a specific medium pull from other media, texts, spaces, and times to produce a unique digital cultural object. What most excites me about the presence of memes in our contemporary life is how readily they can be picked up and used by countercultural and activist communities to advance important forms of criticality. In the following chapter, I look particularly at how feminist memes employ forms of reenactment to critically address dominant ideologies of hyperfemininity and to undermine them in creative and often hilarious ways.

CHAPTER 2

Reenactment, Nostalgia, and Performative Ruptures

In this chapter, I take up the tactic of reenactment that is part of meme specificity. Reenactment is one of the core tactics explored in the book alongside collage, discussed in the previous chapter, and montage, which will be discussed in chapter 3. This chapter traces different types of reenactments found in memes and maps the forms of critical mimesis and temporal ruptures they evoke. This includes both narrative and iconic forms of reenactment, which are used by meme makers to very different ends. I am interested in how meme reenactments recall a longer history of reenactment, especially in feminist performance art from the 1960s onward. To make the connection more apparent, I link feminist meme practices in the present to the work of artists Annie Sprinkle, Pipilotti Rist, and Cindy Sherman. This allows for a sustained conversation across the chapter on the value and uses of mimesis as a form of critical intervention in feminist art. I take time to look at how nostalgia is operationalized as a form of what I call critical mimesis that is found across feminist art and memes in the last six decades. I think across this chapter about a variety of ways in which iconic forms of femininity have been employed in memes to trouble gender ideals from a feminist perspective. These include a consideration of Barbie memes in the first half of the chapter, and in the latter half of the chapter, a look at tactical uses of performances of feminine abjection and excess, drawing on a long trajectory of feminist performance art that equally explores the vexed figure of the ideal woman.

In the winter of 2023, *Barbie* was heralded as the most anticipated movie of the year (Dominick) and was named by *Teen Vogue* as "already the best, and most meme-worthy, movie ever" (Nesvig). This was perhaps facilitated by the fact that in the months leading up to the much-anticipated live-action *Barbie* movie (dir. Greta Gerwig), a promotional movie poster was created for each character that includes a bright sky-blue background and a sparkly, bright neon circle in the middle. For Barbie's poster, Margot Robbie's name is curved above her smiling image, and at the bottom of the circle, a smaller white font reads, "Barbie is everything." In contrast, Ken's poster frames Ryan Gosling in a blue sparkling circle, and just to the right of his face, the same white font reads, "He's just Ken," as a punch line to Barbie's poster. This poster format is replicated for numerous other celebrities in the film and builds the movie's comedic conceit that most characters in the film's diegetic world are either named Barbie or Ken. These cast posters reveal a long list of characters, all named Barbie, whose taglines reveal that they hold esteemed professional positions, including lawyer Barbie (Sharon Rooney), author Barbie (Alexandra Shipp), diplomat Barbie (Nicola Coughlan), Nobel Prize–winning Barbie (Emma Mackey), Supreme Court Justice Barbie (Ana Cruz Kayne), Pulitzer Barbie (Ritu Arya), and President Barbie (Issa Rae). Alongside these impressive posters of the Barbie women are a series of posters of male cast members whose taglines in the posters reveal that they all have the same name: "He's Ken too" (Kingsley Ben-Adir), "He's another Ken" (Simu Liu), "Ken, again!" (Ncuti Gatwa), and "You guessed it. He's a Ken" (Scott Evans).

These movie posters created a meme frenzy by circulating a template for social media users to insert their own images and thus meme it endlessly. This media frenzy took on a life of its own, and nothing in visual culture was immune to the Barbie meme treatment. One viral outcome of this was a secondary set of memes that remixed the original poster's joke, "Barbie is everything / He's just Ken," into a new meme event that celebrated women in famous fictional and real couples or duos. These memes elevated the women in the duo as "everything" and the male counterpart as "just a Ken." The memes that came from this include Elle Woods and her ex-boyfriend Warner Huntington III from *Legally Blonde* (2001), Katniss Everdeen and Gale Hawthorne from *The Hunger Games* (2012), Hermione and Ron from *Harry Potter* (2001), as well as real-life celebrity couples, including Miley Cyrus and Liam Hemsworth, and Princess Diana and King Charles (Richardson). In a moment of playful intertextuality, there was even a set of memes highlighting how great the characters Jo and Amy are over Laurie from director Gerwig's previous film *Little Women* (2019). For every fandom, there was a couple worth meme-ing, with the women vastly valued as the main character of their narratives over and above their supporting male counterparts.

The meme-ified *Barbie* movie posters and the subset of "Barbie Is Everything" memes reflect a compelling relationship between reenactment and meme aesthetics. In the poster, Barbie's iconic image is remixed and, more importantly, *reperformed* in a variety of scenarios that complicate the longstanding gendered associations tied to her character. This is an example of the mimetic reenactment I am concerned with in this chapter. It also makes clear the cultural currency that reenactment as a meme tactic holds in the current moment. The introduction of playful, tongue-in-cheek assertions of Barbie as everything she has never been afforded adds layers of complexity to a one-dimensional figure of patriarchal fantasy. The signifier becomes open to a greater range of connotations and possibilities. As such, the poster and the memes it inspired reflect the mimetic tactic of reenactment, which, I argue, is one of three core medium-specific elements of the meme medium more broadly.

In this chapter, I will explore in detail the tactical use of reenactment in memes and unpack its explicit ties to the concept of critical mimesis. I consider feminist memes' reenactments as a form of critical mimesis via the image of Barbie as well as other iconic figures of femininity. Across all examples, I outline tactics of reenactment that advance countercultural representations of gender. These memes include narrative reenactments of makeup routines that conceal a covert call for resistance en masse, reperforming movie images of femmes fatales, and reinterpreting hyperfemme celebrity culture from previous eras as feminist refusal.

One brief example of the meme-ing of culturally significant feminine tropes is seen in the popular remixes of the 1851 Pre-Raphaelite painting *Ophelia*, by John Everett Millais. In the painting, lush, full greenery crowds all sides of the image of Ophelia on her back and sinking into a riverbed with flowers scattered about. In one popular meme remix from AbsurdistMemer (@absurdistmemer), the text over the top reads, "omfg Hamlet / do I look like I care," while another version form Sick Sad Girlz (@sicksadgirlz) reads, "ill be like 'ive had it' and two seconds later I will start enduring" (see fig. 2.1); the comment "the girlz are enduring" is in the caption. These memes produce an irreverent comedic reversal of the tragic figure of Ophelia. Here she is reinscribed either as bored to distraction by Hamlet's morose monologuing or as an iconic image of women struggling, but "enduring," under the weight of their daily stressors, as they must in our neoliberal culture. In these examples, there is a tactical use of the "scripts" of Ophelia's femininity. Her status as a boy-obsessed, "manic pixie dream girl" who collapses under the weight of

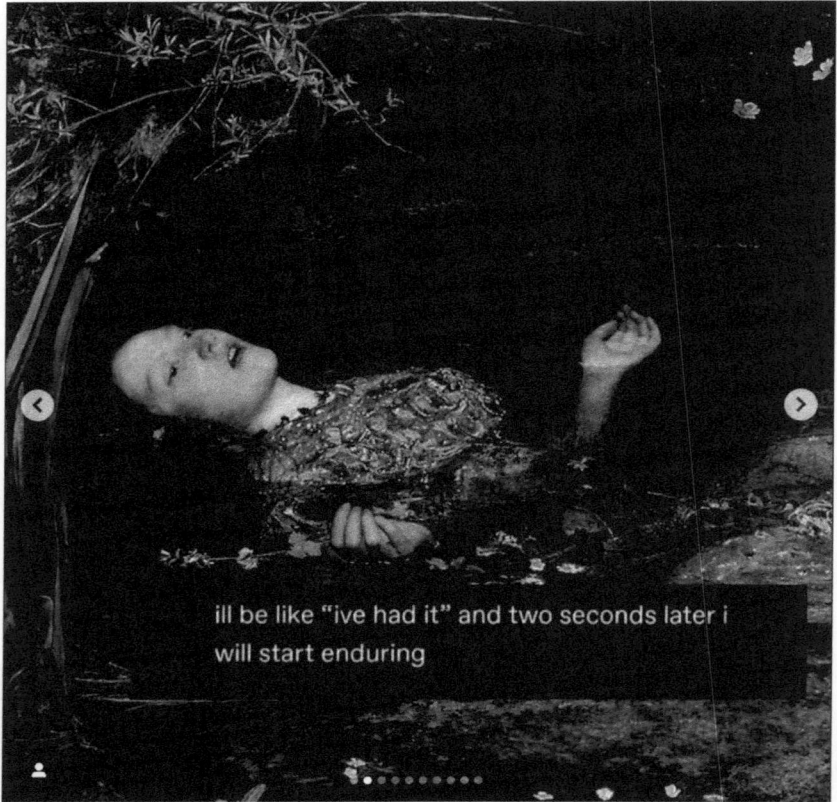

FIGURE 2.1. "girlz are enduring." Used with permission from Sick Sad Girlz (@sicksadgirlz).

her heartbreak is refuted and reinscribed as a woman both annoyed and with agency. The enduring legacy of Ophelia is upended, and the memes call out to like-minded feminist viewers to get in on the joke. This mimetic reenactment of fragile femininity allows the critical distance to engage with these tropes of femininity in ways that sometimes tilt to the humorous, and other times to the abject, nihilistic, or absurd.

The memetic use of reenactment here, with its potential for humor and the abject, is frequently found in other feminist memes that reperform the tropes of femininity in some way or another. It is also an element of feminist meme culture that directly connects it to forms of performance art in previous eras. Like the connections made in chapter 1 between collage-based memes and the work of Dada and photomontage art from the twentieth century, in this chapter, I will make the connection between feminist reenactment in memes and earlier inventions by feminist media makers in the history of art, particularly the work of Cindy Sherman, Annie Sprinkle, and Pipilotti Rist. Before exploring those connections, I want to take the time to unpack a few conceptual connections between reenactment and critical mimesis. Like the connections outlined between feminist meme makers and earlier forms of collage in the previous chapter, the connections I seek to outline here help advance the central thesis of this book, that memes are an art medium that employs formal tactics to advance persuasive perspectives. In the context of feminist digital culture, memes and their tactics of collage, reenactment, and montage offer valuable avenues for disseminating critical positions that counter cultures of misogyny circulating throughout our online and offline spaces.

Memetic Reenactment

My use of the term *reenactment* within meme culture draws on concepts of performativity and theatrical performance and the role they play within digital practices. Reenactment, as a formal tactic of memes, includes the reperformance of existing texts, images, and concepts into new cultural forms. This reperformance indexes the relationship between authors and audiences and the reenacted text's layered, intertextual past(s). While such reenactments have been a consistent part of cultural practices throughout history, I am interested in how they appear specifically in the current digital, participatory, and transmedia environments. In these multiplatform media spaces, the different "assemblages" of our connected media infrastructures produce "flexible" forms of knowledge that constitute a "networked and emergent reorganization of knowledge making" (K. King 1). These assemblages produce and rely on reenactments as both "experiments in communication" and "epistemological melodramas" that create a state of "pastpresents" (K. King 8). These past and present assemblages "very literally mutually construct each other" (K. King 12). There is value in considering the pastpresentness of memes, as it suggests how central the intertextual relationship between different temporalities is to the medium. With feminist memes, it is also an important way to interrogate how past gendered ideologies make their way into the present and are addressed by various levels of acceptance or critique and even sometimes ridicule.

I wish to outline two types of reenactments prevalent in internet memes. These include, first, text-based scripted, or narrative, reenactments. The most recognizable form of textual narrative reenactments delivers a short narrative vignette or script within the meme's frame, often without images. The staged dialogue usually includes character dialogue, timed comedic beats, and a punch line. The second form of reenactment includes iconic reenactments that reperform popular images in meme form. This is often seen through visual reenactments of iconic figures or scenes from pop culture (e.g., movies, TV shows, art, literature, other memes), or remixes of different images from the history of pop culture, art, and visual culture. Often these reimagined images are paired with text-based interventions that alter the status of the iconic object or image in critical, ironic, or absurd ways. Both forms of reenactment add new context to older cultural scripts and, in doing so, participate in forms of critical mimesis that I will define in greater detail below.

An example of narrative reenactment can be seen in the "We Riot" genre of memes. These include a narrator addressing an audience with a beauty or fashion crowdsourcing question until, as the generic meme script notes, "the men stop listening," and then the narrator shares a covert feminist message. In one memorable version, Washington journalist Aída Chávez (@aidachavez) tweeted: "ladies what's your makeup routine? I'm looking for a new foundation, preferably liquid but still matte and now that the men have stopped reading we riot at midnight." Replies to the tweet included "I use a shade called RAGE, and a blusher called BURN IT DOWN" (@lisadubbels), as well as "Personally, I'm into a powder named patriarchy, which I crush with my brush every morning" (@JeanneSeager), "Foundation in a shade with a bluish cast mixed with the blood of my enemies" (@heatherparlato), and "I'm searching for the most effective waterproof mascara that won't smear while justice finally rains down on the patriarchy" (@julianaillari). As seen here with the We Riot meme, the script usually begins with a word like "ladies" to clearly set out who is being addressed. In doing so, it mimics the vernacular of lifestyle influencer–speak that emerged within early 2000s blog culture. It uses this familiar address to suggest the narrator or blog author is a close friend or confidante of readers. The We Riot memes reperform this mode of address with a feminist narrator who aims to have other audiences tune out the frivolity of fashion and makeup discussions so that she may share plans with the "ladies" for a feminist riot. This strategic performance of the postfeminist consumer humorously advances a rebellious siren call to women to organize and revolt (MacDonald et al.; MacDonald and Wiens, "Feminist Memes").

This particular We Riot meme was posted in September 2018 during Dr. Christine Blasey Ford's testimony against then Supreme Court Justice nominee Brett Kavanaugh for sexual assault. The tweet and its 32,000-plus responses parody the consumerist impulses of postfeminism to mask participants' riotous rage in response to the hearings. Together they critically engage the labor required by postfeminism for individual women to be beautiful, replacing it with a meme-based articulation of collective resistance. This communal dialogue mixes humor with rage to articulate a feminist intervention that disrupts present contexts while also gesturing toward an imagined utopic moment of revolt in the future. This and similar tweets recall parallel sentiments present in the #WeRevoltAtDawn tweets and memes that originally circulated in the spring of 2016.

In narrative reenactments like this, the textual voice-over is central to the meme and requires viewers to "act out" the script mentally to get the crux of the joke. This means that two other forms of reenactment emerge from the initial reenactment present in the meme script. The first is in the ways in which it "hooks" an audience and requires a form of "reading" the script to engage with and get the point of the meme. In the act of reading the meme's text, a second reenactment takes place whereby the script is enacted in the mind of the reader. This involves the reader placing their own intertextual lexicon and affective responses onto the initial script, which further transforms its meaning in their mind. Often this scripted form of text-based reenactment meme encapsulates a recognizable aspect of human experience, which can prompt users to share on group chats or in their profile or stories with the qualifier "It's me," indicating how the meme encapsulates some aspect of their identity. If this reenactment of the script resonates enough with the reader, they will likely share it within their networks, thus reenacting the meme script further. This is one of the more interesting sites of reenactment in meme culture, as it metabolizes the intention of the initial meme, filtering it through the interpretations of the reader and resharing it as a meaningful site of identity performance. In this shift from text to performance of one's personality, the ideological force or cultural meaning of the meme embeds itself further as part of our everyday lives as consumers, performers, and agents within digital mediascapes.

Take for instance a meme that circulated during the first holiday season of the pandemic in 2020 responding to the overwhelming burnout, stress, and amplification of sexist double standards around domestic labor. In the meme, on a simple navy background, is the following script:

> That friend: 2020 Holiday season. . . . Ugh. Good thing my daily Pilates and hot pumpkin chai lattes keep me on top.
>
> Me: I'm like 20 mins away from ordering an emotional support guinea pig on a payment plan so keep it down Karen. (Cleaning For the Sitter)

In the side comments, the account adds: "In fact get out. You will NOT be meeting Captain Sir Sprinkles Alot. #Karen," with the additional hashtags

#holidayseason, #holiday, #quarantine, #quarantinelife, #funny, #meme, #sarcasticmeme, #bitch, #bitchmemes, #anxiety, #introvert, #crazymom, #friends, and #thanksgiving.

This meme from Cleaning For the Sitter (@cleaningforthesitter), a snarky, humorous account, critiques toxic femininity, perfectionism, and the outward performances of #winning through self-care and lattes. It locates this within the context of a holiday season unlike those that preceded 2020—where many were facing a radically different experience and all the grief and uncertainty that entailed. What this reenactment script allows for is a critique of capitalist excess and the pressures to perform. This is supported by the "narrator" by her admitting that she is not okay. It offers an inside joke addressed to the audience, giving them permission to also not be okay. Additionally, it locates this critique of capitalism-as-comfort as being in concert with a larger issue of whiteness and white femininity via the imagined Pilates- and pumpkin-latte-loving character of Karen. It plays out for viewers a recognizable slice of life for us to witness and resonate with, while also integrating critiques of white, capitalist, normative culture into everyday digital conversations.

It is because of its recognizable form as a scripted text that the meme can easily encapsulate complex critiques. The quick narrative vignette gets at the heart of this tension within feminist and broader public spaces around whiteness and capitalism, from a site of humor. The punchline "You will NOT be meeting Captain Sir Sprinkles Alot," for example, brings us back to the absurd concept in the vignette that the narrator is going to "stress buy" a support guinea pig, who she will name "Captain Sir Sprinkles Alot." This is both cute and ridiculous, which is what the meme tries to convey about people trying to evoke normalcy in unconventional times. Like Dadaist art, it suggests, in a less avant-garde form, that we have entered the realm of the absurd and should probably stop pretending otherwise.

The second form of reenactment, iconic reenactment, is perhaps even more directly tied to concepts of performance, as it often relies on the visual use of bodies and iconographic tropes that are repurposed to critical or comedic ends. This form of reenactment draws upon lexicons of images from visual culture and treats these images as if they were a script to be parodied, interrogated, and remixed either through a literal reperformance by a creator, or by taking previously circulated images and recontextualizing them with text. This appears as a consistent tactic in feminist media spaces online, because it usefully gets directed at the sexism found within representations of women across history.

Take for instance a meme from Alexandra K Wisnoski (@chaosgirlclub) that includes a picture of Paris Hilton from the early 2000s (see fig. 2.2).

FIGURE 2.2. "Ur in his DMs." Used with permission from
Alexandra K Wisnoski (@chaosgirlclub).

Hilton is at a party, straddling the side of a man's lap. She is in a three-quarter profile, staring directly at the camera, while the man embraces her midsection with his eyes half closed. The photo is taken in a darkened club environment, and there is a purple filter over the entire image to add depth and contrast. The text, white lettering with a punchy pink outline that gives the effect of a neon glow, reads: "Ur in his DMs / I'm in his subconscious deprogramming all his limiting beliefs." The meme is the first in a carousel of ten images, all with various pictures of Hilton and the "Ur in his DMs" refrain. The exception is the final image, which offers a less posed Hilton walking with a loose ponytail and a smoothie, with the text "This is not a meme page it's an intentional community." That final phrase is repeated as the caption within the comments section, hailing Instagram users into a feminist community with the creator.

There are many levels of performance and reenactment contained within this example. First is the reenactment of the posed image of Hilton, pushed into a new context beyond its origins as a celebrity photo documenting the early 2000s party scene (Welkos). It is an artifact that is iconic of a certain idealized form of femininity from a particular moment in time, remixed in the current moment for a different purpose. A second form of reenactment is the purposeful reappropriation of the "DMs" meme phrase and the remixing of it for critical ends. While the meme relies heavily on a reinterpretation and representation of the iconicity of Hilton, there exists a similar level of scripted reenactment, where the meme lays out a cultural script around DMs that it suggests warrants interrogation and reinterpretation.

Here historical images of Hilton, an icon of early 2000s "girls gone wild" culture, were reperformed as a critique of how we situate women as seductive and diabolical but also situate them as rebelliously feminist. The "Ur in his DMs" phrasing is a memetic script regularly remixed and circulated online. It extends from the practice of "sliding into" someone's DMs as an act of flirting. From this vernacular use, the phrase has been extended into a popular meme script where the narrator suggests that while the addressee of the text may be in the desired male's DMs, the meme maker–narrator is one level better— some place of control, or deeper intimacy, with their shared object of desire. The phrase is a flex for the narrator; they are "winning" the competition for the man's attention and are thus superior to their counterpart. The audience is given the chance then to decide who they identify with, the person in the DMs being perhaps "left on read" or the victor, who has greater access because of some cultural cachet they have named as desirable within the meme text. In some online spaces, the meme's narrator is winning because they provide a more desirable form of femininity, they are the veritable girl boss. However, in countercultural spaces, the meme itself becomes parodied, and the reasons why the narrator has made it to a greater level of connection begin to range from the vengeful, to the macabre, to the absurd. In doing so, these memes remix the larger cultural script of women competing for men's attention. This regressive stereotype gets turned upside down. In the example of Hilton, the rationale for going beyond the man's DMs is to reprogram his brain into a more feminist or progressive way of thinking. Matched with the image of Hilton, looking seductively at the camera while dominating the man she is straddling (her ex-boyfriend, model Jason Shaw), the meme suggests that the seductive forms of feminine duplicity associated with the concept of the femme fatale can be used to get close enough to break a man's limiting beliefs.

By considering the range of ways reenactment happens in memes, this chapter explores how temporality is used by meme makers to appeal to viewers and at the same time advance forms of dissonance and criticality through this pastpresentness of iconic images reimagined as resistant ones. As Hester Hockin-Boyers, Leslie Liu, and Danielle Rudnicka-Lavoie note, "gender norms (particularly feminine stylistic conventions) are subverted through memetic practices in ways that open up new possibilities for understanding gender, identity and embodiment" (para. 2). The mimetic practices of subverting gender norms outlined in the above examples are hardly new. Reenactments, both scripted and iconic, are present in earlier forms of feminist performance art and video art, where such mimetic doubling and critical mimesis produce forms of aesthetic rupture. This rupture, like uses of defamiliarization explored in the previous chapter, dislocates viewers from dominant ideas and images of femininity, suggesting new ways of reading and interrogating them. I want to take a moment in the following section to lay out some of the ways feminist performance art has devised practices of reenactment that offer road maps for the kinds of reenactment taken up by feminist memes in the present.

Reenactment as Rupture in Feminist Performance

Reenactment as a concept and practice is tied to historical legacies of performance art, which is a second countercultural historical art movement that informs current feminist meme aesthetics. Performance art uses the artist's body as a medium, placing it into an intentional relationship with both the performance environment and the audience. It does so to reenact social beliefs and conditions and, through this, raises critical questions on the nature of art, communication, expression, and audience/artist relations, as well as on the limits of spectatorship, traditional notions of perspective, and the value of aesthetic innovation within the commodified art market. Like the history of collage, performance art and the related concept of performativity speak to common tactics found in meme culture, including activist, queer, and feminist meme spaces. Relatedly, *performativity*, as I am using it here, is a theoretical concept exploring how our iterative enactments of textual and visual "scripts" both expand and confirm cultural meanings tied to our performances of them. This is useful for considering the forms of mimetic reenactment outlined in the previous section. Performance art as a medium of artistic practice is centered on the body as a tool for countercultural resistance. I wish to consider here the legacy of performance art, and feminist performance art in particular, as a precursor of the memetic tactics of reenactment employed by feminist media in the present.

Performance Art's Legacies

The legacy of performance art I wish to consider in more detail for its relationship to current-day feminist memes emerges from the post–World War II New York art world. This was a moment when artists were contending with the residual trauma of two world wars and the proliferation of bourgeois consumer culture. These social realities produced a severe distrust of Enlightenment truths, a disillusionment with the status quo, and a rebellious approach to the commodification of art among an emerging group of avant-garde artists. The turn to the body as an art medium was an act of resistance against both the catastrophic loss of human life and a refusal to become another commodity within the violence of nation-state capitalism. Performance art is not only an aesthetic rupture but also a response to various cultural ruptures in consciousness occurring around this time.

Allan Kaprow, a key driver in the uptake of Happenings, an early form of performance art, describes them as purposefully situated off the theatrical stage (16) to ensure they were not easily commodifiable (25). Happenings and performance art are the inheritors of earlier countercultural resistance developed in Dada. They offer radical juxtaposition, defamiliarization, and refusal through the collision of performing bodies in spaces outside of the theater proper. They are as much an assault on commonsense norms of the time as they are on the art conventions and traditions that sought to constrain them. My reading of memes as an aesthetic medium suggests that they are as much tied to forms of theatricality and performativity as they are to collage or montage. The composition of reenactment memes forces a theatrical encounter with the audience that destabilizes experiences of self and others in the mimetic encounter. This becomes a useful tool for feminist resistance now as it brings forward earlier experiments with performance art to meme culture so many decades later.

As Rebecca Schneider points out, the interventions made by the "explicit body" of much feminist art from this era emerged "with a certain *en masse* fervor" that was informed by both the ferment of avant-garde aesthetic precursors and a rapidly developing feminist politics (*Explicit Body* 3). For feminist artists in this era, performance art became appealing for how it opened new opportunities to critique the fraught history of women's bodies as objectified commodities in the history of representation and art (Jones; Schneider, *Explicit Body*; Pollock). A clear example of an earlier critical feminist aesthetic is seen in Gunvor Nelson's short film *Take-Off* (1972), which holds an uncanny enactment of Laura Mulvey's foundational call for the feminist disruption of visual pleasure (1975) despite preceding the essay by three years. In the film, a woman performs a striptease where she takes off her clothes, then her hair, her earrings, her ears, and finally her limbs, transforming herself into an alien object that blasts off into outer space. The woman's transformation from burlesque dancer to flying object enacts a visual pun on the term *take off*.

Consequently, the viewer's immediate expectations of visual pleasure are displaced into the realm of the absurd. While the initial minutes of the film provide an iconic image of female sexuality on display, the darkly humorous image of a bald, limbless, flying figure refutes this earlier image through an abject counterimage. There is a tension at the heart of the film, found in the shift between visual pleasure and the negation of such pleasure. The film's transition from erotic stage to outer space moves between and through sites of meaning. The first is the movement from the realism of the filmed image into the fantastical. This produces a liminal transformation between literal body and figurative prop, from objectified image of woman into an abject reinterpretation of what it means to take the "costume" or trapping of femininity fully *off*.

Nelson's film illustrates early feminist art's "ribald refusal to vanish" as well as its disruption "of normative 'appropriate' vision" (Schneider, *Explicit Body*). Such art encourages a reflection on social and cultural inequalities and suggests ways to transform them. The film *Take-Off* reflects a critical use of women's bodies that echoes similar tactics from feminist performance art. Nelson engages in tactics of performance and reenactment that produce forms of visual rupture. I define rupture here as a hostility between two positions, or the tearing apart of what is bound together. This definition includes within it both the action of breaking something and the product of this break, like how memes are both a creative act of doing and a product of that doing, or a thing done. What is bound together in the ruptures of feminist art is a paradoxical relationship between woman as image and women as subjects.

Feminist artists in the 1960s and onward enacted critical strategies of rupture to break down the hierarchy between subject and image. Such strategies reveal the instability of women as a signifier in both dominant discourse and the visual image. This splitting destabilizes the "image of woman," which is revealed to be a false projection. She is no longer a marker of desire and identity via her position as Other but is now presented as an illusion. The terror of ontological uncertainty behind the illusion becomes fully apparent in strategies of rupture and allows feminists to cleave women's subjectivity from the culturally projected image of femininity that it has historically been bound to.

That fictional construct of woman is precisely what gets picked apart and reperformed in feminist art and feminist meme cultures alike. For instance, Annie Sprinkle's performance-based photograph, and proto-meme, *Anatomy of a Pin-Up Girl* (1991) is useful to consider in relation to meme accounts that reenact idealized forms of femininity as a form of critical mimesis. In *Anatomy of a Pin-Up Girl*, a photographic image centers on Sprinkle with her hair in an updo, wearing a red and black leather bustier, wide red lace choker, black elbow-length gloves, black nylons attached to red garter straps coming off the bustier, and thigh-high lace-up red stiletto boots. The image is an index of a desired vision of a sexualized image of a woman. This is complicated by the words written in thick black handwriting all around Sprinkle's body. The writing includes arrows to different parts of Sprinkles's posed image with very *un*sexy insights informing viewers what goes into making such a successful sexualized image of perfect, desirable femininity. For instance, the arrow pointing to the red choker on her neck states, "Choker is really choking me," and the arrow pointing to the cinched waist of the bustier reads, "Lungs restricted. I can't breathe." The text is disruptive, it is an intervention that undoes the script of the image, revealing the kinds of pain and bodily constraints required to meet this required image of heteronormative desire.

The dialogue script "reveals" the secrets behind what goes into making a pinup continue, showing what parts of the pinup costume cause pain (boots are too small, take nineteen minutes to lace up), what kinds of tricks of the eye it requires (black nylons make thighs thinner; bra is too small, to make breasts look bigger), and what it hides of the real body behind the image (her hemorrhoids don't show in this pose; the bustier hides her very big belly). This set of reveals or confessions offers us an inside look behind the false image of femininity. In *Anatomy of a Pin-Up*, Sprinkle demystifies the process and makes it look downright unappealing. It also leaves us asking: Who is this for? What is the point if it hurts and takes so long? What other, less labor-intensive ways could Sprinkle, and other pinup girls use to represent themselves? What would this look like? The mimetic reenactment of the pinup presentation and its accompanying textual deconstruction cathects us as viewers out of the fantasy image of Woman and into another space of more nuanced consideration. It relies on making abject what is valued as appealing in dominant heteronormative culture.

Performative Ruptures in Feminist Memes

The overlap between earlier feminist art and recent feminist memes now speaks to how visual icons can hold cultural ramifications across a variety of social histories. Icons are "concrete images that have rhetorical sway given their recognizability and circulation," which via their resonant meanings can hold deep significance for viewers (Woods and Hahner 77). In this way, "the life of an image is principally social" insofar as it can both evoke uncertainty, disdain, or fear but also "galvanize the chorus" that rallies around it (Woods and Hahner 77). In both cases, the icon's status is premised on a "collective social imagination that personifies the image as acting on others" (Woods and Hahner 78). The icon's circulation, and the way it captures our attention, shapes our world and shapes how we see it. It also determines how we relate to others based on our own personal investments in or repudiation of it. In such a schema, playing critically and mimetically with iconic images opens the space for rupture; feminist art has excelled at taking given notions of what a woman should be and turning those on their head. Feminist memes can often be found doing the same.

This is clearly demonstrated through Barbie as an iconic image that has stood in for a much larger cultural schism around women's role within accepted heterosexual relationship dynamics. Take for instance how the alt-right and far-right media outlets decried the *Barbie* movie for the audacity to have Barbie explore life outside the confines of her relationship to Ken (Shapiro; Monteil). In the "manosphere," men with microphones yelled loudly about how even watching the movie made you a beta male, which in their world is the last thing you would want to be (more on this in chapter 4). Women, on the other hand, started questioning their relationship dynamics with partners after seeing the film. What followed was a surprising phenomenon where relationships crumbled and whether you would watch the movie or not became a first date litmus test (Weiss; Shearing). All this discourse played out across social media sites, news sites, Substack reflections, and podcasts. All of it in response to the reimagining of Barbie by a feminist filmmaker in the twenty-first century, disrupting the safe, predictable icon of Barbie as a feminine ideal. In doing so, she drew ire and galvanized new community formations on both sides of the "gender war" divide.

Feminist memes produce their own forms of rupture in response to such cultural churning, using both textual and iconic reenactment. These memes undermine the persistent paradox of women's objectification and belittling by dominant digital cultural discourse. Within feminist memes, Barbie has held a long-standing appeal that predates the movie's release by several years, and the memes that accompany the *Barbie* movie's release are not the only instance of Barbie existing in meme culture. There have been several meme accounts that use Barbie's image at the center of their content, since the mid-2010s. These include the now largely inactive accounts, Sociality Barbie, Barbie Savior, and barbie birkin. Sociality Barbie (@socialitybarbie) reenacted lifestyle influencer photos, including visits to pumpkin patches and Barbie leaping in silhouette on the beach, while Barbie Savior (@barbiesavior) critiqued white saviorism by reenacting a white Barbie's trip to "save Africa," with all the colonial and exploitative connotations that conjures. barbie birkin (@barbiebirkin) offered a Barbie version of a luxury fashion and travel account. In one of my personal favorites, dyingbutfine (@dyingbutfine), artist Kristel Jax places Barbie in various tableaus with text overlay musing on mental health struggles and existential dread.

I want to consider in more detail some examples from the Instagram account Trophy Wife Barbie (@trophywifebarbie), run by artist Annelies Hofmeyr. This account includes a formally modified version of a Barbie doll, with large antlers emerging from her head, situated in a variety of domestic tableaus with different forms of abjection present. Hofmeyr explains that "the antlers are a physical representation of a label imposed on her and her friends, likening her/them to hunting trophies" (qtd. in Finkel). In the account, antlered Barbie dolls are placed in miniaturized everyday scenes that use holidays and relevant political events to tackle issues like censorship, reproductive justice, bodily pleasure, trans rights, and cancer awareness. Hofmeyr's Barbie, despite the antlers, is still a blonde, thin, stylish image of neoliberal white femininity consumer culture. She is placed in scenes marred by menstrual blood, violent vengeance, and excess; placed beside unexpected elements including oversized glittering genitalia; or poised in uncharacteristic actions like Barbie giving the viewer the finger or collapsed on a couch with messy hair and smeared mascara. Her formal reenactment of Barbie, modified with abject and unbecoming or unladylike accessories, is reminiscent of the forms of rupture advanced by feminist collage artists like Höch, and feminist performance artists in earlier decades.

In the account's first post from 2016, Hofmeyr shares a picture of Barbie in a white fitted satin dress with lace on the torso, her antlers arcing upward and with a somewhat golden hue (see fig. 2.3). There is a sheer wedding veil billowing from her blonde, artfully curled hair. She is holding the head of a decapitated Ken with his eyes crossed out in hot pink tape. In her hand is a yellow plastic sword like the ones that hold skewered citrus in cocktails. This sword, however, is held upright by Barbie and is dripping blood. On the bright pink wall behind her is a splattering of blood. The caption reads, "Yay! My divorce went through today!" From this first post, we see the account's intention to, as Hofmeyr describes, "explore gender issues and the modern female identity while highlighting the limitations of labels" (qtd. in Finkel 2018).

Hofmeyr uses Barbie strategically because dolls are "non-threatening and allow us to project our feelings onto them" (Breslin). Barbie's status as an

FIGURE 2.3. "Yay! My divorce went through today!" Used with permission
from Annelies Hofmeyr for Trophy Wife Barbie (@trophywifebarbie).

icon means Hofmeyr is "able to circumvent censorship and talk about more
challenging topics" (Breslin). The antlers become a defamiliarizing trope that
cues audiences to the disconnect or dissonance between the image of Barbie
upheld as a bastion of feminine ideals for sixty years and the contradictions
and abjection of living under the expectations of femininity in the twenty-first
century. The account is a play on the meme trope of "expectations vs. reality"
filtered through a feminist aesthetic lens.

This relationship between reenactment and nostalgia seen in Hofmeyr's
Barbie memes relies heavily on intertextuality within the iconic image as a
vehicle for establishing this complex and layered sense of time. Like with the
Barbie movie and promotional posters, these memes are imitations of the
well-established lifeworld of the Barbie empire, which since 1959 has embedded a vision of femininity into the Western cultural imaginary. At the core of

this intertextual mimesis of feminist Barbie memes is the displacement of heteronormative hyperfemininity. Barbie's idealized femininity articulates values of whiteness, thinness, and a capitalist-consumerist lifestyle.

The sheer variety of Barbie memes and different critical interpretations on femininity suggests that visual culture, especially iconic aspects of it, can experience an "afterlife" (Hale 510) through performative and intentional forms of digital mimicry. These memes reveal a broader cultural practice of critical mimesis within memes. Barbie memes reperform the script of femininity attached to Barbie and, as I discuss later in the chapter, other nostalgic and iconic images of women. They reenact the long-standing scripted images of idealized feminine whiteness, thinness, and wealth, establishing a temporality to the intertextuality of Barbie as an everywoman. The temporality suggests that the pastpresentness of the Barbie image perhaps needs to be interrogated in the present and probably for critical ends. Barbie is *everything* the past required of women—and the memes suggest that perhaps we should know better by now. Meme culture in this instance draws on and plays with the anachronistic visual markers of Barbie, often out of step with feminist reimaginings of womanhood in the present, to advance current conversations around constricting gender norms tied to neoliberal consumer life. This, then, is a clear example of how the reenactment of cultural icons and scripts in memes produces forms of critique, or what I, drawing on the work of feminist performance scholarship, am calling critical mimesis.

Critical Mimesis

Feminist memes and the aesthetic legacies they draw offer us insight into the tactic of critical mimesis through their use of reenactment in different forms. Mimesis as a practice brings together the act of "artistic representation" and "general claims" or interventions "about social behavior" (Potolsky 2). Mimesis is social commentary in representational form. Mimesis wants not to reproduce reality but rather "give a persuasive . . . simulation of it" (Potolsky 4); it is distinct from reality yet integral to how our reality is shaped. The connection between memes and mimesis raises necessary questions about how we as social media users employ digital texts that we make and share to comment on the social and cultural landscape we live in.

There is a theatricality within mimesis that is present as well in memes. Memes encourage a centering "of the relationship between art and its audience," one that is clearly "grounded on the relationship between spectacle and spectator" (Potolsky 8). I wish to foreground this theatrical element of memes between spectacle and audiences further. Meme makers craft imitations of social and political life as a means of furthering different types of in-group discourse, opening the site of the meme up to paratextual conversations. The value of mimesis is that it offers us forms of "pleasure and knowledge" as well as "fictional distance from things" so that we can "learn from [such] representations" (Potolsky 37). This distancing through mimesis is vital for taking the time to consider and discuss the complex and ever-changing flow of contested ideas, vitriol, violence, and political restrictions directed at women, femmes, trans, nonbinary, and genderqueer communities. This requires different forms of conceptual collapsing, reenactment, and techniques of defamiliarization that the meme form is well equipped to provide via mimesis. Feminist and queer memes broadly employ reenactments of gendered stereotypes to offer the kind of distancing needed for adopting critical perspectives on "common-sense" gendered ideologies circulating in dominant culture.

Returning to the We Riot genre, in this case, the memes enact feminist rebellion through narrative scripts that address the audience directly and provide short comedic vignettes that invite paratextual replies. The script is written and performed as it is encountered, remixed, and recirculated. The tone is set in the original tweet, and it is matched by those who choose to join in. In this way, it not only produces a textual script to be read and acted out in one's mind but then invites audiences to take up the task of extending the script as performers and producers. Followers pick up the context of the thread's parody, adding to the script in a variety of humorous ways. See for instance chat lunatique's (@heatherparlato) aforementioned response to the original question from Aída Chávez, "ladies what's your makeup routine?": "Foundation in a shade with a bluish cast mixed with the blood of my enemies." And @datingdecisions's follow-up question: "Anyone know of a good eyeliner that literally allows looks to kill?" Each of the responses offer a mimetic enactment of dominant social expectations of what women are (and perhaps should be) talking about): makeup, beautification, personal self-improvement to maintain status as visual objects. They also imitate Chávez's parody of this, recognizing the humor and the impulse toward riotous actions against patriarchal constraints. Indeed, the thread evokes the most unladylike impulses: to kill, burn, and mark themselves with their enemy's blood. It is through the suggested enactment of a violent feminist resistance that the memes index cultural pressures and desires faced by women.

A somewhat related feminist meme trend is one that takes up the figure of the bog witch as a more preferable route to freedom than that suggested by the heterosexual Disneyfication of neoliberal "girl boss" culture. In a narrative reenactment meme from Roxi Horror (@roxiqt), a series of statements are ordered sequentially, corresponding with the fictional "Me" characters of the meme at different stages of her life. "ME, 10" states, "I want a prince to marry me so I can be a princess," while "ME, 20" wishes "to be the queen of my own castle," and finally, "ME, 30" concludes with the punchline "I want to be an old witch that lives in a swamp." The trajectory here, from idealized vision of feminine happily-ever-after to being one's own queen, is upended and ruptured by a figure that is not accepted or well contained by dominant culture—that of the bog witch. The meme thus uses a reenactment of the well-worn script of little girls wanting to be princesses, to provide a critical mimetic pathway to rupture and refusal of the original script. While the bog witch is not welcome within the smooth flow of cultural expectations, her freedom is found (and yearned for) in her being an objected, cast-off misfit; no one will mess with the bog witch.

This rejection of dominant femininity for a more disruptive and uncontrollable version of womanhood is reflected in Pipilotti Rist's earlier performance art video *I'm Not the Girl Who Misses Much* (1986). In the work, Rist performs a version of femininity that is steeped in long-standing cultural stereotypes and value systems, to resistant ends. Rist's five-minute video riffs on the Beatles' song "Happiness Is a Warm Gun" (1968), written by John Lennon about Yoko Ono, which begins with the line "She's not the girl who misses much." In the video, Rist, a conventionally attractive young white woman in a stylish black dress, tap-dances frantically around an empty space, singing, "I'm not the girl who misses much." Due to the pixelated quality of the video, Rist is a blurry figure moving in and out of frame, sometimes tap-dancing, sometimes sliding down the wall slowly until she is almost off-screen, and other times making maniacal faces up close to the camera lens. The video manipulates the speed of Rist's movements, speeding it up, slowing it down. This causes her singing to sound at times like a high-pitched chipmunk and other times like a heavily sedated man. Rist's low-cut dress does not always contain her breasts, which fall out and become another form of excess or lack of containment in the video. The video offers different forms of reenactment and critical mimesis that undermine an idealized image of woman.

First, in the audio Rist offers an homage to Yoko Ono and her art. The aesthetic choice of a pixelated video screen equally indexes the early video art of Nam June Paik. This visual reenactment of early aesthetic movements creates a dialogue or trajectory between Rist and them. Second, Rist shifts the song lyrics from "She's not" to "I'm not," which produces a sense of agency in the reenactment that is not available in the original wording. When Lennon writes that Ono doesn't miss much, is it a positive assessment or is she breaking some rule by noticing instead of accepting and acquiescing? Rist's shift to "I'm not the girl who misses much" confronts the first iteration, taking responsibility for being the type of girl who sees the mirage for what it is. The video pairs this with an image of femininity that is utterly rebellious in its excesses and abject performance. It also plays on cultural tropes such as the notion that to refuse cultural logics of femininity means that one is mad, or unstable, or needing containment. The fact that Rist chose an empty white space, intentionally or not, indexes asylums and the long history in the nineteenth century of women "hysterics" being admitted and contained in mental hospital settings when they wouldn't comply with the gendered expectations of their times (Beizer; Didi-Huberman). In acknowledging that she knows what's expected of her, she points to how she doesn't miss much. Rist thus offers a form of critical mimesis that indexes cultural contradictions of femininity in order to undo them.

Earlier feminist art's interest in "social and identity politics and the deep interrogation of subjectivity" (Jones, *Body Art* 8) is also present in feminist memes exploring social movements, representation, and agency under capitalism. Most pertinent is how feminist memes employ women's bodies as performing and performative subjects to push forward critiques of the objectification of women in the current moment. I see similar efforts occurring in the work of feminist meme accounts like Trophy Wife Barbie's that show abject bodily excess. In an interview reflecting on the video, Rist reveals that it initially struck a chord with many viewers who would tell her how much they saw themselves in the video. The formal tactics of critical mimesis in the video produced affective resonances with audiences. This mirrors a similar way that memes draw in and impact viewers and how this helps them achieve their popular status. There are shared aesthetics between the memes and feminist media art I consider, which actively work to ensure forms of intersubjective relationality through an intentional address of the audience. This is a clear example of critical mimesis that is shared across earlier performance reenactments and those found in memes.

Critical mimesis in memes relies on this intertextuality to gesture toward the layered forms of meaning that textual or iconic reenactment carries within it. It is also bolstered by the layered sense of temporality or 'pastpresentness' that such reenactments bring forth. Memes are never simple or straightforward acts of communication. Built into their very specificity is a framing of communication as a performance, or a reenactment of past scripts, cultural references, times, spaces, affects. The layered meanings inherent in meme communication inform how we make and engage with memes, suggesting we are all in on an elaborate reperformance of culture that we willingly reproduce and tarry with.

The Feminist Performative Gestus

Extending the discussion of mimesis within performance studies, Elin Diamond defines it as "both the activity of representing and the result of it—both a doing and the thing done" (*Unmaking Mimesis* v). Diamond calls for us to "embrace this doubleness," as it reflects the existing self-reflexive nature of feminism (v). For Diamond, this is because woman "in mimesis is always more and different than she seems" (v). By this logic, woman as a subject is always more than what she performs. This encapsulates well the counter-practices of feminist digital media outlined in the Chávez Twitter thread, as it indexes the need to consider the role of the historical and the corporeal within forms of mimetic critique. Online performances of rage and refusal are of course tied to offline protests. The intersecting dialogues occurring across these spaces are important to consider, especially in determining how discourses function through the exclusionary logic of platforms. The We Riot memes are not exempt from this critical limitation—the types of femininity that they mimic are dominant beauty standards tied to cis, white, hetero, upper-class positions. Mimetic action operates as a vector that enacts representations consciously. In this duality, Diamond sees possibilities for disruption that reflect the Brechtian "gestus" contained within her understanding of mimesis (Diamond, "Brechtian Theory").

Diamond defines gestus as "an action" that makes "visible" for the spectator the prevailing "social attitudes" of a work (Diamond, "Brechtian Theory" 89). In theater, the "gestic moment" both "explains . . . (and) exceeds the play," illustrating for viewers the "ideologies that inform its production" (90). A large part of how memes operate within social media platforms is that they are offered as bite-sized theatrical scenarios that play out some relevant social drama, putting it on display for spectators to encounter in the privacy of their own personal algorithmic curated content. Through the gestus of critical mimesis, memes enact scenarios for the viewer that merge contexts, affect, performances, and jokes. In doing so, new modes of temporalities emerge that discursively make meaning of what is on display and metabolize it into the miasma of our daily meme consumption. When meme producers rely on abject, excessive, nonnormative scripts within their mimetic representations, they open the potential to disrupt this process to critical ends. The memetic use of this tactic does not emerge from a vacuum; rather, feminist artists have been parodying idealized versions of women's image for decades, as the examples from Rist, Nelson, and Sprinkle make clear.

Gestus and Abjection in Feminist Memes

Memes also include a Brechtian gestus in their formal logic. Feminist meme makers, like other feminist artists before them, imitate standardized images of femininity to disassemble them for critical insights and gestures of refusal. This often requires some form of abjection that, in its excess, surpasses the idealized images and places viewers in a place of discomfort. The culturally abject, most often tied to women and femme-coded bodies, includes body fluids, dirt, foods—often tied to bodily areas that are thresholds or boundaries between inside and outside or self and other. These inside and outside thresholds of blood, mucous, and saliva contained and expelled by the body mark the border between subject and object and hold vast cultural meaning (Kristeva, *Powers* 143). The abject reveals the impossibility of clean borders and the tidy separation of binaries. This use of abjection is one way to evoke the Brechtian double gestus Diamond refers to.

In Hofmeyr's work through the Trophy Wife Barbie account, this comes across in the antlered Barbie's excesses of blood, violence, masturbation, insatiable sexual desires, saggy skin, fat rolls, unmitigated consumption of alcohol and food, smeared makeup, and love of swearing and flipping the bird. This Barbie is the avatar of everything a good girl does not do. Hofmeyr's reenactments of an antlered Barbie evoked a range of abject imagery for critical ends. In a frequently shared and reposted image on the account, Barbie sits on a toilet in a bathroom with the walls covered in blood. Barbie is in a hot pink T-shirt, looking down in a deflated resignation at the blood dripping from her hands and the side of the toilet. Further blood is shown on the white cotton underwear at her ankles and in the puddles of blood beneath her feet. The image caption reads "Heavy Period Feels" for anyone not yet clear on the source of the crimson excess covering all surfaces of the room and doll.

The meme reenacts a miniature tableau, with objects in the room resembling DIY versions of everyday items found in a bathroom. The tableau indexes the reality that some bodies menstruate, and this is messy and often uncontainable despite societies' ongoing efforts to sanitize and hide away this evidence. The image works with abjection to confront viewers in ways that exceed the more popular use of memes as entertainment. It instead makes visible the contradictions and inadequacies of social attitudes around menstruation. This again points to the connection between the performative gestus and forms of discursive, intentional undoing through critical mimesis. In this way, Hofmeyr models a way out through vice and through the "failings" of the body that cannot uphold the requisite perfection placed upon it by social standards. Again, this performative representational refusal is reminiscent of forms of feminist media art from previous eras that worked with abjection to assert a refusal of patriarchal norms of women.

Another helpful illustration of memetic uses of abjection and performative excess is found in one of the more popular Barbies to come out of the *Barbie* movie—that of Weird Barbie, played by queer comedian Kate McKinnon. In the movie, Weird Barbie lives on the outskirts of Barbieland and is rarely engaged unless a Barbie begins to look less than perfect. Once this happens, Barbies make a pilgrimage to Weird Barbie's very colorful cubistesque house to seek council. Weird Barbie gets her name from the fact that her hair is short and choppy and her face has scribbles across her forehead and a black circle outlining her right eye. In short, she looks like a Barbie that young kids have enacted failed fashion experiments on. Weird Barbie wears a neon pink short satin mini dress with layers of tulle crinoline and vibrant green snakeskin cowboy boots and is often found in her house doing the splits against a wall or on the floor in a strange bodily configuration. She in no way upholds the standard of perfected femininity, and there is a subtle suggestion that because of this, she has gained a certain form of wisdom and freedom. Weird Barbie was a popular Barbie in memes surrounding the movie's release. In the official release poster, Weird Barbie's body is turned to the left with one booted leg up in the splits with her head turned straight toward the viewer with a piercing stare. The punchline caption reads, "This Barbie is always in the splits" (see Sharf).

The first layer of doubling that Weird Barbie introduces is an alternative iteration of Barbie that does not comply and yet is, crucially, still a Barbie. She looks strange, her body does strange things; she bears the markings of those who play with Barbies and yet have become somewhat frustrated with the monotony of feminine perfection and express that through creating with their Weird Barbies images of both refusal and failure. As we know from Jack Halberstam, such failures offer us a queering of our heteropatriarchal capitalist systems (*Queer Art*). Weird Barbie is both an iconic image of woman and a critical doubling that shows us the impossible contradictions of trying to emulate that iconic stature. In the immediate days after the release of *Barbie*, a meme circulated that shows a still image of McKinnon as Weird Barbie, looking pointedly and imploringly at someone off-screen with the text caption "POV: You watch the Barbie movie and Weird Barbie is the character you most identify with" (Kleivset, "Weird Barbie"). The meme shows us the tactical

FIGURE 2.4. "Weird Barbie." Screenshot from Birgitte
Kleivset's (@smeigedag) Instagram account.

reenactment of a textual script that must be acted out (and identified with)
by the viewer, as well as an image of nostalgic and critical reenactment of the
iconic image of Barbie in the modified form of Weird Barbie, both on-screen
and as an image captured and used as the basis for the meme's textual intervention (see fig. 2.4). What it also does is locate a temporality that gets reac-
tivated in the memetic present. It gives us a "slice of life" vignette, enabling
viewers of the meme to recall an experience of watching the *Barbie* movie,

and suggesting via the trope of the "POV" that a particular viewing experience is being recognized and renarrated in the present as a form of creating resonances and online community in-group bonding. The memes act almost as a confessional; the creator and viewer align themselves with Weird Barbie to stand against more standard expectations of the dominant forms of femininity we should be identifying with.

I am interested in Hofmeyr's, Kleivset's, and other meme artists' uses of abjection and excess and how these echo earlier uses of it in performance art to challenge gendered categories such as proper and improper or clean and unclean for activist ends. Exploring the bodily taboos around abjection in feminist memes and art subverts the gendered hierarchies that situate women as excessive, irrational, emotional, and full of different kinds of leakage that threaten the rational order of the patriarchal world. Nelson's film addresses cultural taboos against women's sexual agency by veering into an illogical scenario that pokes fun at the male gaze. Rist performs an unwilling subject of masculine desire, turning it into one of excess and psychological leakage. Sprinkle demonstrates just how much labor is required to uphold that gaze and how painful it is for the bearer of it. Hofmeyr adds to this and rejects the separation of discrete boundaries by centering blood, women's pleasure, and affective states in her work. In placing earlier forms of feminist art such as Nelson's film, Rist's video, and Sprinkle's performance art in dialogue with feminist memes like Hofmeyr's in the present, I hope to illustrate that feminist uses of reenactment advance different forms of critical mimesis by pointing out cultural contradictions and ideologies.

Across Hofmeyr's images, these two concepts become the guiding force for the images and the account's brand. This is seen for instance in the popular image of antler Barbie in perfect feminine makeup and clothing, head slightly tilted to one side, and with both hands giving the middle finger to the viewer on either side of her perfect smile. The tagline for this post is "When people tell me to smile," with the hashtags #TrophyWifeBarbie and #shitjustgotreal. For Diamond, an important effect of the gestus in feminist theater is that it "undermines the stability of the spectatorial 'self,' for in the act of looking the spectator engages with her own temporality" ("Brechtian Theory" 90). Equally, the gestus of critical mimesis in feminist and other critical meme cultures places versions of dominant culture on display to undermine and satirize them. It does so, often, through a form of reenactment that relies on audiences being interpellated by a set of recognizable intertextual references that it proceeds to alter for the purpose of evoking a critical dialogue within the spectator, who feels destabilized by their affective or conceptual reaction to the remixed or reimagined image or scenario on display. This back-and-forth between the forms of temporality evoked by mimetic meme images holds layers of intertextual timeliness in their frames. How these are encountered and altered by a spectator at a specific moment in contemporary cultural flows is precisely what consistently locates audiences into an awareness of their own temporality while consuming memes.

Reenactment reveals memes as a form of "culture creation" that operates at "multiple levels," including "through the self and through the other" (Woods and Hahner 49). They are a form of "communication" but also "a mode of deliberation" (49). Memes merge "action and invention" that "require and encourage participation in their creation" (52). This includes developing a means of "enticing" users into "audience engagement" through their formal properties and tactics (52). The Barbie memes and others considered up to this point in the chapter have demonstrated multiple levels of cultural baggage and self-expression embedded in feminist digital culture. Through the layered and nuanced meanings contained within, memes offer feminist audiences a mode of deliberation that asks us to actively participate in the meaning making we ascribe to them and to determine what we do with them once they are in the world. In this way, feminist memes that employ tactics of reenactment are not one-offs to laugh and scroll by quickly; they can sometimes engage us in ways that compel us into action. Feminist memes employ reenactment, and all the ironic, sometimes abject and excessive, critical perspectives they include, to address the standard roster of women icons in inventive and resistant ways. They give us a lexicon of images of refusal and rebuttal to use in our own digital attempts at political and social change.

Iconic Reenactment and Social Change

What makes memes significant is that when done well, their intentional mode of direct address "speak[s] to a contingent audience of strangers who may number in the millions" while also managing to "amplify the scale at which" their invitation to invention and action "might occur" (Woods and Hahner 52). Building from Woods and Hahner, I wish to extend and complicate the view of memes as enthymematic rather than mimetic, as advanced by Bradley Wiggins. Wiggins suggests that memes are not mimetic, because they are "marked not by imitation but by the capacity to propose or counter a discursive argument through visual and often verbal interplay" (1). I would argue that memes are both enthymematic and mimetic, especially in their visual interplay, because they contain the possibility of critical resistance through the performative reenactment of iconic texts. Take for instance the work done by

Hofmeyr and other meme accounts that satirize the image of Barbie, which demonstrates how the tactic of reenactment employs mimesis as a form of performativity. Performativity, in its original linguistic sense, argues that to make an utterance of any kind is to introduce new lexicons as well as new cultural possibilities. Each utterance expands how we understand and use language in all its various forms, including verbal, written, gestural, and visual (Austin; Butler, *Gender Trouble*).

The reenactment of iconic figures is a form of performativity, as it introduces new cultural and discursive possibilities in the lexicon of that figure or image. One of the discursive possibilities is a complete refusal or upending of what an icon represents in its dominant form, remixing it for creative and political ends. Continuing the Barbie-themed analysis, I want to consider for a moment an example from Kristel Jax's dyingbutfine account, which uses the image of Barbie as a means of getting at some of the social contradictions currently faced by young women. It relies on irony, the ugly, and a sense of embodiment in its address of the audience. Jax, a Canadian performance artist and musician who explores mental health issues through a variety of media art, includes memes on her account that position Barbie in different posed scenarios accompanied by ironic send-ups on the absurdity of cultural expectations of women. For example, one of her memes uses the figure of a "weird" Barbie, even though the meme precedes the movie by two years, to critical ends. The meme was posted in response to the viral "Fall Plans vs. Delta" meme trend from August 2021 in response to the Delta variant of COVID-19. Like earlier COVID-themed narrative reenactment memes from the start of this chapter, this meme emerged at a moment when meme audiences and producers needed a release valve for the social pressures of being pandemic citizens. In the meme, the left side of the frame is a smiling Barbie with glitter stars in her perfectly styled hair, and the text reads, "Fall Plans," at the top of the image (see fig. 2.5).

On the right side is a low-resolution picture of a "weird" Barbie with a truly terrible chopped-off, short "home" haircut. The text above this Barbie includes a slew of anxiety-inducing terms, including "gig economy," "systemic racism," "rent," "wealth hoarders," "data surveillance," "mass evictions," "rising food costs," "overdose deaths," "anti-vax grifters," and "resource extraction," among others. This meme explicitly names the growing list of concerns facing global citizens within the context of a "nailed it" framework. What this example shows is how critical mimesis in memes can be used to poke fun at the neoliberal white femininity that Barbie exemplifies and at the late-stage capitalist culture it lives within. The arrangement of the anxieties listed into an overcrowded mess of words evokes an embodied response that mirrors the

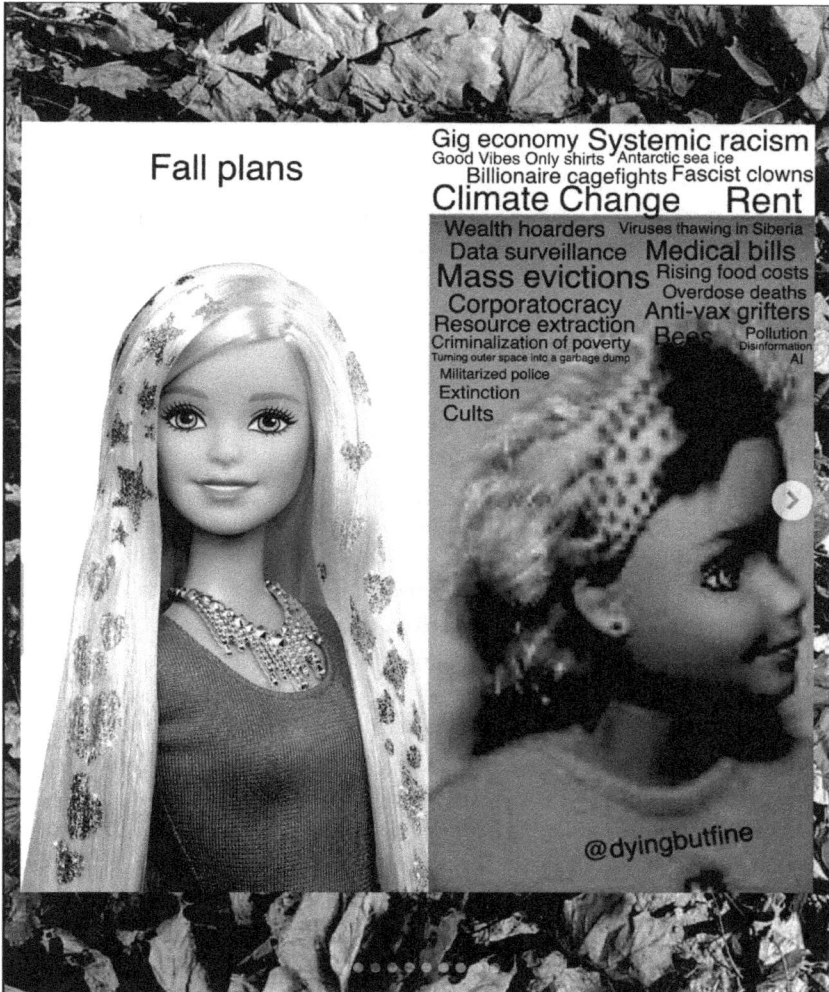

FIGURE 2.5. "Fall vs. Delta." Used with permission from
Kristel Jax for dyingbutfine (@dyingbutfine).

level of concern the text names. The meme employs a popular viral template and a use of irony and the ugly to name a list of social ills the account seeks to actively resist.

Similarly, the We Riot tweets all begin with mimetic enactments of femininity, through their references to makeup routines. They index how being a woman in public requires a performance of acceptable femininity (Butler, *Gender Trouble*; Bartky; Bordo). The references in the We Riot tweets to blusher, powder, serums, and mascara as the site of women's discourse is both a cultural parody and a strategic, playful entry point for women's mobilization as a critique of postfeminist ideology. The crucial point in this is how both meme examples enact a performance of femininity that is undermined by declarations of revolt. If, as critics like Schneider have suggested, "women are dismissed because of association to mimesis," then this becomes the starting point for newly articulated forms of refusal or a shadow feminism that operates beneath the radar of dominant culture (Schneider, *Performing Remains* 153; Halberstam). Broadly, women are an "emblem of reproduction" that is always tied to notions of this feminine masquerade and the forms of duplicity it connotes (Schneider, *Performing Remains,* Doane). Feminist meme makers, like performance artists before them, know this and use it to their creative and critical advantage.

The memes of Weird Barbie, Delta Barbie, and Hofmeyr's antler Barbie considered so far index how the historical and the corporeal elements of women's public performances play a central role in enacting mimetic critique. As demonstrated above, they also overlap with prominent artists working in spaces of excess and abjection in their art between the 1980s and 1990s. Barbie memes like Hofmeyr's show how fictional constructions of femininity within dominant discourse normalizes a preferred version of Woman and thus erases all other enactments of Woman, showing how one must exist as a woman in ways that are entirely arbitrary. It is useful to consider how these examples include different strategies of "challenging normative femininity and deconstructing restrictive gender roles, broadly categorised as . . . the ugly, the ironic, and the embodied" (Hockin-Boyers et al., para. 3).

Memes like this help to articulate the emotional currents of our culture within specific points in time. Temporality as an operating force in reenactment memes is "often created in direct response to an event as a discursive way to add commentary or to argue a position" (Wiggins 14). As a tactic, when memes "address a real-world event or issue" they "also imply a media narrative" (xvi). This relationship between event and memetic time is often articulated via the acting-out of narrative and iconic cultural scripts, as I have shown above. Wiggins argues that while "the topic," and the topical nature of the event memes are responding to, "may eventually fade, the function of the internet meme does not" (14). The function referred to here is of memes as media responses that critically engage social or political events to participate in further forms of public processing and meaning making. The memes explored in this chapter suggest how as a medium they exist within larger lineages of critical mimesis operating across feminist media histories. Further, it is not only events that memes engage through critical mimesis but also tropes or dominant discursive constructs such as the one considered here—idealized femininity.

The Barbie meme zeitgeist of 2023 can be read within a broader timeline of feminist reinterpretations of femininity and the dominant cultural responses that seek to contain them. Being a feminist scholar oftentimes means feeling like you are in a space of eternal return; what was fought for in the past is still being fought for in the present, *plus ça change*. This is equally true of the recurrence of certain meme templates in our cultural imaginary at different points, especially when they align with discourse emerging from a given event. I would argue that this illustrates well how temporality is central to meme aesthetics. In concluding this chapter, I wish to consider temporality in relationship to critical mimesis and tactics of reenactment a bit more closely, via feminist and queer theorizations of time, especially as they inform the political, the resistant, and the aesthetic. It is through mapping out the interaction between reenactment, critical mimesis, and temporality that I hope to illustrate how feminist and queer activist memes employ iconicity and nostalgia to destabilize but also reimagine long-standing cultural scripts of femininity. This analysis requires a sense of temporality as nonlinear, which earlier eras of feminist and queer theory provide a useful framework for.

Memetic Temporality: Performing Nostalgia in Feminist Memes

The image of woman in society "bears the brunt of time's meaning," as she "is called on to represent many measures of time" (Felski 21). Feminism is well suited to explore the complex temporalities ascribed to women, because as a figure she "binds together our visions of history and eternity, tradition and modernity, permanent revolution and eternal return" (21). Reenactment in performance, memes, or elsewhere helps feminists build on this overdetermined representational temporality that is assigned to women and call it into question. For Elizabeth Freeman, the enactment of overdetermined cultural histories becomes "a way to lay bare the rules of gendered performance" ("Introduction" 161). Each intervention by feminist artists and meme makers is an iterative, performative attempt to expand the script on what Woman signifies and complicate its more dominant forms. As the examples throughout this chapter reveal, this conscious reenactment of the tired scripts of dominant gender ideology produces important and evocative critical encounters for the viewer.

As with my analysis of the critical reperformance of Barbie memes above, I want to consider in the closing section of this chapter feminist memes that reappropriate other forms and iconic imagery of hyperfemininity found in our cultural imaginary for critical ends. This can include the feminist remixing of classical paintings of women from earlier centuries or the use of campy, sexualized images from pulp novels in the 1950s and 1960s as well as repurposing paparazzi photos of postfeminist icons like Paris Hilton and Britney Spears from the late 1990s and early aughts. Bringing these past images of femininity into the present is another way these memes enact critical mimesis. These memes formally employ appeals to nostalgia to center their critique.

Nostalgia is "often associated with the quaint, the kitsch, the declining and most importantly, the consumable" objects that "mediate our relation between a past and present moment" (Eichhorn 259). Yet, as Emily Apter notes, nostalgia makes it possible "to submit to time's ravages" insofar as it "loosens periodicity's possessive perimeters around spots of time and releases arrested images into the future" (Apter 14–16). This, I believe, is what makes the reappropriations of past visual histories in memes so compelling. As we have seen with the use of Barbie in memes, there is a reaching-back toward an icon that has visual appeal, not because, like neoconservative traditionalists, they want to go back to the way things were in a "simpler" time of gender binaries and roles but because they want to reimagine those moments in more complicated ways. There are many feminist meme accounts that open this temporal collapse of different moments and eras of ideal femininity. In most, there is a reenactment of iconic imagery that is often paired with text-based forms as reenactment at the same time.

Take for instance the accounts notthirsttraps (@notthirsttraps) on Instagram and @not_thirsttraps on TikTok, which are run by Los Angeles–based artist Polina. The Instagram profile image is a self-portrait of the artist in a nun's habit with a cigarette hanging out of her mouth. She is staring, with her head cocked, at the camera in three-quarter profile and giving the middle finger. This gives a sense of the kind of irreverence and rebellious feminist excess the account provides. It also seems to evoke the trope of the "naughty nun" figure that was popular, from pulp novels to porn, from the postwar era onward. The account includes both meme content remixing celebrity photos with text commentary and staged images of the artist in various scenarios. The running theme across these memes and images is that they are all performing the script of a "thirst trap," or a photo used to encourage attention and engagement, often of a sexualized nature. In a slide deck that uses the same visuals as the account's profile photo, the artist frames herself in full length wearing the nun's habit, a long black wig, black thick-rimmed glasses, and props including a Bible or alternately a cigarette dangling from her mouth. The camera is positioned in front of the artist. She poses in a full-length mirror, in the background of the image, that offers a second angle of her poses. This produces a doubling of her image that is used for critical ends. In some of the photos the mirror reflection reveals that the nun's habit is open at the back, showing the red mesh lingerie and red calf-length boots underneath.

The madonna/whore dynamic in this "reveal" becomes the foil for a set of textual interplays. These include one image where the artist is staring down the camera with the Bible held in her hand, her exposed back facing us. The text reads, "me and my two personalities trying to co-exist in peace" (notthirsttraps, "to be perceived"). Similar images include the text "to be perceived / is to be misunderstood" and "my online persona" overtop of the lingerie half of her outfit, and "my offline persona" over the image of her as nun reflected in the mirror. In a similar play between perception and reality, the account posts a slide deck with a set of pictures of models "reading things" (notthirsttraps, "don't bother me"). Using this theme as the backdrop, the text offers humorous suggestions of things being read: "us rewatching our stories as if it is the greatest cinematic short-film of all time," "googling their birth chart & psychoanalyzing their existence," and "sorry for oversharing, i'm just practicing which version of the story i'm gonna use to create shock-value when i write my autobiography" (notthirsttraps, "don't bother me").

All of notthirsttraps' images are modified by the addition of text in an image-macro format. While they are clearly memes, they also feel like a twenty-first-century crossover between the works of Sprinkle, Rist, and Sherman outlined in this chapter. Like Sprinkle, the notthirsttraps account performs an expected version of sexualized Woman that is self-aware and highly reflexive. The text in the posts often include the artists' musings on her mental health and on the gap between what people perceive of her in the image and who she is. In the posts of herself, she explains how much she struggles between her online persona and her everyday self and with her reliance on viewer attention as self-medication. None of this is presented as a problem but more as a fact, exposing what it means to perform for the attention economy of social media platforms. Her work illustrates how feminist meme accounts, "rather than negate spectacle, openly play with its signifiers," producing an experience of "networked communication as ironic encounter" (Zaiontz and Cochrane 149). Using avatars of celebrity women's images to create an open play of signifiers is a compelling tactic of activist memes that employ "strategic platform uses for . . . authoring ironic memes" (144). This use of avatars and an ironic distancing for the purpose of criticality is a clear part of the trajectory of reenactment across performance art and meme culture.

I wish to consider one final comparison, between the earlier performance art of Cindy Sherman and contemporary feminist memes employing hyperfemininity to illustrate the temporal ruptures of reenactment in feminist media. My analysis hinges on theories of temporality found in Rebecca Schneider's discussion of reenactment in *Performing Remains* (2011). Schneider considers photography not only as documented records but also as "durational events" that hail the viewer into the role of witness (*Performing Remains* 140). The image and the event it records are placed in a "cross-temporal . . . 'between'" that situates the photograph as "an ongoing live event" (140). The two examples I discuss below can be read as forms of performance art that rely on photographs and, in particular, self-portraiture as performance. While the mode of circulation is different for these—fine art galleries and social media platforms—the use of the performative photograph as the images' theatrical stage for confronting the logic of hyperfemininity is the same.

The *Untitled Film Stills* series by Sherman is composed of seventy black-and-white eight-by-ten photographs of Sherman posed as various generic characters inspired by films from the 1950s and 1960s (Ricci). Working from a "vocabulary of popular culture in postwar America," the series offers a "powerful . . . reflection on the themes of identity representation and stereotypical femininity . . . in Western culture at large" (Ricci). Schneider describes Sherman's *Untitled Film Stills* as a "duplication of movie stills" that "both resist and underscore the live power of images as composed and recomposed in passage across bodies, across media, and across time" (*Performing Remains* 138). Sherman's characters "emerge from embodied memory and from a culturally shared sense of what it means to 'do' femininity" (Meagher 9). The bodies Sherman performs emerge from what Bourdieu conceptualized as *habitus* and perform "repositories of culture" that hold the values, morals, and marks of their society (Meagher 8–9).

One of the most iconic images in the series, *Untitled Still #14*, frames Sherman in a full-body photograph. She is shown in a somewhat sparse domestic space, wearing a short, belted black dress with lace, pearls, and makeup, with hair in a stylish bob. She is looking slightly off camera, and her head lightly rests on her hand, with an expression situated somewhere between curious and wary. While she stands just right of center, she is reflected in a mirror hanging behind her above a credenza. The reflection frames her silhouette from behind and reflects a table off-screen with a drink on it. Her body position is cautious and coy, as if she will startle and run off at the slightest provocation. And yet it is an alluring pose, calling the viewer forward into the mise-en-scène. Similarly, in *Untitled Still #50*, the mise-en-scène evokes a cinematic landscape where Sherman is framed just right of center in a wide shot with her gaze looking off to screen left. This time she is photographed from slightly above and is seated in a low-lit living room that evokes a film noir aesthetic. Her dress is more dramatic, an iconic femme fatale costume with a veiled hat slightly obscuring her gaze. She is holding a drink in her lap and resting against the couch with a slightly pouty, unhappy, yet defiant expression. In a third photo, *Untitled Film Still #43,* the setting is radically different, with Sherman in a mountainous desert landscape where she is seated on a low-hanging branch of a large, craggy tree. The framing is again full-body, a wide shot that includes the distant mountains of the vast landscape. Sherman is again looking off-screen left while positioned slightly to the right of the frame. Her costume change is notable, as she is wearing a white cotton dress with slim straps and a sweetheart neckline. She is barefoot as she lounges with one leg on the tree and the other dangling toward the ground. She offers that same distant, defiant expression as in *Untitled Film Still #50,* but it looks less imposing with the open-air backdrop of the desert. Each of these images performs a cinematic trope. They represent "genres without referencing any recognisable film, and yet, every element—framing, costumes, facial expressions, and so forth—is so embedded in the collective memory that [it] arouses a sense of familiarity" (Ricci). Sherman notes she arrived at the portraits "not through conscious selection of specific roles, but through play and improvisation" (Meagher 1). Sherman performs these images to illustrate the exaggerated fakeness of femininity idealized by culture. Here femininity becomes a surface with no depth, and she makes it look strange in order to show how the ideal image of woman is produced through the gaze of the media apparatus and how this is different from women's actual identities.

Sherman's series reveals women as icons that perform a gendered form of visual pleasure that is hardwired into our collective media imaginary. It is easier to identify a femme fatale, an ingenue, or countless other tropes than it is to represent a complex character beyond these generic kinds of flattening. Sherman's *Untitled Film Stills* series are echoed in memes from the account notthirsttraps, which also employ images of women to wage critiques against social expectations of women. Both Sherman and the notthirsttraps artist Paulina use the body as a site of performance that illustrates the relationship between women's bodies and cultural expectations of them. The images produced by the artists also illustrate the complex ways representation and reproduction influence our relationships to viewing women's bodies as part of our visual cultural landscape. In this, the work becomes a frame for looking at contemporary relations between representation, media, individuals, and the cultural discourses of gender they move within.

Like Sherman's work, the images from notthirsttraps' accounts rely heavily on a visual lexicon from media history. Unlike Sherman's reliance on visual tropes from 1950s and 1960s cinema, the notthirsttraps account builds from the 1990s and early aughts onward. The icons and celebrities found across the account vary, but there are repeated posts using images of Lana Del Rey, Kim Kardashian, Holly Madison, Bridget Marquardt, and Kendra Wilkinson from the Playboy Mansion reality TV show *Girls Next Door* (2005–10), Britney Spears, the cast of *Sex and the City,* and Paris Hilton, among others. The artist also uses movie stills as the backdrop for several of her meme carousel decks, where different text is placed on the stills, building an argument over the sequence of posts. A post from January 2024 uses stills from *Eternal Sunshine of the Spotless Mind* (2004), *Almost Famous* (2000), *Girl, Interrupted* (1999), *Buffalo 66* (1998), *Dazed and Confused* (1993), and *Lost Boys* (1987) (notthirsttraps, "this is just a list"). A through line of these movies is that they have women lead characters who are at times unstable and struggle with their mental health or use drugs. They are not perfected or idealized women but more complex characters. In each movie still, the text says, "If she says [Title] is her favorite movie, then . . . ," with a closing point that sets out what "kind" of girl this imagined person in question is, revealing what the movie says about her personality. For the first slide of Christina Ricci sitting in a bowling alley looking somewhat angrily off-screen left, the text reads, "if she says buffalo 66 is her favorite movie, that girl been thru some shit" (notthirsttraps, "this is just a list"). What is interesting is the way that the posts locate specific characters and performances and build genericized reads on the women who like them. It is not a reperformance of an image but a remixing of the image through textual interruption that determines a class of women and girls who consume these cinematic narratives. The meaning is made through what a woman's movie preferences say about her, but also, in their textual interpretation or proscription, the memes reperform scripts of "that girl" discourse in a tongue-in-cheek kind of way. The caption notes, "this is just a list of my favorite movies," suggesting that the artist is all these women combined, and this shows their fluid, nebulous, idiosyncratic nature. This is part of the account's intervention, that reenactments of feminine stereotypes, as a means of disrupting them through ironic textual interventions, reveal their fabricated nature. It does not destroy or do away with these images but instead complicates them and asks us to reconsider their potential significance within meme remix culture.

Throughout the account, there are memes that speak to the entire project as a piece of performance art. The artist posted a meme using the "Expanding Brain" template, which includes the caption "i love entertaining the masses." In this meme template, the right side of the image has X-ray-style pictures of a brain inside a human skull that, with each progressive image in the sequence, expands even further, with new information provided by the meme's text on the right side of the image ("Galaxy Brian"). notthirsttraps modifies this image with two visual panels, one of a nonexpanded brain and another of an expanded brain shooting blue light with different text combinations including "she's being slutty on the internet," on the normal-sized brain; "this is peak performance art," on the second image, of a larger brain; "i am an object / i am a subject," with an image of a brain shooting out blue light; and "what if they don't like me? / i literally don't like anybody," on a final image of a brain as a galaxy (notthirsttraps, "i love entertaining"). Here the artist performs a series of dialogues within the backdrop of the recognizable meme to expand audience understandings of the account's intentions and the persona she performs. This, in some ways, is the meme version of *Untitled Film Stills*: the language and iconicity of memes is reperformed as iconic for an audience that knows the meme's intrinsic style, genre, and connotations. The meme template here is as recognizable as the femme fatale in Sherman's work. In both there is a collapsing of temporalities and a reappropriation of older, popular forms of media and images for new purposes.

As the discussion on reenactment in the context of feminist meme and performance art suggests, there are layers of intention embedded in the critical use of hyperfeminine figures on display. The irony and playful subversion of the work allows viewers the vital critical distance to consider a range of questions around tensions between performing idealized femininity in a context of capitalist visual culture and using these platforms, as well as their affordances and constraints, to point out the shortcomings in the representational systems we move within. Together these examples of feminist memes from notthirsttraps help get at the crux of the double gestus of mimesis and how it operates both then and now to advance feminist discourse around the idealized feminine body. This is very similar to what Sherman aims to achieve in *Untitled Film Stills*.

Critical Temporalities in Feminist Digital Culture

Considered together, the examples from performance art and meme culture woven throughout this chapter demonstrate the "four forms of time that shape and circumscribe feminist thought," which include redemption, regression, repetition, and rupture (Felski 21). These four forms are "metaphorically resonant" and "saturated with affect" (21) and "often intertwined and hard to separate (27). What they suggest is how feminist articulations of time in media connect "the subjective and the social, the personal and the public . . . [the]

links between our own lifetime and the larger historical patterns that transcend us" (22). The slogan "We are the granddaughters of the witches you didn't burn" is an example of redemptive time that "relies on the . . . power of hope" in our futurity, a power that includes "joyous anticipation and the thrill of expectancy" (22). While asserting a collective resistance in the presence, the very fact that there are "granddaughters" of a movement also suggests hope for the future and what these lineages can foster. The statement asserts a collectivity that is both expectant of future successes and joyful in its resilience. In contrast, regressive time is dispirited in its nostalgia for past moments that were somehow better than our present, creating a sense of "lost hope" (22). It is hard here not to think of regressive gender narratives tied to the Christian right and the desire to return to a time of more limited roles for women, primarily within the domestic sphere. This is what underpins "trad wife" culture, where largely white influencers produce lifestyle content that displays domestic labor (baking bread, growing food in gardens, homeschooling children) as an ideal aesthetic. There is nostalgia in the visual cues and in the professed joy of the simpler pleasures of motherhood and homemaking. What is left out is the kinds of wealth required to undertake this labor but also an acknowledgment that this may not be appealing to all. It is simply asserted as a preferable return to a past paradise.

Both redemption and regression "carry an in-built emotional and moral response"; however, rupture and repetition "arouse more complicated and contradictory sentiments" (Felski 22). Repetition in time can be either comforting or a site of dread and constraint. Rupture offers responses ranging from the terror of "instability" and uncertainty to the freedom of nihilistic joy (22). Repetitive feminist time builds on redemptive time but situates the notion of progress "as a wager with the future, as a nascent hope, rather than a complacent certainty" (23). It recognizes that "feminism cannot do without an orientation to the future" but also acknowledges the outcomes of this as "changeable," wherein "a destiny that seemed written in stone could be erased and written anew" (23). Repetitive time in some ways is the form of time that has haunted feminism the most in the last decade. The outcome of the 2016 US presidential election was a bitter pill for some women who had been upholding a redemptive narrative around the upswell of fourth-wave feminism emerging around 2012. The forms of feminist activism that followed, including the viral uptake of Tarana Burke's MeToo movement, took broad advantage of meme tactics to articulate a desired feminist future while also naming the forms of structural oppression that seek to both deny that future and regress to an even more constrained past. Repetitive time is "viewed with distrust, or even with horror," around "the oppressive regimen of natural or man-made cycles" where women "remain trapped in the deadly grip of cyclical time" (25). The way this debate has played out within the battle for reproductive rights is most instructive.

However, for the purposes of this chapter, the most interesting form of feminist time is that of rupture. It is a "distinctly modern idea" arising from avant-garde movements, which "sought to break absolutely with the past" and "dreamed of the pristine newness of permanent revolution" (Felski 26). This is a compelling view of rupture, as not just about a break in time, space, or meaning but also as a temporal form invested in imagining new forms of expression that can be revolutionary. It draws attention to the relationship between revolution and a temporal sense of newness. It also alerts us to the risk of forgetting those revolutionary gestures that came before us. It is perhaps wise then to situate the temporality of different feminist histories as a continuous stream of revolutionary gestures in the present. These collective gestures can inform how we refuse and resist. I believe that feminist reenactment memes offer both a temporal rupture in their reperformance of Woman as image and a sense of continuous feminist histories that reminds us of how far we may have come (if indeed we have) and how much we need to do. What these memes do well is to pick up on the important and "rich residues and layerings of past time in the present moment, the complex interplay and disjuncture of the old and the new" (27). What makes these memes so rhetorically powerful is that they do not "deny the haunting power and presence of the noncontemporaneous" (27). Rupture and repetition in feminist reenactment memes "connect in myriad ways," as "the old and the new are interdependent" rather than "antithetical" (27). Gender performativity in meme reenactment as a form of cultural resistance indexes a series of complex inter- and paratextual negotiations with time, history, and nostalgia, all made apparent via meme aesthetics in the present. Feminist memes that perform femininity in their content reveal a tactic of resistance through reenactment. Like explorations of the spatial collapse encouraged through the tactic of collage in the previous chapter, I hope to have demonstrated here that the tactic of reenactment, especially the reenactment of heavily weighted iconic images of femininity, can produce equally effective forms of temporal collapse. Through these complex forms of intertextual interplay and an endless chain of semiotic connections and contortions, feminist memes reperform the visual and textual scripts of dominant femininity to critical ends. In doing so, they help us as audiences to understand how stubbornly timeless constraining cultural expectations of femininity truly are. They also offer us humorous and irreverent ways to respond in turn. In the following chapter, I look at one final tactic that I believe makes memes truly unique—that of montage. What is important about moving into a consideration of montage in memes is how much it already contains the impulses of collage and reenactment within its formal approach. As such, while being the focus of the following chapter it is also the summation of my overall argument around memes as a medium that is tied to a formal aesthetic based on the bricolage of times, spaces, and movement into a coherent whole.

CHAPTER 3

Montage and the Memetic Assemblage of Attractions

In this chapter, I extend arguments made up to this point in the book around memetic specificity by considering the tactical use of film forms like montage editing as well as cinematic tropes within meme culture. This builds on my discussion, in the previous two chapters, of memetic uses of collage based in visual art practices as well as that of reenactment stemming from performance art. Here I am interested in how memes repurpose cinematic images and use principles of filmic montage to advance forms of feminist and queer affect for activist ends. I situate the use of film form as a key aesthetic touchstone of memes within the larger kaleidoscopic landscape of digital visual culture.

This chapter also takes up the conceptual outcomes of memetic uses of film form, like in my exploration of how collage and reenactment complicate our experience of time and space in meme culture. As I have argued, collage in memes leads to a collapsed sense of space, and reenactments via critical mimesis reveal a layered sense of temporality, or mimetic time. Both these tactics produce significant ruptures around our experience of space and temporality in the digital era. Building on these arguments, this chapter shifts attention to tactics of mimetic movement, considering how memes use montage, or the assembling of disparate moving images, to create critical interventions. What this tactical use of movement leads to as well is forms of assemblage that are conceptual—a connecting of disparate ideas and affective states—but also that assemble countercultural communities. Across previous chapters, I have linked memes with larger trajectories of resistant art, including a linkage between memes and the visual art histories of Dadaism and collage-based photography as well as postwar feminist performance art. In this chapter, I link memes with experimental cinema and moving image culture as well as feminist zine culture. Both experimental cinema and zine culture exist in close formal proximity to the medium specificity of memes, as all three use juxtaposition, reenactment, and assemblage as part of their formal approach. Useful to exploring the concept of assemblage is how both experimental cinema and zines assemble communities of practice or subcultural connections that, beyond their formal interventions, also create meaningful alternative spaces from which to resist dominant culture. I link these to memes because, as this book has aimed to demonstrate, memes also assemble communities of makers and audiences that connect over a shared cultural set of referents. These cultural assemblages are perhaps the most significant outcome of any medium employed by activists and countercultural artists.

In my investigation of the link between memes and film form in this chapter, I depart from my focus up to this point on image macro memes. I looked almost exclusively at image macro memes in my analysis of collage and reenactment, as it has been the dominant from of meme production up to this point. In what follows, I consider a wider range of memetic forms that have emerged in the last five to eight years to include moving image and sound as part of the memetic object. These include carousel decks, CapCut superimpositions, and in-camera video editing techniques found in stitches or duets. I am interested in the use of moving images and audio and in the practice of assembling or editing these together into new forms of filmic montage impact that advance current modes of communication and counterculture resistance.

Take for instance a sequence of images framed as a "mood board" that was created in honor of filmmaker Kenneth Anger posted by the Instagram account Queer Death Stories (@queer_death_stories_) in May 2023. In the commentary, Queer Death Stories (QDS) gives a brief synopsis of the avant-garde filmmaker, citing him as an important gay artist, author of *Hollywood Babylon,* a Satan worshiper, and an iconic "Gay Villain," which the account notes is "absolutely one of my favorite gender bends." In the sequence of images, clips from Anger's film *Scorpio Rising* (1963) are meme-ified in various ways. Still shots from the film are placed at the start and finish of the carousel, which includes additional stills and video clips that, linked together, evoke a mood of queer rebellion. The scene is set clearly with the first image, which is also the iconic opening title shot from Anger's film. It is a close-up image of a black leather jacket with the words "Scorpio Rising" spelled out in rhinestones on the back. This is set in front of a deep red background (see fig. 3.1). The

FIGURE 3.1. "Me." Screenshot from a Kenneth Anger mood board
by Queer Death Stories (@queer_death_stories_).

image is altered by the addition of a meme script for us to read out during
our encounter with it. On the bottom left of the frame the text reads, "Them:
Explain why you're like this," while the response, on the top right of the frame
says, "Me:" just above the rhinestone lettering on the jacket, as if to suggest,
"I'm like this because I am a Scorpio Rising." The meme uses Anger's title for
Scorpio Rising as the punctum of the meme's joke. The iconic queer film is
remixed as an astrological typology. It is a form of defamiliarization that also
allows the meme to retain the appeal of Anger's queer aesthetic, embedded
in a new context. Notably, the meme-ified image also queers and defamiliarizes the standard template of a "them/me" meme script by placing the script
out of sequence. Whereas usually the image frame would include the "them"
script somewhere on the top left and the "me" response somewhere below for
sequential reading, here this is reversed. We see the "me" asserting itself in the
top right corner, establishing a visual trail from right to left and top to bottom, requiring us to linger on the words "Scorpio Rising" in the center. There
is also a dangling text below the "them" script, with the word "Insert" placed
in an open parenthesis with nothing following it. It leaves open the possibility
of what the instructions beyond "Insert" would be and when the parenthesis
would be closed.

This opening meme is representative of the delightful and bewildering inscrutability of the entire carousel sequence. The second image is an old video clip of Madonna being interrupted by Courtney Love during a 1995 MTV interview. In the video, Love throws things at Madonna, who is sitting up on the interview stage. Madonna claims that "Courtney is in dire need of attention right now" before they sit together uncomfortably, acting out a "mean girls playing nice" script for the at-home audience. It is a remarkable archival object of celebrity history, with competing forms of femininity on display where both are playing some version of a campy villain. The carousel deck also includes still images of skeleton flowers that look like small translucent glass versions of forget-me-nots; Chihiro and No-Face from *Spirited Away* (2001) having tea with Yubaba's twin sister, Zeniba, with the accompanying text: "You can't tell me the vibes weren't immaculate"; a still from the *Beetlejuice* cartoon, of Lydia with the text "my revenge will be artistic and personal"; and an interview with Sister Boom Boom, a.k.a. Sister Rose of the Bloody Stains of the Sacred Robes of Jesus, an iconic member of the gay activist collective the Sisters of Perpetual Indulgence. Peppered throughout are clips from other Anger films, including *Rabbit's Moon* (1972) set to the 1975 song "It Came in the Night" by the Digalongamacs, and an image from *The Inauguration of the Pleasure Dome* (1966) with a dance remix instrumental of Lana Del Rey's "Summertime Sadness" with the words "Kiss me hard before you go" superimposed on Anger's images. Together the slides evoke a sense of playfulness, longing, and irreverence. They collapse many textual references into one another, producing a "mood board" of queer-villain-with-immaculate-vibes as, in the words of QDS, the "best kind of gender bend." The slide-deck-as-mood-board provides viewers with an intermedial interplay and invites them to linger and luxuriate in the collisions between images from different eras. This assemblage promises a sense of unsettling excitement, indulgent refusal, and chaotic eros. What drew me to the "Anger mood board" carousel by QDS was how it employs tactics of montage and assemblage to frame and circulate memes on its account.

Memetic Montage in Carousels, CapCut, Stitches, and Duets

In this example and the others in this chapter, I consider three different sites of memetic "movement" that exemplify an aesthetic assemblage via the use of montage. These include different formal approaches I have referenced throughout the book, including carousel decks, CapCut superimpositions, and video stitches or duets. The first, carousel decks, I defined briefly in the introduction and discussed examples of throughout the last two chapters. Within the context of montage and movement, what is interesting about carousel decks is how they present the viewer with the option of *moving* through curated content to experience thematic pairings of media assembled by the carousel creator. What first emerged as a tactic to ensure algorithmic attention has expanded to include sophisticated curation practices by content creators that reflect a sense of formal and conceptual assemblage. Arguments are built across the interconnected dialogue that emerge from a curated carousel slide deck. The linkages between discrete media in a carousel deck operate via the logics of montage, as meaning is created through their associative merging. This is seen clearly in the assembled sequences outlined in the QDS carousel above.

Carousel decks allow for a more sustained engagement with a single account and have become a popular way of ensuring audience interaction and a form of account branding. These carousels function as "visual clusters" that offer a "loose association of images based on formal characteristics" that produce a "relation to and among each other on a level of content, emotion, or personal meaning" (Hanßen 125). Importantly within digital networks, these visual clusters are tied to "the expectations of community members and . . . references to a collective cultural memory" that provide them with "a historicity" (125). This historicity is "produced and manifested over time by a community" and "repeated in everyday practices" including "style" and "rhetoric" (125). These visual clusters "leave behind their original contexts" and "enter into new ones and represent completely different concepts" (128). Carousel decks on Instagram offer a compelling insight into the semiotic chain of meaning derived from placing together a series of up to twenty still and moving memes to create an argument or themed collection. These small-set curated archives produce a similar effect to montage insofar as it produces a narrative and sometimes formally dynamic connections between slides in the deck.

Meme movement tactics are also found in the use of video editing to create short form videos on social media platforms. TikTok short-form videos are memes insofar as they combine a variety of viral textual and visual elements that mimic image-macro components but in moving image form. TikTok as a culturally dominant form of visual media has inspired platform adoption of video content by competitors. This has prompted Instagram to emphasize Stories and Reels in response, which include a variety of moving image and audio components. Most interesting of these is the growing use of editing software, such as CapCut from ByteDance, to superimpose moving images, text overlays, and sound on still or moving image backgrounds.

I see this as a second site of exploration for the development of moving image memes. This use of superimpositions is an expansion of GIFs, transforming them into textual overlays on static or moving backgrounds. When accompanied, as they often are, by text punchlines and audio soundtracks, the combination becomes an animated audiovisual version of the more standard image macro meme. These superimposed moving images largely remix pop culture images, isolating the bodies of the chosen performers into bite-sized movements that are taken out of context and sutured into new spaces. With additional components of text and audio overlays, these videos produce a whole new set of referents to comedic and critical ends.

The third type of movement I consider includes any sort of video performances by content producers on-screen, including original content or reperforming viral dance and video trends. The most interesting of these for the discussion of montage and assemblage are stitches and duets, which use common video-editing tactics to create a more interactive and responsive form of meme content. In stitches, the assemblage occurs with one content producer editing themselves into another account's content, usually to offer a reaction or commentary to the original post. In a duet, a split screen is created so that one content producer can interact with another producer's content. Unlike a stitch, a duet lets the reactions unfold alongside the original content simultaneously so that both the original post and the response post are on-screen together. The use of stitches and duets within influencer content can be a way to boost brand recognition by interacting with a more popular account. It can also be a way to create collaborations across content producers that are mutually beneficial.

Often, these are humor-based or used to show the creator's remix of a viral trend. In more activist-oriented content, they can be used to showcase and critically intervene on forms of sexism, racism, and trans- and queerphobia as well as conspiracy theories and rampant forms of disinformation. This allows for a form of informational activism that is quite effective in utilizing the platform affordances of stitches and duets to advance critical arguments against harmful ideological content. All these different examples of meme assemblages push the tactics of collage and reenactment into new aesthetic forms, producing video assemblages that utilize such tactics for deeper forms of engagement, including humor and relatability, to assemble niche audiences together into a more coherent whole.

Assemblage and montage are complementary and somewhat parallel tactics to the use of collage in reenactment explored in the previous chapters and are arguably as central to the meme medium. In some ways, they encompass key elements of these previously considered tactics. What is collage if not an assemblage of disparate visual and conceptual elements? Further, all forms of assemblage in some ways are a reenactment of previously situated images, media, and concepts, displaying them as a new form with transformed associations. *Assemblage* and *montage* are also seemingly overlapping terms; it is not always clear where the definition of one begins and the other ends. I believe, when analyzing the relationship between memes and the legacy of the moving image as a countercultural tactic, these differences between assemblage and montage need to be teased out to see their individual value. In what follows, I explore the use of montage and the use of film as a remixable visual lexicon. I also consider how groupings of memes tied to a particular community can collectively help advance sociocultural forms of assemblage that create a space for countercultural convergences. To do so, I begin with an exploration of montage theory and how it applies to memes before delving into theories of assemblage and what memes offer us culturally as a way of binding us together. This theoretical progression leads me to argue later in this chapter that memes are not just formal assemblages circulating across platforms but also as social or cultural assemblages.

To explore the formal connections associated with montage and assemblage, I outline the use of the three tactics of carousel decks outlined above—CapCut, stitches, and duets—to analyze how they interact with different platform affordances and how that impacts cultural discourse. I will extend this analysis through a discussion of how memes offer a digital form of the "cinema of attractions" (Gunning, "Attractions") in the twenty-first century. I do so to highlight the important disconnects and ambivalences around capitalist cultural production brought forward within more activist uses of memetic visual gags. In the latter half of the chapter, I turn toward assemblage within meme culture. Here I extend the argument built across the book, around memes as an aesthetic medium of collage, reenactment, and montage, to consider how, together, these aesthetic aspects of memes produce a mode of cultural assemblage that both echoes and extends earlier aesthetic-political movements in the 1990s such as Riot Grrrl zine culture. I make a connection to digital zines as meta-memes in the present that, like their predecessors, circulate across different media channels to inspire future forms of political action, especially around queer, feminist, anticapitalist, and ecological movements. In this way, the chapter moves from formal considerations of movement in memes to how memes are recognizable communicative figures in current social and political movements.

The Aesthetic Interventions of Montage and Assemblage

Montage, like collage and performance art, is central to the twentieth-century avant-garde countercultural movements. The tactic of montage within film is an important precursor to the kinds of meaningful visual and intertextual assemblages created within carousel decks and video meme content. To better understand the montage, or the assemblage of moving images, I want to consider the concept of montage developed in early twentieth-century avant-garde film culture by Sergei Eisenstein. Montage is an aesthetic tactic that directs the viewer's attention through assembling discrete visual elements into a coherent and often sequential whole. This principle of montage provides a precursor to understanding the use of moving images as a critical and aesthetic intervention by meme makers today.

As Eisenstein argues, film montage offers "a means to 'link' [on] . . . the screen—various elements (fragments) of a phenomenon filmed in diverse dimensions, from diverse points of view and sides" (111). As such, "the choosing, the selecting and the foregrounding of the significant elements" can be found in all forms of visual representation and make up montage relations found across media practices (Aumont and Hildreth 53). In montage, meaning is communicated by "putting each fragment into relationship with those that surround it" (Aumont and Hildreth 51). Eisenstein argues that viewers, by "taking in all these elements" together, "will obtain . . . the impression which the author wishes to induce" (111). Montage can help creatively transform realistic images into meaningful sites of perception (111). Montage is tied to formalism and the avant-garde impulses of early revolutionary Russian aesthetics. The significance of montage is about not only the individual parts being brought together but also what they produce in their juxtaposition (Bordwell).

Montage was also used to "build a narrative (by formulating an artificial time and space or guiding the viewer's attention from one narrative point to another), to control rhythm, to create metaphors, and to make rhetorical point" (Bordwell 9). For David Bordwell, these elements of montage in film are transferable to other art forms because the "fundamental principles [of the] assemblage of heterogeneous parts, juxtaposition of fragments" as well as "the demand for the audience to make conceptual connections" create "radically new relation among parts of a whole" no matter the format (10). In this way, montage as a tactic offered broad appeal to a range of other artists who have sought "socially useful and revolutionary" artistic practices, including at the time montage theory emerged, Constructivists and Futurists (Bordwell 13). Such associations and lineages make clear how closely tied montage is to avant-garde interests in collage and defamiliarization. It is equally an element of memes, where visual and conceptual expressions are built into the connections between discrete images that follow each other in sequential form, such as with the carousel slide deck.

Montage in Meme Carousels

In his discussion of memes as forms of assembly, Kyle Parry notes that memes "are not like art exhibitions," where "the components are gathered in single places like the rooms of museums," because memes can "be in many different places at once," including across platforms and personal archives on phones and computers (136). I would argue that the increased use of the carousel deck to display a curated set of memes complicates this, as it reveals an intentional move by meme makers toward gathering memes in a single place for exhibition that groups memes in a thematic whole. Carousel decks rely on taking existing meme media out of its "original" context where the carousel curator first finds them, thus creating a rupture or dislocation of the text. It then further produces assemblages from these dislocated texts to create a new set of meanings. New relations and associations are built in the interplay between the elements of the slide deck, creating a way of viewing memes as discursive assemblages. These larger units of memes can often advance complex arguments and, as such, are a favored tool of popular activist accounts on Instagram.

In a carousel deck from April 2023, the queer femme artist disssgrace (@disssgrace) posted a series of collaged images with text overlays, expanding the format of the carousel deck to advance activist and anticapitalist ends. The carousel starts with a slide that reads, on the top of the image in black type on a white rectangle, "I dream of who I am," with a follow-up in the same text box—"outside of capitalism"—on the bottom of the image. The accompanying image is of a hand underwater on the bottom left third of the frame, reaching toward a cluster of bright pink flowers on green leafy stems floating upward toward the rippled surface of the water, with a burst of sun illuminating the upper third of the image with softly distorted reflections of the pink flowers below. The images in the carousel were created by the artist using generative AI via the popular platform Midjourney. This is a particularly useful tool for achieving surreal images through digital technology, as it tends to produce highly unnatural and dreamlike landscapes. The additional five slides in the deck create new and seductive dream landscapes that each contain part of the longer written text shared in its entirety in the caption:

> I dream of learning who I am outside of capitalism
> who am I outside of capitalism?
> what do i like to do?
> what are my passions
> when i am not focused on survival
> outside of consumerism
> what are my interests?
> what would I choose to do for fun?
> for the sake of doing it?
> what could be my potential outside of survival?
> what could i achieve? What could i create?

This includes a passage from the first slide, which is in a medium close-up, with the flowers and water filling the frame so that there is little perspective outside of the hand grasping toward the flowers. The placement of the hand in the center ensures that this is where our visual focus should rest. There are gaps of pale green-blue water between the flowers, and these somewhat circular openings become a visual match echoed across the carousel. The cut between this image and the next successfully ruptures the viewer's gaze as it shifts to a wide shot of a large fantastical vista with a shiny white marble structure that looks as if it's dripping and rippling like waves and waterfalls frozen in mid-motion. There is an inviting pool of water in the center, with circular cutouts that match those of the first image, which reveal a lush green scenery and sky beyond. This is further ruptured by the shift in the third slide, where we are back to a full frame of pink flowers and a young woman's face emerging in a medium shot from the center of the cluster of blossoms. There is a visual back and forth in terms of a medium to wide shot that creates a dynamic movement for the viewer that is grounded by a distinct final slide. This last slide includes the last two lines of the text cited above: "what could be my potential outside of survival? / what could i achieve? What could i create?" It is split up between the top and bottom sections of the image, surrounding the center image of an intricate rainbow-hued spider's web dripping with gossamer shimmer. The web takes up most of the frame, with a soft, out-of-focus background in mostly black-toned shading. Like the rest of the carousel deck, the image is captivating and sensual. It beckons viewers into an alternative space where we can experience wonder outside of capitalism. It is a place to rest and ask questions that are utterly defamiliarized in the spaces that constrain us.

The poetic visual and textual form used in this carousel work well together to prompt us to look outside our constructed surroundings and imagine different futures. This aspect of disssgrace's work is seen most clearly in a related slide that imagines queer worlds of possibility. This is made explicit on the first slide, which states: "yearning for a world where queer futures can flower." The suite of slides is constructed as spaces full of colorful maximalism that evoke a sense of fecundity and potential through the rich layers of texture, colors, warm lighting, and comforting, inviting objects and scenarios. The final slide in this carousel is from the inside of a greenhouse. At the center of the greenhouse is a black square pool surrounded by lush greenery that makes up the rest of the frame. In the background at the perspective line is a massive black canvas painted with vibrant fruit and flowering foliage. The text written at the bottom of the image reads, "visualizing what we can build together / outside of capitalism," in black text on white rectangles (disssgrace, "yearning"). The collaged meme-scape reveals what could be possible if we worked toward queer futures. It presents us with an image full of growth, beauty, and space to thrive. It is maximalist and sensual—two visual cultural referents that tend to push back against the contemporary aesthetic of clean, white, smooth-surfaced domestic spaces and idealized bodies that are micromanaged into optimization. It is worth considering the kinds of work done by this image and its outlining of a space of possibility, particularly within a capitalist platform like Instagram. It is an image of growth and fecundity, as suggested by the plants, but these are housed in an inviting contained space that suggests boundaries or protection. Nothing about the image is smoothed out or perfected, instead it is textured with rich contrasts. There is queerness in the joy that it brings, in its excess. It does not conform or confirm a heterocapitalist normativity but shows us other ways of being.

One form of montage found across the different slides in this carousel deck is that when moving between them, the viewer creates new associations that are not present in the discrete frames on their own. Visually, when read together, they build a visual landscape of contrasting angles and visual cues in the move between one image and the next. Conceptually, they also build a shared argument around queer futurities outside of capitalism that is sutured together by their proximity. Further, there are montage elements found in the formal composition of each specific meme in the carousel. The composition of visuals and text produce a dynamism within the still frames as much as in the movement between them. These two types of montage in memes are significant for how they draw viewers into carousels as assemblages of cultural errata and ask us to contemplate the meaning of the whole. By framing them on display through the carousel format, we are witness to a purposefully selected grouping of visual and often audio cues similar to what would be offered in a short film. The carousels contain a narrative—or, if not something that coherent, at least a theme playing out rhythmically over the specific arrangement of clips and images. They build toward something, and in the encounter, viewers take away a meaning or affective experience of some kind. A meme carousel thus exhibits a problem, a question, an insight for broad consumption, and in doing so assembles us into publics that are addressed by its display.

Assemblages as Extended Montage Form

My use of assemblage considers how groups of material artifacts become associated through contextual—and I would add conceptual, proximity—to meaningful ends (B. Brown, "Re-Assemblage" 268). Assemblage is both an aesthetic formal practice and a concept that can describe artifacts or practices from an analytic position (B. Brown, "Re-Assemblage"). Assemblage as an aesthetic tactic can be found across different media and art forms, including literature, painting, sculpture, collage, performance art, and film (B. Brown, "Re-Assemblage"). It can also be a form of epistemology that is an "aggregation of experiences and the associative relation of ideas" that inform our understanding of the world (B. Brown, "Re-Assemblage" 280). Most interestingly for Bill Brown, drawing on the work of the philosopher G. W. F Hegel, assemblage can be framed as the way "our perception organizes properties (color, size, shape) . . . into an entity that . . . is in fact a community" (B. Brown, "Re-Assemblage" 280). In the latter half of this chapter, I will focus on this shift from aesthetic and formal practices of assemblage to their organization as forms of community. In some ways, assemblage best encapsulates a variety of overlapping threads traced throughout the book to this point. The term draws together the different formal aspects of meme specificity. The modes of collage, performative reenactment, temporal collage of sorts, and montage I explore as fundamental to meme specificity are themselves forms of assemblage. Bricolage, remix, and intertextuality run as a through line between these different formal tactics.

As noted in the introduction to this chapter, assemblage has a clear formal lineage and is used to describe "material practices that range from scrapbooking to quilting to intricate photomontage to monumental assemblage" but also structural and cultural forms such as "those practices through which the city is assembled" (B. Brown, "Re-Assemblage" 276). This definition quickly moves from the formal to a more broadly tactical understanding of assemblage as having a range of scope and impact, from the art artifact to how we gather and make meaning in large environments. This is precisely what Kyle Parry considers in his book *Theory of Assembly: From Museums to Memes,* where he argues that "assembly" is a "dimension of memes that needs attention" primarily as it will help us better understand the high-stakes ways in which memes affect social and cultural discourse for better and for worse (137–39). Assembly "has become increasingly powerful and pervasive . . . as a type of expressive artifact and communicative practice . . . but also as one among many strategies practitioners can creatively combine," the effects of which can both "mobilize publics" and "do harm" (Parry 1–2). Assembly thus can be understood as a "cultural form" and a "widely practiced form of cultural production" (4). It is equally a "thing and something people do" that is centered on "expressive gathering," which "places expressive relationships front and center" (3–4). Importantly, memes as assemblages "cut across all manner of platforms, times, and places" and have greatly expanded "in accessibility, frequency, and influence" within in the digital era (3). The term *assemblage* also indexes the way memes assemble publics and circulate forms of discourse that produce movement(s). The two elements of memetic assemblage—the formal and the sociocultural—cannot be separated from one another. In their combination, they make memes an intensely significant force within our contemporary digital landscape.

Assemblage as defined here can juxtapose images within different temporal and contextual landscapes, to resistant ends. For instance, it can turn older images into something new for political purposes. I am interested in the use of older cinematic images in the newer context of carousel decks. In these new formal spaces, cinema icons become referents for thematic, aesthetic, and political purposes. Here memes remix film images away from previous cultural moments and into new sites of meaning. A great example of this is found in a carousel post from the queer film meme account @lezzieborden, run by Toronto artist and scholar Alex Hall. It uses stills from one single movie, Gregg Araki's 1996 cult classic, *Doom Generation,* to offer viewers a "queerpocalypse blessing" in honor of the start of autumn (Hall, "Initiating"). Notably there is no text added to the film stills in the carousel montage. Instead, Hall relies on text already present in the selected film stills and on the interplay between images in the slide deck to advance her thematic and aesthetic intentions.

The first image in the slide deck is a compelling image of the three main characters in the film, alluding to their love triangle in the narrative with Rose

McGowan, who plays Amy Blue at the center. The next slide is a wide shot of Amy Blue entering a thrift store and framed by a large yellow sign above her that reads, "Prepare for the Apocalypse," with the word *apocalypse* emphasized in red lettering. Amy is the central draw of this image, in her unmistakable "bad ass" costume of sunglasses, black mini dress, and combat boots. The images from the film posted in the middle of the slide deck all punctuate the growing love triangle and further the queer eros embedded within the film, which was dubbed cheekily as a "Heterosexual romance" by the director, Araki, in promotional materials (Araki; Chen).

The last three slides include a close-up of a cash register glowing with the green numbers 66.6 (a running joke involving the total of each convenience store purchase the trio make in the film); a darkly lit, soft-focus close-up of Amy with a cigarette dangling out of her mouth, looking like a femme fatale villainess; and finally an image of Amy staring someone down off-screen, in her signature black dress and a beat-up leather jacket, with a black sign behind her that reads, "shoplifters will be executed," again emphasized in red lettering. The choice of images in this mini-montage does not tell the complete story of the film but offers a sequence of visual pleasure, queer eros, and a strategic use of signage from the original movie to reproduce the image macro meme format without altering or remixing the film stills. The text signage from the film stills, when read in this montage, provides a sense of doom, precarity, and uncertainty. It does not create a punch line so much as a queer apocalyptic sense of end-times gallows humor. This fits in well with the overall approach of the Hall's @lezzieborden account, which provides a queer appreciation for horror and the iconic women characters that make up the genre.

What is notable in this sequence of stills from *Doom Generation* is how they are reappropriated and used in the meme montage to serve a different audience and different media form. And yet they still retain the overall intentions of the earlier cult classic film, preserving a clear appreciation for the original text. Film stills here are a site of meme remix, bringing aesthetic legacies from earlier queer cinematic eras to a wider and contemporary audience. I would argue the temporal collapse explored in the previous chapter is extended into the reenactment of cult cinema, as it is used for queer nostalgic ends. Elizabeth Freeman notes that the "sensation of asynchrony" found in nostalgic, overdetermined histories of signification is "a queer phenomenon" ("Introduction" 159). Queer nostalgia is an affective temporality that functions "as a means to express or enact ways of being and connecting that have not yet arrived or never will" (Freeman, "Introduction" 159).

Feminist and queer temporalities and histories are attentive to the affective experience of nostalgia and to utilizing these for formal and critically

FIGURE 3.2. Instagram grid. Used with permission from Alex Hall for @lezzieborden.

persuasive ends. In queer temporalities, this nostalgia includes "the feelings of uncanniness, untimeliness, belatedness, delay, and failure" (Freeman, "Introduction" 162). Feminist and queer subjects are often positioned out of normative "time" for not adhering to dominant cultural milestones that mark how heteronormative life should be lived, with these milestones themselves steeped in a nostalgia for a fantasy "simpler" heteronormative past. Nostalgia can equally be present in the forms of hauntings and longings feminist and queer communities can feel for lost or distant trajectories of past movements and role models. Kate Eichhorn describes this as a nostalgia of reaching backward toward feminist models of the past that can help us better understand where we are going (253). There is a power in sitting with the iconicity of earlier movements of our queer and feminist histories. This in part may be why images from queer classics, like the *Scorpio Rising* memes from the start of the chapter or the uses of *Doom Generation* in the meme carousel explored above, are so evocative and successful in communicating a queer temporality in meme form.

When I was revisiting this post for analysis, Instagram offered me its own curated assemblage of other posts from the Hall's @lezzie_borden account, which, when taken together, offer an uneventful yet meaningful set of assemblages that I'd like to discuss further. The grid (see fig. 3.2) was assembled by an algorithm to encourage further engagement with the platform, yet it works well for offering a snapshot of how the account's queer activist content makes curious and engaging semiotic chains of meaning by chance. In the suggested content grid, there is an image from *The Craft* of the four main characters conducting a séance. Beside it is a still from *Scream* (1996) that has a huge Indigo Girls poster looming behind Skeet Ulrich's character turning and saying to someone off-screen, "The Exorcist was on. Got me thinking of you." There are also thumbnails for a variety of women-centered horror films, to complete the grid. There are many ways to analyze this assemblage as a networked constellation. The six-image grid reveals a goth-themed, nostalgic form of queer and feminist aesthetics that is both unsettling and inviting. The grid has hallmark horror films from the 1990s that evoke this nostalgia but also provide tongue-in-cheek nods to the forms of toxic masculinity the films call out in their narratives (with Ulrich as the evil protagonist in both of the first two posts on the grid). While this montage provided by Instagram's algorithm may not have been intended to produce such a rich text, it shows the potential within capitalist platforms to accidentally produce sites of queer affect and aesthetics. Like the histories of cult and experimental films, visual art, and performance art suggest, there is potential in co-opting mass media spaces to inform and draw dispersed publics into countercultural wholes. This is a point that I will return to in the final section of this chapter, where I explore the potential of sociocultural assemblages encouraged by activist memes and previous countercultural media communities. This is the ultimate point I wish to build to in the book. The combined tactics of collage, reenactment, and montage in memes work not only to provide us with meaningful digital visual texts, but they also bring us together in meaningful cultural assemblies. Before unpacking this claim further, I want to take some time to think more specifically about the linkage between memes and cinema. Just like I laid out the relationships between memes and collage and between memes and performance art, here I want to more fully map out the ways in which memes follow a clear trajectory from some of the earliest impulses of film form.

Memes as a Cinema of Attractions

To expand on how cinema and cinematic techniques figure into current meme aesthetics, I turn to the concept of the "cinema of attractions," developed by Tom Gunning, to describe aspects of early cinema that aren't readily encapsulated by the popular, yet not wholly accurate, division of film into narrative and documentary forms. Gunning offers a reread of early cinema history that explores a crucial yet overlooked component of the film medium: a form of "attraction" that predates the narrative dominance found in cinema from the 1910s and onward. While this presence of attraction is emblematic of the earliest decade of cinema, it finds its way into narrative genre conventions as well as more avant-garde approaches to cinema throughout the twentieth century (Gunning, "Attractions"). I want to suggest that memes are a legacy of the cinema attractions and hold many of the same properties and impulses that mark this earlier media form. This is part of what connects memes to the medium of cinema and, in conjunction with collage and reenactment, is part of what makes memes a unique medium.

Gunning starts his famous essay with a quote from avant-garde artist Fernand Léger around the "potential" of the film medium, and Léger's dismay with how it has been used by more commercial productions ("Attractions" 381). What drew Léger to the cinema's "radical possibilities" is akin to what Gunning defines in the essay as the cinema of attractions, or its "ability to *show* something" (382). This often includes a look at the camera by those on-screen, which ruins "the realistic illusion" of film (382). This visual, rather than narrative, and spectatorial address is, for Gunning, significant, as they show an aesthetic aspect of cinema that is often overlooked. The cinema of attractions "displays its visibility" and is "willing to rupture a self-enclosed fictional world for a chance to solicit the attention of the spectator" (382). Attractions offer "less a way of telling stories than . . . a way of presenting a series of views to an audience" that are "fascinating because of their illusory power . . . and exoticism" (382). This is interesting to contemplate in relation to memes, and especially memes that operationalize our nostalgia for movies and cult movies in particular, to draw in social media viewers.

In his discussion of the cinema of attractions, Gunning considers the work of Georges Méliès, a vaudeville magician recognized as having a significant influence on the development of trick photography in his early films. He translated a lot of his previous stage magic to the screen and created fantastical films where the plots are often secondary to the jump cuts, superimpositions, and on-screen pyrotechnics. The word *trick* is key here because it suggests two elements that are useful for discussing memes. The first is how the concept of a trick is tied to another term: *gag*. A meme, on a fundamental level, is set up via a gag that forms the punch line of the joke it displays, often through visual means. Tricks and gags take many forms in memes, and they have multiple intentions. Sometimes the gag is textual and runs as a joke played out within the frame. Other times the gag is visual and provides a dissonance between text and image that conveys humor. In a different way, memes are constantly playing with the limits of their digital form and visual lexicon and producing new tricks or displays to compel their audience. This can be seen easily in the evolution from a simple "Cheezburger cat" image with white text from the early 2000s to the overlay of moving images of popular cultural videos with text and sound twenty years later.

Gunning builds his use of the term *attraction* from Eisenstein, who, like other avant-garde modernist artists, held an "enthusiasm for a mass culture" coming out of cinema that provided "a new sort of stimulus" for audiences less connected to high art ("Attractions" 385). This form of cinema, dedicated to attraction, display, and direct audience address, held political potential. Eisenstein wanted to take mass media like cinema and "organiz[e] the popular energy" around it "for radical purpose" ("Attractions" 385), much like how in Hall's use of *Doom Generation* and other queer horror classics, even outside of the context of the original film, the still images offer a visual power that articulates new forms of desire and affect in the present. Memes share with the cinema of attractions an emphasis on visibility and spectacle over sustained narrative coherence. While certainly there are distinctions between them, including the scale of spectacle of early attractions-based cinema in comparison to those contained on our portable devices, both hold the potential to grab the viewer's attention and evoke forms of rupture and criticality in the viewing experience.

I wish to bring forward one additional point by Gunning that I believe helpfully situates memes as a medium of attractions that extends those early cinematic impulses of display and purposeful spectatorial address. In early cinema, the sites of exhibition, or the movie houses, "exerted a great deal of control" over how films were shown, and this could include "re-editing the film" as well as offering supplements like "sound effects" and "commentary" ("Attractions" 383). This strikes me as similar to memes being circulated and shared on specific accounts, especially social media accounts dedicated to displaying curated meme carousels, but also specific platforms. Memes are constantly being re-edited, modified, reimagined in new contexts, often including commentary either within the frame or within the post as well as, in more recent years, soundtracks as part of the gag to help further facilitate the intended meaning of the meme or its remix. They also inform or adapt to the platform affordance they are exhibited within and make conscious use of tricks and spectacle to be promoted further within the algorithms of a given site.

Cinema of attractions and how it circulates offers a "different configuration of spectatorial involvement," largely via "gags or visual pranks" whose "temporal structure of anticipation and eventual pay-off" offer their own form of "mini-narrative" (Gunning, "Attractions" 37). I see this as equally reflective of carousels use for political purposes, where the mini-narratives they produce evoke a deeply satisfying pay-off for audiences. Take for instance a

Pride-themed carousel roundup by Still We Rise (SWR, @stillwerise) in which a theme of rainbow paraphernalia orients a series of comedic posts. This includes a meme by @ChiefJimHop on how to foil a homophobic neighbor by placing dabs of rainbow paint on their windshield wiper so that they create a windshield rainbow the next time they turn their wipers on. There is also a repost of a meme by @nihilistgf_, which shows a burning police car stopped in the middle of a city street, with an animated rainbow bursting out of the roof, displaying the text "my gender is whatever this is," perfectly summing up a nihilist and rebellious performance of gender (SWR, "SWR Weekly"). There is a video clip of Adele telling off an audience member who screamed "pride sucks" as well as a tweet by @stephnmholden that says, "no cops at pride just an entire women's roller derby team skating around knocking over homophobes"; a photo of a United Church marquee that reads, "Happy Pride Month! Jesus had two dads and we think that's fabulous"; a picture of Ernie and Bert from *Sesame Street* reading quietly in a dimly lit room on separate arm chairs with the text "imagine being against gay marriage when its literally just this"; and, perhaps the most gimmicky and most iconic, an image of Mike Pence stepping off a plane and running to a podium, with AI generated images of him shaking glitzy pom-poms and a large rainbow-colored bow on his head. The spectacles and gimmicks are many and varied in this carousel slide deck. There are also nods to intertextual queer-coded icons like Bert and Ernie, reimagined here as fully and openly queer.

The grouping of memes evokes a queer irreverence that carries with it both refusal and joy. The very evocative image of a roller derby team pushing over homophobes is the kind of queer imagining that is funny for its improbability but also for the delightful and playful image it evokes. In the editing of these into the "queer edition" of the SWR meme roundup (a recurring feature on the page), the account takes up the social media imperative for public accounts to post during social events such as Pride month. This is a gimmick of sorts often used by corporations to signify allyship with a given event or community. SWR employs the gimmick to more resistant ends and presents a series of memes that themselves use a range of gimmicks to share their intentions clearly with viewers.

From Cinema of Attractions to Memetic Gimmicks

For Sianne Ngai, the gimmick is an aesthetic phenomenon that is specific to capitalism (*Theory*). It is key to how we make aesthetic value judgments of different kinds of visual content. The gimmick is a cheap trick, recognizable for what it is and what we are supposed to take away from it. It becomes a shortcut, a metonym for cultural experience and expectations. Gimmicks thus "embod[y] [a] significant temporal contradiction of capitalism . . . a perpetual present . . . and a relentlessly ongoing historical continuity" (Ngai, "Theory" 487–88). However, what is interesting is the ambivalence embedded in our relationship to the gimmick; it is something "we marvel at *and* distrust, admire *and* disdain" (469), it is both "enchanting and repulsive" at the same time (472). While I've written about the obvious link to the gimmick in hyperconsumerist media such as the "holiday film" (MacDonald and Wiens, "Back to the Future"), I find this concept interesting for different reasons in the context of memes as a form of digital attraction. The SWR meme roundup knowingly employs the meme roundup formula despite its capitalist uses by platforms to encourage algorithmic favor. This suggests a possible commitment to transforming the practice into a site of queer reimagining.

I believe this connection between the legacy of the cinema of attractions and Ngai's more recent considerations on the role of the gimmick in popular media offers a great deal of insight into the medium of memes. It helps situate the broad appeal and use of montage within carousel curation as well as the CapCut superimpositions. It situates these within the realm of the trick or gag that demands audience attention. The idea of "attractions" means very different things for early cinema forms of spectacle than it does for media today. Yet, Gunning's attention to not only form and content but also modes of delivery and display relates to questions around why memes rely on spectacle and different forms of attraction. It would be useful to ask how spectacle in memes is dictated by platform affordances and algorithmic determinations of the social media they circulate within. Here I look more closely at both the intentions behind attractions and how these can be employed for resistant ends. Memes of course are not just attractions, or intentional spectacle. Rather they mesh these impulses with others, like those outlined in previous chapters, including irony, defamiliarization, and forms of humor that allow for detached criticality. One place where this is abundantly clear is in the practice of superimposing cut-out images onto disjunctive backgrounds using media editors like CapCut. The outcome is a meme that moves and has audio to punctuate the more standard relationship between image and text from image macro memes.

These superimposed moving image memes are an extension of the earlier popular format of the GIF (or graphics interchange format), used to express a reaction to a statement either in a group chat or in a public post. The frequent use of affective performances of the body in GIFs stands in for the person posting the GIF as a response or reply. Our use of GIFs to express our own affect forges a "union of the provoking content with the response . . . as though one were taking on the facial expression of someone else" (Parry 142); they become an avatar for our emotions. Think here of the popular Cap-Cut meme of Bill Hader gesturing comedically as if to say, "oops, my bad," while still smiling impishly, thus not demonstrating any remorse. The clip comes from a *Saturday Night Live* skit from 2014 about a robot named Alan that was never aired (Di Placido). It is often paired with upbeat and whimsical music, including the Oompa-Loompa song from the original *Charlie and the Chocolate Factory* movie, as well as a sound clip from "Makeba" by Jain. This is overlaid with any number of different textual scenarios, from skipping work, to avoiding household chores, to stress shopping. Another popular one is the image of Pedro Pascal sheepishly but contentedly eating a sandwich that is overlaid with captions on a variety of topics, including resisting diet culture, representing social anxiety, and the AI appropriation of artist images. There is one with a cut-out figure of Michael Scott from *The Office* standing on a chair holding a boom box stereo overlaid with lyrics from Rage Against the Machine's "Killing in the Name Of": "Fuck you, I won't do what you tell me." This is often paired with text overlays that suggest some kind of rebellion or another—in the workplace, in a relationship, from a teenager toward their parents. Another one is of a shrunk-down image of a woman performing on a stage with a microphone, superimposed on a variety of background still images, singing a song with the lyrics "surprise, surprise" in a rising crescendo. This one is placed ironically on anything that would be a surprise to literally no one.

These superimposed video memes displace us from the original temporal contexts of the video clips, remixing them into an untethered, acontextual, and semiotically unique representational object. In the process, the image is pared down to a core emotion—happiness, laughter, apathy, rebelliousness—as a site of expression. Further, the video clip is often presented as a shrunk-down, cut-out, miniature version of the original image, in a new frame with different scaling. It is a fully defamiliarized image that then gets reconstituted for novel purposes via new background space, audio, and text. I'm interested in the use of what I see as a cinematic lineage of superimposition in this form of digital meme content. This includes a temporal displacement, where the video builds on a scripted cultural lexicon in a different way than a Barbie meme does. The layering of the video clip, as a cut-out, shrunk-down, miniature version of the original image in a new frame, displaces a sense of space that would also ground it in its original context.

Take, as another example, the meme template that has the "cut-out" image of two actors in a postapocalyptic scene of burnt-out buildings and general destruction in the background, with the text often showing some absurd thing to laugh about with someone the viewer is close to, despite the dire circumstances of the apocalypse. This meme uses the gimmick of green screen superimposition to affectively hail a close kinship and intimacy between the people sharing it. The meme acknowledges that we are often in what feels like apocalyptic times, with ongoing climate crises, geopolitical tensions resulting in wars and genocide, and increased risks of violence and hate in our everyday and online spaces. It puts us "there" even if we aren't technically there. It also locates who we want to be there with and tries to ease this process with a form of gallows humor. In this way, it is an aesthetic assemblage of sociocultural realities, distilling them to the humor and absurdity memes are so proficient in articulating. It allows us to delimit our intimate kinships and open the release valve on our fraught realities. Tactically what is interesting is how the physical displacement and collaging of different spaces together is compelling, as is the literal cutting-out of the moving bodies from video clips and the pasting of them into the new landscape, with new text to alter the scene being performed as a meme. This displacement and suturing, as an extension of montage and collage tactics, advances conversations that are less easily circulated in straightforward ways. The format becomes a foundation upon which complex cultural reckonings can take place. In this way, the tactics reflect a lot of the impetus and tactical media uses developed in feminist zine cut-and-paste aesthetics from the 1980s and 1990s. This is a connection I will return to in a later section of this chapter.

The Critical Gimmicks of Meme Parody Video

One other place where this use of montage is used to produce cultural reckonings in meme culture is found in reels or short videos where creators reenact displaced audio into a new theatrical interpretation of the original audio, for humor and critique. Reenactment, as was discussed in the previous chapter, allows for forms of critical distancing by the performer. Within parody videos, it is a quick way to direct the audience's attention to the slippage or break between the original audio's intentions and the critical or humorous interventions made by the video's creator. The dissonance or incommensurability between audio and reenacted video is the focal point of the gimmick or comedic gag. While the use of parody has long been a part of moving image culture, the extent to which it is being employed on social media platforms through meme culture is notable. It is a form of juxtaposition, tied to reenactment and the suturing together of distinct audiovisual elements, that is particular to the

FIGURE 3.3. "Soup anyone?" Still image from a video by TikTok account for Arin Knox (@arinsquirel98), reposted by Kelly Oxford on Instagram account kellyoxford (@kellyoxford).

meme medium. This is especially the case when we contemplate its mode of delivery via social media platforms as an ad hoc microcinema.

I want to consider a video on TikTok by two young women doing an interpretive performance of an incoherent Donald Trump's speech about the activists' use of soup cans for violence. The content creator, Arin Knox (@arinsquirel98), uses low-fi camera filming with natural lighting and an unadorned set to act out the script in a way that completely undermines the original point, showing the argument up for the farce it is. They punctuate different words in Trump's monologue with gestures, using props and bodily gags as well as facial expressions to build the comedy of the performance. There is a purposeful use of editing that ensures dynamic images are sequenced to work humorously against the speech. The reenactment video moves from wide shots to close-ups to emphasize the word "soup" which is repeated many times in the speech. The actors interpret this by holding the soup in the palm of their hand like a game show host showing a product placement (see fig. 3.3). At other times, they offer close-ups of their face miming the words. This creates a comedic slippage, where the decontextualization of the words becomes even more absurd. In the performance, they defamiliarize the voice-over through a

Brechtian "reenactment" that brackets the performance as one of critique. For instance, they turn a passage by Trump, rambling about what happens when cops catch up to the "devious activists," into comedy. They reenact the "catching" action through one actor placing a mesh shopping bag over the other's head in a slapstick manner. The shopping bag mimics a net, and the timing of the actors' facial expressions successfully turns this into a deeply comedic beat in the video. One of the reasons this is so successful is because of their use of film editing, or montage techniques, that keeps the movement between images dynamic and compels viewers to continue watching the full performance. There is joy and pleasure in watching the performance. The overall effect allows for a critical detachment rather than suturing the viewer into the post.

Even more significant is that this video, originally posted on the TikTok account of the video creator, was shown within a carousel roundup curated by an Instagram influencer @kellyoxford. As argued above, the carousel slide format of sequencing thematically connected still images, memes, and video content does not just produce a formal type of montage; it also produces social montages of culturally specific themes. It assembles discrete clips that, when joined, make a coherent conceptual whole. The practice of carousel decks on Instagram uses the platform's affordances to create an attention-grabbing attraction, or gimmick, that encourages longer-durational engagement with a given account, thus keeping the account in circulation within larger Instagram algorithms.

Stitches: Gimmicks That Speak Back

In concluding my exploration of cinematic gimmicks in queer and feminist activist memes, I want to look at the meme tactic of stitches, where a content creator records themselves reacting to content previously posted online by another account. Sometimes this includes showing a clip of the other content and then following up with a video reaction to it. Other times the creator will superimpose their own video image on top of the original and react in "real time" to the post. This montage tactic is used extensively in contemporary meme culture, taking off in popularity with the rise of TikTok. What it offers is an opportunity for a creator to build a conversation with other content and other creators. I have seen it used for everything from critical queer and anti-racist commentary on celebrity culture (Blakely Neiman Thornton, @blakely-thornton), to popular science communicators debunking disinformation and wellness conspiracy content (Food Science Babe @foodsciencebabe; Samantha

Yammine, PhD @sciencesam; Mallory @this.is.mallory), to men pushing back on different iterations of toxic masculinity circulating online (Professor Neil @professor_neil, Moses Williams @unexpectedlyfun). Stitches are a way to quickly establish one's brand as a creator through how you respond to the kinds of videos you stitch with and what position you take. It can help creators to quickly build communities of viewers and rapidly disseminate a critical position to large audiences.

For Parry, memes "perform some kind of take" on a topic via an assemblage of formal elements and media (144–46), offering a "form of a form" that suggests "the world is reducible to a set of situations or scenarios" (146). Memes employ simplified signifiers that drill down to the crux of the subject or issue being engaged to distill sometimes complex cultural concepts or emerging discourse. This is why the gimmicks found in the stich format are so useful for disseminating forms of critique. Take for instance the account Professor Neil, which stitches clips from the manosphere to debunk their overtly misogynist and racist claims. The account is run by Canadian academic Neil Shyminsky, who draws on a range of expertise in popular culture, cultural history, and politics, using personal anecdotes, research studies, and facts to counter the harmful discourse in the videos. The overall effect is an accessible breakdown of how the stitched videos perpetuate harmful ideologies and misinformation, and one gets the sense they are sitting in on an engaging university lecture, if only for a minute. Shyminsky uses platform gimmicks to great effect in his posts. Often, they begin with a clip of some influencer saying outrageous or alarming things, with the text "Stitch Incoming" in pink bubble letters at the top of the frame. This is followed by a medium close-up of Shyminsky in a domestic setting like a kitchen or a den with a bookshelf in the background. Sometimes the original manosphere clip is cut off just after some absurd claim, and the stitch cuts to Shyminsky saying, "Hit me with it," as if he's dreading, but resigned to, what he's about to hear and mentally preparing himself for the task of deconstructing the sexist messaging after the clip continues. He then proceeds to break down the logical fallacies of the clips through a critical lens that uses different rhetorical strategies, including an appeal to expertise via citing peer-reviewed studies on an issue, as well as his own anecdotes from real life that create a greater emotional connection with the viewer. The stitch as clapback against hypermasculine ideology is productive and educational and opens spaces for further discussion amongst audiences. In this example, and many other activist uses of the stitch, the formal properties of editing are used to merge two disparate videos. This allows for an assemblage of forms as well as cultural texts to produce critical commentary and political interventions. Taken as a collective effort to stem the swell of toxic and increasingly hysterical "hot takes" in conservative, misogynist, homophobic, racist, and alt-right spaces, these stitches as political intervention use meme tactics to produce a critical counterpoint within digital mass culture.

Meme Assemblages as Critical Mass Culture

In a consideration of public protest in the last decade, Alana Gerecke and Laura Levin consider "what is at stake in gathering and moving together" in public and "collective . . . choreographic arrangements" and ask how this "re-shape[s] the social, the aesthetic, and the political?" (5). Their work situates the last decade as an "era of assembly," a distinction that is useful for addressing the different ways people presently gather to protest and resist (Gerecke and Levin). This era of assembly encapsulates the various physical social gatherings that mark movements like Occupy Wall Street, Idle No More, #NoDAPL, Black Lives Matter, #MeToo, and reproductive justice protests. Assembly extends beyond offline spaces of protest, bringing them into the virtual spaces of the internet. It is useful to think about the collective, choreographic arrangements of online assemblies and how they also do the work of reshaping the social, the aesthetic, and the political. Memes function in and as assemblies on formal and political levels that contribute to the uniqueness of memes as an aesthetic medium.

Gerecke and Levin build on Butler's argument in *Towards a Theory of Performative Assembly* that our presence as visible subjects requires we both name the forms of power that situate us as subjects and do so in "critical alliance" with others equally constrained by such power (Gerecke and Levin 50–51). Freedom from this power "does not come from you or from me, but from what is between us" (Gerecke and Levin 52). For Butler performative acts of assembly critique power and set forth the possibilities of freedom for marginalized populations to assert the right to livable lives. This can be extended to performative acts of assembly that occur in online spaces of gathering such as social media platforms. Digital activists engage in performative acts of political critique in their memes but also in the acts of assembly that circulate those memes. These employ the tools of platforms, which are a site of differential forms of power digital activists seek to resist. Such assemblies risk the trappings of the platform, which can easily slip into forms of individual promotion. Digital activists work against these kinds of algorithmic gatekeeping, which are built into the design of capitalist platforms, and the technological erasures of activist content that they include. Despite these real barriers to the circulation of activist content, there is ample evidence to show that this work continues to develop and showcase tactics that can "establish new forms of appearance . . . to overcome that differential form of power" (Butler, *Performative Assembly* 52). This solidifies the work of those engaged in the act of performative assembly, through what it critiques and how it engenders new forms of expression (Butler, *Performative Assembly* 52). This, I believe, is a key site where memes contribute meaningfully to our social worlds. Activist meme makers are exploring and pushing the limits of the possible within our digital visual cultural landscapes. They innovate new forms of expression from the digital tools at hand. The appeal of their products—memes—have produced an unending number of performative assemblies and thus opened a new and productive avenue for cultural critique.

Many of the politically oriented memes I have studied in this book offer, in the words of David Blakesley, "a rhetorical situation in which interactions among an anonymous creator, the meme and meme iteration, and the viewer combine to create 'he total act of making meaning'" (qtd. in Huntington, "Pepper Spray" 79–80). And yet these memes' rhetoric also encompasses the context of events to which the memes respond and source texts from which the memes appropriate and remix. These associations lend memes their rhetorical power (Huntington, "Pepper Spray" 79). Many activist memes gesture toward a better future, one that is woven together through shared affective desires. In the final section of the chapter, I extend my examination of memetic aesthetic tactics of collage, reenactment, and montage to consider how memes, as a combined formal assemblage, can also produce meaningful modes of social assemblage. Using recent theories of assemblage, I consider how social assemblages appear in the historical practice of feminist zines from the 1990s. I then link this to similar formal and political assemblages in current spaces of feminist and queer activism. To make this link, I take up renewed production of digital and physical zines by activists and activist collectives working in both an online and offline space.

Zines as Precursors to Memetic Aesthetic Assemblies

Zines from the feminist punk and Riot Grrrl subcultural spaces of the 1990s are an excellent example of cultural assembly that hold both aesthetic and political elements within the larger movement. Formal or aesthetic assemblage as well as forms of cultural assembly can be seen in the ethos of the Riot Grrrl movement as well as in the aesthetic tactics they advanced via zine experiments. As Janice Radway notes, "the term *zine* is a recent variant of *fanzine,* a neologism coined in the 1930s to refer to magazines self-published by aficionados of science fiction" (Radway 140). The term as we understand it today originates "with the '70s punk scene, because zines proliferated at that time as a means of reviewing and promoting punk bands independently of the mainstream music industry" (O'Brien 90). The work of zine making brings forward a related feminist and queer DIY aesthetic practice that shares a great deal of overlap with the original impulses of bricolage to use the available materials at hand to create critical cultural artifacts. Zine makers sought "to resist commodification formally by practicing an aesthetic that was decidedly not reader friendly. They produced collaged pamphlets with chaotic, cut-and-paste layouts that defy linear scanning, sometimes resist traditional narrative sequencing, and even refuse pagination altogether" (Radway 141). The low-stakes production of zines as cut-and-paste analogue assemblages of photo-copied ideas and images allow "creators to control" their content as "it is not created to serve the interest of others: zinesters do not have to bend to, or tap into, market trends and pressures" (Ramdarshan Bold 223). They also offer an easy and accessible entry point: "Anyone—no matter what their background or skill—can create their own zines and thus participate in literary culture" (226). They advanced a "collaborative, participatory, approach to cultural pro-duction" that productively alters how "people, especially marginalized com-munities, see themselves situated within a wider social context" (226).

Zines, a space of vital critical resistance, can also be seen as "an inher-ently hopeful medium" that "make[s] visible the desire for community and human connection," and their "materiality produces embodied community" (Piepmeier 235). In this way, "zines instigate intimate, affectionate connections between their creators and readers, not just communities but *embodied* com-munities that are made possible by the materiality of the zine medium" (214). Feminist zines' commitment to a collage-like materiality "creates commu-nity because it creates pleasure, affection, allegiance, and vulnerability," and, importantly, "this is one of the causes and consequences of the humanized connections that zines enable. It is one of the most mysterious and important elements of this embodied community" (230).

This echoes the sentiments shared by Kathleen Hannah writing on her role as the reluctant de facto leader of the Riot Grrrl movement in her memoir *Rebel Girl.* She outlines how a group of women students began meeting so that they could find a space to develop their artistry outside of the constraints of masculine-dominated art school discourse at the time (83). She notes,

> it was such a relief to hear other women talk about how the faculty didn't know how to deal with photography outside of the Ansel Adams model

of using the golden ratio. It was exhilarating to show each other work in progress and get the critiques and encouragement we weren't getting in our classes. . . . We started bringing in an article each week to discuss, which is how I learned about artists like Jenny Holzer and Barbara Kruger. Both were feminists who used text about identity and power in their work. . . . the idea of merging text with photography fascinated me. (83)

Describing what stood out to her about Kruger, Hannah points to how she "recontextualized old advertising images by placing her iconic red-and-white text on top" (Hannah 83). With Jenny Holzer, it was how she turned her feminist phrases "into everything from sculptures to hats to t-shirts to postcards to flyers" (Hannah 83). What was appealing about both Kruger and Holzer was how they "turned streets, subways, and mailboxes into impromptu radical museums" (Hannah 83). These inspired much of Hannah's earlier photo collage art as well as the zine aesthetic that grew from this in the zines tied to her band, Bikini Kill. Once the band started touring, Hannah would send postcards to women she had addresses for, "asking them to come to our shows and bring more girls," with the invitation to "Draw Hearts and Stars on your hands . . . and if you see a girl with hearts or stars, go ask her if she got a postcard too, strike up a conversation" (169). Hannah notes how well this worked and precipitated an influx of women at shows. She invited them onstage at show breaks to share their zines (169). This gives a sense of how networks of circulation spread within Riot Grrrl zine culture as a form of performative assembly. In a related way, our recirculation of memes that match our own personal politics, identities, ideals, and communities offers a similar form of signaling. By sharing memes on our personal accounts or resharing in our stories or privately with our contacts, we are building connections and identifying ourselves with some sort of subculture. It becomes a badge or way into a community, and once in the community, we are opened to networks of cultural sharing around that community's interests.

Hannah's reflections draw a picture of a Riot Grrrl assemblage that includes combining affect, politics, ethos, and practice to produce what has become an influential and significant moment within the history of late twentieth-century feminism. It is a good example of sociocultural assemblages that emerge from a set of intentional practices but also take on a memetic life of their own as they circulate and expand into larger collective forms of action. Assembly in this sense is perhaps most clearly understood as "*a way of looking at the world*" insofar as examples of assembly "do not narrate or represent the world, but instead rearrange it" by "bringing other things into view"; as such, it is also an act of assemblage (Parry 28; emphasis in original). This is a useful frame for activist memes, as they are representative of forms of assembly and practices of assembly but also in the sense that in their concomitant efforts, they rearrange the world with a gesture of always looking toward a horizon of new potentials.

Early Riot Grrrl zines, like *Jigsaw* created by Hannah's bandmate Tobi Vail, established an aesthetic template that merged handwritten and typed text with cut-and-paste images. These were assembled into a whole, sometimes with additional text overlays adding critical commentary. For instance, in issue 3 of *Jigsaw*, there are the "official" texts typed out on each page including the cover, which identifies the zine as for "newMODROCKERS and the jigsaw underground," just above a cut-out vintage image of a group of four women standing closely, staring directly at the camera. Their 1950s hair (wavy pin curls) and outfits (wide cuffed jeans, varsity and leather jackets) evoke a sense of a vintage girl gang. This is supported and is supplemented on the bottom by a follow-up descriptor: "angry grrrl zine" (Vail and Klein 1991). This is not just a music zine for mod rockers but a feminist one with an orienting politics. This cover operates similarly to the way that different lines and levels of text in image macro memes complicate or extend each other—where the second line of text often undermines or shifts the first line of text. In the *Jigsaw* cover, this proto-meme format offers an example of aesthetic tactics that operate in the service of cultural assemblage. It calls like to like and creates a space inside the pages for feminist community formation. The zine's text is confessional and intimate in tone, as if Vail is having a conversation with readers in a consciousness-raising group meeting. These political passages are interrupted on the top and bottom margins by the words "girlfriend," "slut," and "feminist" written in thick black marker and accompanied by simple doodles of hearts, stars, flowers (prototypes of emojis, in some sense). There is a suturing or editing together of the typed text and the three terms *girlfriend, slut, feminist.* Read together, they assemble a very particular public—that of young feminist artists on the Pacific Northwest coast of the US—who were being actively and sometimes violently marginalized by the visual art and music scenes for daring to be living and creating in public spaces. The words *girlfriend, slut,* and *feminist* capture well the kinds of complicated negotiations this public assembly managed while demanding a set of livable lives within a deeply misogynist and racist set of power differentials operating in their cultural spaces at the time. These zines reveal the forms of world making that assemblage media tactics enable. They are performative in the sense that they articulate into being new possibilities. As Butler notes, performative assemblies, such as those created by Riot Grrrl zine culture, hold to account operations of power (*Performative Assemblies*). They also enable the emergence of new forms of appearance to counter such power. In the context of the nostalgia that haunts my personal reading of Riot Grrrl zine culture, assemblage is as much a merging of temporal layers of meaning as it is a merging of tactics and bodies.

Zine assemblages from past activist moments, especially as they reappear as a site of interest in the present, reflect this sense of temporality. They also activate a layered sense of the term *movement* to include temporal movement, political movement, affective movement. Here I want to reflect on a passage by Elizabeth O'Brien describing a visit to the Papercut Zine Library:

> I am reading about some punk band in Cleveland, about the music industry's fascist ways, about how some girl who works in retail hates her stupid job. . . . I lose myself in the dissonance of so many words, so many voices that add up to something big . . . anybody who wants to can belong here. I belong here. (99)

What stands out for me in this passage is the multiple ways that assemblage can occur in something as simple as sitting within a zine archive. As artifacts of past cultural assemblages, earlier zines and their commitment to the personal and the intimate reveal a politics of the everyday, but told through a chorus of voices that, as O'Brien recognizes, "add up to something big" (99). I think memes can be understood in a similar way. If one sifts through their own personal meme collections—either gathered by screenshots, saved on a platform, or shared in group chats—an equally fluid yet affecting set of experiences emerges. Not all memes are informational, or personal, or work with aesthetic intentions to move the viewer, but a lot of memes tied to activist accounts do. Memes, as a form of aesthetic assemblage, in their aggregate, produce cultural assemblages that draw networked communities together that sift through our digital ephemera and make meaning of the detritus. Memes, as a formal cultural artifact and a social and communication practice, circulate and share content as a way of advancing conversations, politics, identities. In doing so, they engage in forms of rearticulation that allow new modes of appearance to emerge that speak back to how differential power operates in our digital and offline lives.

Aesthetic Assemblages as Memetic Legacies

I want to consider the legacies of these earlier zine assemblages in the present. Zine aesthetics are reemerging as a popular form of communication both online and offline in the twenty-first century. They can take many forms, including memes and meme carousel decks that employ a cut-and-paste aesthetic, as well as popular activist accounts sharing zines via digital platforms but also translating those to material zines for followers to purchase. The intentional use of zines in digital space is made explicit on many zine accounts circulating on Instagram. In a post from February 2022, the account Cyclista Zine (@cyclista_zine) posted an image that has a collaged background of their zine pages with a cutout tweet laid overtop from the fanzine account, which states, "Stop doomscrolling / Start zine reading." The accompanying text in the comments from the account reads:

> These last few days of watching the news has really reaffirmed why zines and zine making are critical for our collective care. F*ck imperial state propagandist machines. Sharing zines in stories today on care and more. We know not all folks are able to break from the news cycle but zines can offer some sort of relief from doom-scrolling and provide the tools of resistance. Don't give into western propaganda and imperialism. Stay radical. #zines #collectivecare #zinemaking #independentmedia #bipoczines #bipoczinesters #diy #feministzine #feministmedia. (Cyclista Zine)

This commentary zeroes in on the ethos of this and other activist accounts that operationalize a zine aesthetic within digital platforms. Earlier eras of feminism used zines as a way of side-stepping media hierarchies tied to capitalist aims. As such zines and their digital counterparts are forms of countermedia that assemble audiences in ways that do not contribute to the consumption of news media doom cycles. Instead, they ask us to consider how, together, creators and their audiences can resist. The hashtags are significant here where they locate this politics in feminist community activism as well as emphasizing both the vital necessity of independent media and an orientation toward collective care. Like the additional text in *Jigsaw* noted above, hashtags situate a media text within a larger collective conversation that ultimately coalesces around the hashtag. Importantly, hashtags also extend the reach of a text, delimiting the shape and contours of the assemblage that is called together through its interpolation. Through this, hashtags allow for feminist activist media to assemble communities of users together from a place of collective care and intentionality.

The centering of collective care as a point of action can be seen in how zines operate in their transition from digital back to material spaces offline. For instance, artist and activist Rachael House (@rachaellhouse), whose work affirming queer existence is exhibited widely, including in the Victoria and Albert Museum, posted information on a zine she was part of in

2021 "protesting violence against women." In it there is a collage image by Queer Anarchy Now! that states, "Listen to your daughters. Educate your sons" (House). The zine included art and comics by a range of contributors and included the hashtags #listentoyourdaughterseducateyoursons, #protest-zine, and #feministzine. Notably the zine could be purchased by donating to the Housing for Women organization in the UK. Queer Anarchy Now! also houses several free posters on their personal website that can be used by anyone for activist ends, often with queer, feminist, anticapitalist, and antig-enocidal messaging (see fig. 3.4). House's zine and the Queer Anarchy Now! posters encapsulate well the use of zines, zine-related protest posters, and their promotion on social media as a means of producing collective care by redi-recting funds toward nonprofit organizations helping those most affected by the issues forming the focus of the zine's political intentions and knowledge sharing.

This is also reflected in the work of artist Katie Kiesewetter, whose zines include a fully free downloadable copy of her "Feminist Art Punks" sylla-bus for people to print out and use as a guide for both learning about Riot Grrrl politics and aesthetics and for making one's own feminist zine. The syl-labus presents material on the history of Riot Grrrls as well as information and links to Riot Grrrl formations in the current moment. It offers themed weeks on social justice, intersectionality, and bodily autonomy rights. There are readings and research lists, midterm and final assignments, as well as a series of sketchbook exercises and final project prompts. The downloadable syllabus is formatted as a zine. In the introduction to it, the creator notes this work comes out of her MFA project at the University of Iowa and is the dream course she has always wanted to teach. She shares the well-crafted syllabus with the public as a "radical act of care, challenging the Academy™ and ideas surrounding who has access to knowledge and artifacts related to knowledge-production" (Kiesewetter). The syllabus is an assemblage of Riot Grrrl zine politics, academic practices (freed from institutional constraints), art, and activism, all circulated through digital means. This is the outcome of a series of different kinds of aesthetic and political interventions developed at different moments in time, collapsed together to make what I believe is a practice of social assemblage. While social assemblages are an apparent ele-ment of cultural practices across different eras and movements, the current uses of collage and montage, and the assembling of image and text in a variety of forms that move between the digital and material, is notable and deserves further exploration.

A clear example of the coming together of aesthetic and social assemblage is found in the work of the For The Wild collective, a women-run group "of

SEX WITHOUT STIGMA

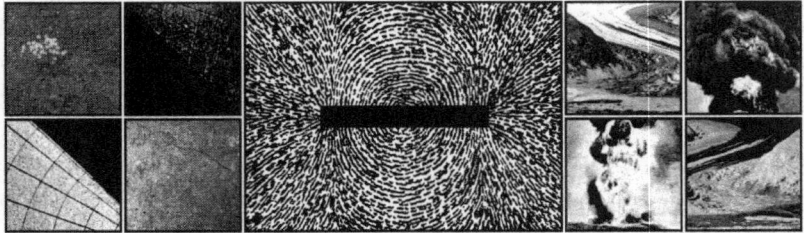

SEX WITHOUT SHAME

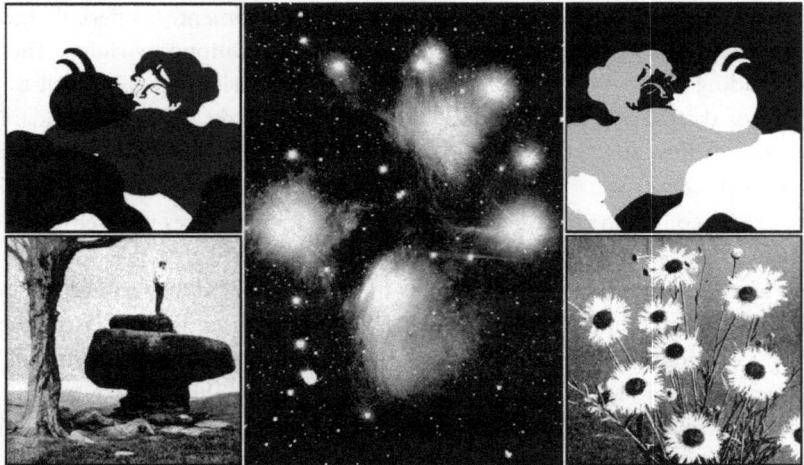

RESIST HETERONORMATIVITY!

FIGURE 3.4. "Resist Heteronormativity." Used with permission
from Black Lodge Press for Queer Anarchy Now.

dedicated creators, alchemists, and forever-learnings who are committed to land-based restoration, social reconciliation, storytelling, responsibility, and education" (https://forthewild.world/). A subheading on their website tags this work as "An Anthology for the Anthropocene," and their work includes an Instagram account, a podcast, monthly zines, and for Patreon subscribers, additional materials including playlists and community dialogues. I first came across and wrote about the account while studying carousel decks in the context of eco-activism online (Wiens and MacDonald, "Dwelling as Method"). Here I wish to extend this work and explore their political use of zines in more detail. The collective releases a zine monthly, with six published to date. Each zine is themed and includes work and writing by a variety of artists, activists, and thinkers.

In the "Practical Wisdom for Times of Renewal" zine released in April 2024, the For The Wild collective offers thirty-seven pages that include an opening prayer, original digital photographs, artwork and illustrations, a ritual, reading lists, reflective prompts, and text excerpts from guests of their podcast (Shiva, "On Becoming"). The focus of this issue was on acts of renewal in our relationship to the earth. While eco-activism was at the core of this theme, the writing and dialogues in it spanned a range of topics from technology, to ecological sustainability, to culinary care. The collective introduces the text excerpts as "call[ing] into deep conversation what it means to be involved in growth, both as we tend to the land and soil that nurtures us and as we grow new systems of humanity that exist in better reciprocity with the Earth" (Shiva, "On Becoming" 5). The text by Indian ecological activist Vandana Shiva titled "On Becoming Untameable" starts with a provocative passage around the need to return technology to its position as a tool that requires our collective assessment and consent to be used in society (6). Shiva warns that if we miss these steps in our relationship to technology, "you are moving very quickly into the use of tools as dictatorships," placing it "in the hands of the masters rather than . . . at the service of nature and humanity" (6). The textual components of the zine are placed on a warm yellow page and look as if they have been block-printed, giving them a texture and adding some shading to the ink-like lettering. These texts are interspersed with screen prints of nature, including sketches of bees and flowers. There are also vivid photographic images of women placed in natural settings, seemingly being consumed by plant growth. The overall effect is one of contemplative resources to accompany a reader on their explorations into the many interesting angles one can take on eco-activism. The sheer merging of so many different ideas, images, textures, and colors provides an assemblage of forms and concepts that advance a larger political vision. I find this a compelling example of where current zine aesthetics and practices, as a form of social and formal assemblage, can take us as activists.

The way current activist content creators are merging contemporary political issues with the ethos of Riot Grrrl and DIY zine culture from past decades is an important element of activist tactics at present. One important aspect of digital culture it addresses in thoughtful ways is the ephemerality, the fleeting nature, of meme culture. Digital zines are extending memetic tactics beyond the curated slide deck that Instagram affords, moving into the production of independent digital artifacts that can be easily circulated but that also have an intentional structure and design and are accessible, locatable, and archivable. The consequence of this is twofold. First, social media accounts and content creators that make zines are producing content independent of the platforms and their algorithms, regaining a certain amount of agency to direct traffic to their websites and other spaces that retain their projects. Second, with a zine, there is an increased amount of space to share complicated social ideas and activist tactics. These offer more sustained spaces of engagement for those audiences who desire to move beyond the quick peeks offered by memes, GIFs, stitches, duets, and carousel decks. As the content by For The Wild and Kiesewetter illustrate, this form of activism found in the move from internet memes to zines contains an impulse toward joy, pleasure, care, and community. These, I believe, are the best kinds of insights and commitments to emerge from activist meme practices in the current moment.

The Import of Memetic Assemblage within Digital Culture

Memes are producing new forms of cultural assemblage in the digital era that require careful analysis around how their formal aspects greatly inform their discursive effects. The impact of memes is not in dispute—we have a rich field of scholarship dedicated to this. What is needed is in-depth considerations of the specific modes employed by memes to achieve their consequential impact on social configurations, identity performance, and the dissemination of ideas, values, and beliefs. The carousels, videos, and digital zines considered in this chapter, I would argue, collectively function like daily micro gallery visits, media binges, or film programs. They offer us readily accessible sites of media consumption that, given the ubiquity of our devices, cause the content we consume to interact with our everyday worlds. This integration has formal, conceptual, and social implications.

Via memes' formal specificity, time and space become abstracted so that in their displacement from offline reality, we can get at other perspectives or suggested ways of seeing. This provides forms of spatial and temporal collapse as well as opens the space for reenactment that produces critical mimesis. This is not relegated to image macro memes and their reliance on static image and text. As this chapter's examples suggest, these tactics are equally present in memetic uses of video forms such as montage, parody reels, and stitches. It is vital that scholars well versed in the tactics and effects of moving image media from previous eras take seriously the kinds of legacies that reside in current moving image production on social media platforms. These videos, for better or for worse, are the current lingua franca of moving image content for some online subcultures. It is important that we map the forms of avant-garde film that have historically employed different types of visual collaging, performance, and rupture largely for political means.

Aesthetically, memes are illustrative of Umberto Eco's notion of "open work," or the "unfinished, unresolved, in process, participatory" work of culture grounded by a "collective, almost authorless shareability" (Merjian and Rugnetta 4). As Henry Jenkins notes, for Eco the "cult film is made to be quoted . . . because it is made from quotes, archetypes, allusions, and references drawn from a range of previous works" (*Convergence Culture* 98). It is useful here to think about meme culture as a legacy of counterculture with its deep ties to intermediality and intertextuality. What interests me most in this connection is how much memetic cultural practices have integrated montage, collage, and reenactment as mediatic conditions that allude to visual and textual ephemera outside memes, and the interdiscursive textual play between them.

If memes are both social practices and forms of cultural discourse, it is arguable that they are also events. This distinction indexes the performativity and the liveness of the medium. Memes are uttered or articulated within a particular cultural moment tied to the deep contextual threads of time and place. This is part of the temporal and spatial conditions of memes that we need to read closely, as it grounds their use of formal innovations. Within digital culture, this sense of time is diffuse and ongoing, multilayered and recurring. Additionally, the space of memes is unstable and unfixed, hard to locate or ground as it moves across platforms and digital space. And yet memes still can be located, even if part of mapping memes and their historical trajectories means locating them in perpetually new locations and contexts.

The event-ness of memes indexes their performativity—they act out culture alongside the personal performative scripts of those who stage and circulate them. The borders of the meme frame are the stage for this personally and culturally contextual performance. This frame is both a mise-en-scène and mise en abyme that is dependent on the form of presentation the meme takes. It is incumbent upon scholars to study how memes develop new ways of performing culture back to us. This includes considering the way different platforms frame meme content in its larger interface and how that impacts our interaction with the textual aspects of the memes. Memes, as viral practices that circulate and are taken up, reinterpreted, and redistributed, are media examples of what Butler calls "improvisation within a scene of constraint" (*Bodies*). While it seems perhaps fraught to apply a hallmark of gender performativity theory to a media object, it is worth considering for a moment how this helps frame the interplay of cultural texts and the structural constraints of platform design.

What I have aimed to unpack in these last three chapters is the ways memes utilize aesthetic practices of collage, reenactment, and montage to create a unique medium of expression responding to, and reflective of, the current digital moment. I have mapped the longer histories of each of these tactics and where they show up in earlier moments of countercultural media and art. I do so to demonstrate that memes as an aesthetic medium come from somewhere; they are a remix of formal experiments that came before them. Just like those earlier countercultural practices, activist memes are well suited to push back against dominant culture even when circulating within the spaces of mass media and capitalist platforms. They take the tools of social media and find the spaces of possibility for critique to break through. I believe that in this way activist memes have successfully encouraged the formation of critical cultural assemblies, creating discursive networks that can rapidly respond to the seemingly unending terror of our news cycles and geopolitical realities in thoughtful, supportive, and sometimes necessarily humorous ways. Having established the clear use of these three tactics as well as their historical lineages and potential for devising coalitional networks, I want to turn in the concluding chapter that follows to the value of pleasure and joy in activist meme culture. In the chapter, I work through concepts of joyscrolling and pebbling as practices of digital care, consider the value of pleasure activism for activist meme culture, and explore the value of queer affect in sustaining us as activist meme communities far into the future.

Embracing the Pleasure Activism of Joyscrolling

I conclude this book with a meditation on the joys of meme-ing in a world full of hate and division. I have spent a lot of time in the previous chapters outlining all the ways activist memes can produce critical and resistant forms of communication that challenge the status quo and assemble communities that seek other forms of being outside of the sexist, racist, homophobic, ableist, and capitalist structures that confine us. What I wish to turn to now is the pleasure we find in memes even in a cultural landscape of uncertainty, fear, and pain. We wouldn't spend so much time scrolling and consuming memes if they didn't offer us something beyond activist dictums, rally cries, and quick bits of wisdom. We dwell with memes because they are entertaining, engaging, resonant. Even those that evoke plainly the stark realities of the moment often do so with a dose of humor around the illogical, upside-down world we encounter. I spend the remainder of these pages, then, contemplating the specificity of joy and pleasure in memes: how it operates, where we can find it, and what it ultimately means for us. This chapter turns at times reflective and personal, which seems appropriate for a scholarly study on such an intimate element of our contemporary everyday communication practices. I invite you then to ponder on the possible joy of memes for a bit longer, and I hope that the questions I open here and elsewhere in the book encourage further conversation among us fans, scholars, makers, and consumers of memes.

Bernie's Mittens and the Performance of Joy

My first conscious encounter with the social media phenomena of "joyscrolling" occurred when Bernie Sanders once again became a viral meme during President Joe Biden's inauguration on January 20, 2021. A photo was taken early on that day of Sanders sitting on a folding chair on the generic white steps, snuggled down in his familiar green winter coat, arms and legs both crossed, with a pair of vividly patterned mittens on. Sanders is wearing a mask but has a concentrated and somewhat contemplative expression on what is seen of his face. The "Bernie Mittens" memes began almost immediately and spread across social media for many days and weeks after the inauguration. The remixing included a plethora of pop culture reimaginings with Bernie at the center. This included the Bernie image on the album cover of Pink Floyd's iconic *Dark Side of the Moon*; Bernie hanging upside down with a couple of bats on a tree; Bernie in the chair at the center of a Ming dynasty vase; Bernie ascending to the Heaviside Layer, a remix of the climax to the musical *CATS*; Bernie sitting just behind Han Solo and Chewbacca on the Millennial Falcon, under the sorting hat at Hogwarts, on a road trip with Cheech and Chong, in the car with Wayne and Garth, embedded in a famous Banksy screen print on a concrete wall, in the Georges Seurat painting *Sunday on the Grand Jette*, in various versions of the Last Supper, in detention with the kids from *The Breakfast Club*, with Forrest Gump on a park bench, in the living room of the *Golden Girls*; Bernie replacing Baby in the iconic scene from *Dirty Dancing* where Patrick Swayze's character reaches out his hand in invitation while saying, "Nobody puts Baby in a corner"; Bernie waiting outside for an Amazon delivery. The list goes on. You could even get a meme generated of the Bernie image in front of your house (I know, because I have one). The meme generated over a million dollars for charity based on merchandise sales tied to it ("Bernie Sanders Mitten Meme"; Rathke).

Beyond collapsing Bernie into other times and spaces, some simply captioned the photo as a means of interpreting the meaning and affect behind Bernie's demeanor and remixed that into other internet meme comments, including popular phrase "this could have been an email" (McCluskey). Others used Bernie's pose as a site of reenactment, taking up the Bernie Mittens persona themselves in a variety of personal, everyday contexts like sitting on a beach or music rehearsals, where Bernie is seated beside musical instruments. In the image, Sanders wears a coat from Vermont-based company Burton, and the infamous upcycled mittens were gifted to Sanders by a teacher from the state, prompting the Vermont Folklife Digital Archive to openly call for submissions of "Bernie Memes" for a digital archive that currently contains more than fifteen hundred images ("Vermont Folklife Archive"). The collection's images were uploaded by meme makers who could add context and commentary to their submissions. As such, it offers an accessible snapshot of how capaciously the Bernie Mittens meme has been remixed and reimagined. In viewing the collection, one gets a sense of revelry and joy.

While most Bernie Mittens memes abstract quickly away from the original context of Biden's inauguration, there is in its origin a kernel of what makes the image of Sanders from the event so appealing. This kernel is both about the subject of Sanders himself but also the context of the image as being tied for many to a collective sigh of relief that the inauguration was happening at long last. The inauguration was just three weeks after the January 6 storming of the capitol. Those in the United States, and those of us watching with deep discomfort from elsewhere, were negotiating differing forms of dread and concern over an apparent erosion of respect for democratic processes that had amplified under Trump's presidency and came to a spectacularly unsettling apex that day earlier in January.

As I have noted elsewhere in this book, memes have been a central cultural aspect of American election politics since at least the early to mid-aughts, where they played on outsized role in circulating pro-Trump and pro-MAGA discourse, leading some to claim that Trump's election triumph was the outcome of the great 2016 meme wars (Donovan et al.; Woods and Hahner). Memes have continued since 2016 to be central to how Americans express their politics, as was made abundantly clear as well in the 2020 and 2024 election cycles. I have written elsewhere about the rise in popularity of witch memes in 2017, with many of the early viral memes coming from collective efforts (both real and performative) to "hex the patriarchy" and do binding spells to minimize Trump's damaging effects for marginalized and vulnerable communities targeted by his hate-fueled politics (MacDonald and Wiens, "Feminist Memes"). In November 2020, there was a large outpouring of memes from both the left and the right that cast the differing sides in clear relief. Over the four years between 2016 and 2020, the left began to meme differently, and Twitter was a significant site of meme-based discourse around Biden and Trump including in left-leaning digital communities. This is clear in the left's co-optation of the "Let's Go Brandon" memes used as code to insult Joe Biden. In its remix by the left, Joe Biden is reimagined as "Dark Brandon," hyping a masculine image of Biden that "out-alphas" the MAGA image of Trump. Such emergent vernaculars are gleefully humorous in their form of "trolling the trolls."

This countertrolling of alt-right discourse became even more prominent in the weeks after the 2024 election, in particular by feminist and queer activist accounts responding to a renewed set of threats against bodily autonomy for those most vulnerable to conservative policies (especially those outlined in the Heritage Foundation's Project 2025 document). There has emerged a strikingly noncompliant and rageful tenor to memes pushing back on the popular manosphere influencer Nick Fuentes's ill-advised proclamation "your body, my choice" after Trump won. The response was swift and uncompromising in its refusal of such violent and egregious rhetoric. This included many memes that employed Artemisia Gentileschi's painting *Judith Slaying Holofernes* (1610) (see fig. 4.1), itself suspected to be Gentileschi's response to her own sexual assault. Other memes had images of a woman serving a man's head on a platter. All included a text overlay of Fuentes's statement remixed for vengeful and resistant ends. Indeed, this is made clear in the memetic use of a classical sculpture of Medusa standing with a man's head in one hand and a sword in the other. It was remixed to include the text "Your body, my ch—" overtop of the image, reenacting a scenario wherein the vengeful witch Medusa cut off the uttered threat midsentence, silencing the unnecessary debate it elicited, once and for all. This is in keeping with a poem posted to Riot, a.k.a. @riotaddams's Threads account that stated, "Roses are red, Violets are blue, Nick Fuentes the witches are coming for you." There is a sense in these memes that activist communities have been here before (and certainly we have, even as recently as 2016 and the repeal of *Roe v. Wade* in 2022) and are quicker to anger and ready for the fight. The memes reflect both fatigue and disgruntled resignation that we will continue to resist.

This was apparent even on the eve of the 2024 election, when a popular meme template circulated that showed two images side-by-side in the meme frame. On the top of the left side was the text "Voting for Hillary in 2016," and on the right, it read "Voting for Harris in 2024." Below the text were comparative images of various actors where each of their characters on the left was chipper, perky, full of hope, and the one on the right resembled a character in a postapocalyptic world. The meme included a version of Winona Ryder from the start of the film *Heathers* on the left and holding an ax on watch for Demogorgons, from her role in *Stranger Things*, in the image on the right. There is also a comparative image of Donald Glover smiling in a suit as Troy from *Community* on the left and, on the right, shirtless and holding an assault rifle from his video for *This Is America*. The comparison continued, with Linda Hamilton in her role as Sarah from the start of *Terminator* on the left and as a fully jacked version of the same character in a desert landscape, also holding an assault weapon, on the right. Other celebrity memes in this genre included before-and-after pictures of Sissy Spacek in *Carrie,* Charlize Theron in *Mad Max: Furiosa,* and Sigourney Weaver in *Aliens.* This trend, toward disheveled

FIGURE 4.1. "Your body, my choice." Posted with the caption "Fixed it." Used with permission from Siobhán Gordon for @siobhaneen_queen_of_dreams.

character on high alert with weapon on the right side of the meme template, says a lot about cultural sentiments on what it means to have survived over these particular eight years of American politics. It suggests there was a great toll on people, a dystopian tip of the landscape we inhabit, and a need for vigilance as well as a preparedness for the inevitable fight or violence facing us. While this may sound hyperbolic, it is reflecting the affective temperature of some spaces of internet culture in both stark and playfully humorous ways.

These and the other memes considered in this concluding chapter exemplify the joyful use of meme culture to gather community in the face of tensions and dissolution of political certainties. They also speak to the continued interest by meme makers around the joyfulness found in spreading and encountering humor in our online spaces; joy operates as a vector for processing collective confusion and concerns. Parry notes that definitions of memes must consider the specific networks and collectives they emerge from and move within as well as "the joy and investment" they can elicit (138). Enter the Bernie Mittens memes, which offer through their visual lexicon and associated meanings a sense of hope, normalcy, steadiness, and consistency as well as a lack of theatrics—or, more specifically, Trumpian hysterics. The image of a curmudgeonly older gentleman looking a bit bored while he sits waiting was comforting in its banality. Notably, as a figure and a post, the Bernie Mittens meme is not particularly ideological; it is quite a neutral and quotidian image of a less than inflammatory public figure. Even if one disagrees with Sanders's politics, it is undeniable that he is broadly respected as a lifelong politician open to working along bipartisan lines for his stated commitment to the public good. The Bernie Mitten meme is an example of how "internet memes evoke festive laughter because they build on not only one comic event or themselves in solitude, but on a myriad of texts, references and online 'discourse'" (Gallup 27). The Bernie Mittens meme event reveals an important but overlooked aspect of our collective experience of internet cultures of production and sharing—that of joy.

Joyscrolling in a Time of Cultural Uncertainty

Joyscrolling, as the opposite to more recognizable practices of doomscrolling through negative news cycles, describes intentionally consuming media that offer us pleasure rather than outrage and despair. It can be something that happens because of the viral content circulating within one's media landscapes, or it can be a purposefully orchestrated experience one cultivates through curating their social media algorithms. Discussions of the term seem to emerge around six to eight months after pandemic lockdowns, where social media users were faced with an uptick in their daily media consumption alongside consistently distressing news environments. Some journalists noted how they themselves and others were actively searching content "showcasing adorable pets and babies along with influencers doing funny impressions, dances, and skits," causing the term *joyscrolling* to emerge as a buzzword in late 2020 (Radin). As an intentional rebuttal to how algorithms can skew to the negative, joyscrolling opens a path to more generative experiences of internet content (Radin). As Musgrave, Cummings, and Schoenebeck argue, Black women and femmes offer a clear example of this intentionality, curating "digital lives" that center "dynamic self and collective expressions of healing, communality, self-care, personal reflection, creativity, joy, culture and knowledge production" into a mode of "digital alchemy" that advances the principles of #blackgirlmagic in everyday online interactions (109). There is a Joyscroll UK email listserv that will bring joy to your inbox once a week as well as a related weekly roundup post on their Instagram account JoyScroll (@joyscroll. uk). The Icelandic Tourist Board took a cue from the trend and created a now defunct website, Joyscrolling.com, with content from national landscapes and wildlife.

The concept of joyscrolling as it is seen in the Bernie Mittens memes aligns well with Sparby's definition of mimetic behavior as different "actions and behaviors recapitulated in new but relevant contexts" (17). Memes like those of Bernie that circulated around events like the inauguration evoke joy. Through remixing, such memes and the viral events they turn into circulate that joy into a new set of temporal and spatial contexts, creating new cultural meanings. Not only was the inauguration a site of celebration or at least relief, it occurred in a temporal moment of tensions within the US but also globally, including widening divisiveness in politics and the strains of maintaining a capitalist status quo during a global pandemic. The internet public was already worn down by so much fear, distrust, miscommunication, state violence, division, disinformation, grief, and exhaustion. Sanders, his pose, and the mittens offered a way to focus on a silly small visual delight and push it into as many contexts as possible as if its proliferation could alter or wash away the dread that met us on our scrolling journeys, if only for a minute.

This came also at a time when Bernie memes more broadly were already well established and, while largely joyful, could sometimes evoke divisiveness in the tense "side-ism" of contemporary American electoral politics. Bernie Mittens memes are the antithesis of all of this. They are silly, inconsequential, quotidian, and comforting, like the mittens themselves. Putting Bernie in a variety of settings (like one's home via Google Maps) meant that we could all be Bernie in that moment, waiting out a long but necessary work event that we had to attend. The appeal of the meme's message is arguably that sometimes we don't need to dwell (and often flail) in the seriousness and chaos of world embattled by unending far-right vitriol, climate catastrophe, global pandemics, and economic crises but can also take time to gather in joy or place a focus on the mundane and the delightful. In the attention economy of platform capitalism and a social media landscape that thrives on discord, rage, and divisive entrenchments in political silos, this itself can be a form of joyful refusal, a way of opting out of what the internet trades in—fear and loathing.

In *Glitch Feminism*, Legacy Russell outlines how those marginalized by dominant culture have a historically significant relationship to remix, which she defines as the practice of "finding a way to innovate with what's been given, creating something new from something already there" (133). Russell argues that using cultural ephemera in ways that they become "reclaimed, rearranged, repurposed" moves us toward "building the world(s) we want to live in" and encouraging an "emancipatory enterprise, creating new 'records' through radical action" (133). To continue this line of thought further, and to close out the book, I want to explore joyful meme content in relation to contemporary activism's embrace of pleasure, joy, and connection as a necessary part of resistance. Take for instance a simple yet incredibly popular remixed meme template of a cute animal such as a cat or frog, with the script: "Me: no problemo! Narrator: but it was all problemo" (my favorite being an animated frog from Eimear [@flotsamm], "Some memes"). When this is reshared with a user's public as part of their own persona, it indexes a common tendency to minimize any form of tension or conflict despite the internal strife it may cause. This is relatable and performs, through humor, some of the struggles of contemporary work life. Even in a simple example like the "no problemo" frog, there is a sense of pleasure that I believe is highly productive for social movements seeking to push against the swell of unregulated online hate and abuse the internet contains. There is a need here to assert that we are not alone, thus building important connections and forms of solidarity so crucial to activist practice.

Pleasure Aesthetics

My formulation of pleasure and joy via aesthetic practices like memes is directly indebted to adrienne maree brown's writing on pleasure activism. She opens her book *Pleasure Activism: The Politics of Feeling Good* with a quote from Toni Cade Bambara defining art making as a job of making "the revolution irresistible" (a. brown, *Pleasure Activism* 1). In this, we already see the close connections between activist pleasure and the role of art and representation. brown's articulation of pleasure activism ties pleasure and joy closely to desired experiences of aliveness and liberation (1). Pleasure is essential as a form of politics, most significantly for "people who are surviving long-term oppressive conditions" (7). She locates pleasure in the space of "happy satisfaction and enjoyment," and pleasure activism is oriented toward actions that "reclaim our whole, happy, and satisfiable selves from the impacts, delusions, and limitations of oppression and/or supremacy" (11). In practice this means we "seek to understand and learn from the politics and power dynamics inside of everything that makes us feel good," including art (11). Some of the key principles that emerge from this include the idea that what we focus on and what we do shapes and grows our visions for a better future (12). brown also suggests that our joy has transformative effects on our world, and we need to endeavor to make "justice and liberation feel good" (12). I would argue this is precisely what countercultural internet content seeks to do, and I wish to consider further how pleasure aesthetics emerges in digital culture as a notable strand of activist tactics.

In the book, brown revisits the often-cited Audre Lorde quote that "self-care . . . is an act of political warfare" and notes that while "we know how to meme and tweet those words, living into them is harder" (a. brown, *Pleasure Activism* 17). She notes that what is needed is for us to learn that such acts of love are themselves acts of "political resistance and cultivating resilience" (17). What does this mean, if we consider the memes created within a pleasure activist space of love and care as cultivating resistance and resilience? Is this even possible, and if so, what does it even look like in practice? I want to sit for a moment with an example from @hopehealingarts that for me highlights the sense of pleasure aesthetics I aim to articulate. Run by Hope Carpenter, the profile describes the account as a "sanctuary for sensitive creatives" and "healing in community," and herself as a "soft meme magician." She is also a "dv survivor turned victim advocate" studying for her MSW. The account's aesthetic is full of soft pink and purple hues, and the meme slide decks she creates use still images from nostalgic cartoon series, including *Sailor Moon, My Little Pony, Pokémon, Winnie the Pooh, Care Bears,* Disney's animated *Robin Hood* and *Bambi,* and more obscure references such as *The Last Unicorn.* These characters are situated in carousel decks with themes that speak to healing from trauma, breaking abusive cycles, accepting states of vulnerability, and building meaningful connection. The text and image pairings are soft and full of care.

It is a remarkably different tone and approach to that of lifestyle influencer content, not only in tone and aesthetic but also in how it is upfront about struggles and pain; nothing is perfect in the world it represents, and it affirms that that is okay. It also removes any sense of neoliberal competitiveness, exceptionalism, or overcoming of that which holds one back, all part of a more "boss babe," "lean in" culture. Instead, it is an account rooted in collective care. The pleasure in the memes comes from the joy of being invited to sit with these cartoon figures, which bring a form of childlike play as Carpenter dispenses words of encouragement through them. In a carousel post from late 2023 that uses *Sailor Moon* still images, Carpenter writes "a love letter to all the moods and feelings moving through me" and invites audiences to use the comments to complete the phrase "in the mood to . . ." The first image is a split screen with a close-up of Luna, the cat mentor for the Sailor Guardians, looking upward with tears streaming down her face. In the bottom

FIGURE 4.2. "A love letter to all the moods." Used with permission from Hope Carpenter for @hopehealingarts.

image, Sailor Moon holds Luna in a close embrace (see fig. 4.2). The text broken up across the two images says, "how do we get through this? / together." This was reposted the day after the 2024 election, suggesting that even within our own remixing of culture for specific political ends, they may indeed be repurposed when the occasion calls for it, even months and years after their initial creation.

From the start, there is an assertion that in our greatest struggles we need communities of support to hold us through the pain. The punctuation is notable for how it starts as a question, but in some ways, this uncertainty and fear indexed by the question mark is overwritten by the period at the end of the word *together*. There is no ambiguity but rather a certainty that the way through is together. This is emphasized by how comforting the image of Luna and Sailor Moon is. The second image is a still showing Sailor Moon in some form of transformation, with a pink gem encapsulated in a glowing sphere emerging from her. The text reads, "in the mood for a revolution powered by the heart." The rest of the deck uses images of Sailor Moon in a fairy ball gown, speaking with a younger girl, as well as images from a similar backdrop, speaking to a young woman. In both these sets of images, the text speaks to current versions of the narrator giving permission to offer comfort and care to younger versions of herself for the purpose of healing. There is also a slide where Sailor Moon embraces Luna again, this one in quite a different aesthetic of reds, that reads, "in the mood for personal and collective rebirth."

Linking this thematically (both visually and textually) to the earlier slide of Luna, this image-text combination suggests that the transformation for us as individuals and as a collective requires collaboration and connection. The image of Sailor Moon with the gem emerging from her body is repeated and expanded, stating in the text overlay, "brb, harnessing my sacred anger as a fuel source to bring a better world into being." In Carpenter's curated carousel deck, the visual pleasure of softness and nostalgia is blended with a caring message that offers a break for audiences from the grind of bad news cycles, doomscrolling, and the sometimes toxicity of social relations under late-stage capitalism. Carpenter's account is not unique in this; there is a growing genre of "soft" memes that offer a pause from the darker, angrier, or destructive parts of our social media feeds. What is important is how, aesthetically, these memes and meme accounts produce forms of beauty, visual ease, and joy as a means of communicating their message. It is effective, as the aesthetics match the intent within the texts overall.

Visual Pleasure, Spectacle, and the Feminist Queering of Memes

In the essay "Spectacle, Attractions and Visual Pleasure," Scott Bukatman offers a comparative reading of Tom Gunning's theory of the cinema of attractions alongside Laura Mulvey's theory of visual pleasure and considers the potential relationship between the two foundational texts via Brechtian alienation and Eisensteinian montage (81). While the comparison undermines (and I think misreads) Mulvey's argument, it does give her credit for opening a discussion around how cinema, and cinematic figures such as women, operating as objects of desire can exceed cinematic narrative constraints. Bukatman suggests the takeaway from Mulvey's writing in conjunction with Gunning's theory of attraction allows "spectacle [to] be harnessed to serve the interests of ideological resistance," allowing "the attraction" to "return as an untamed form" (81). This references Gunning's argument that an early cinema of attractions, built on visual appeals rather than narrative ones, was subsumed or "tamed" by the dominance of classical Hollywood cinema in the decades after early cinema's more experimental forays. As you will recall from the previous chapter, the cinema of attractions operates via spectacle that engages audiences with cultural products that are highly visible and enact forms of rupture (Gunning, "Attractions" 382). This sort of spectacle can be used in the service of both Brechtian alienation and Eisensteinian montage. While I don't agree with Bukatman's assessment of Mulvey, who he situates as an iconoclast, he does quote a very important passage, where she argues:

> It is said that analyzing pleasure, or beauty, destroys it. That is the intention of this article. The satisfaction and reinforcement of the ego that represent the high point of film history hitherto must be attacked . . . the alternative is the thrill that comes from leaving the past behind without rejecting it, transcending outworn or oppressive forms, or daring to break with normal pleasurable expectations in order to conceive a new language of desire. (8)

This attention at the end of the quote to a new language of desire, which emerges as an alternative to more status-quo forms of representation, breaks with normal pleasurable expectations. It does so not to repudiate visual pleasure but to imagine what it could look like if women moved from a state of to-be-looked-at-ness and into one of "dialectics" and "passionate detachment" (Mulvey 13). In her final sentence of the essay, Mulvey argues, "women, whose image has continually been stolen and used for this end [visual pleasure / the male gaze], cannot view the decline of the traditional film form with anything much more than sentimental regret" (13). Mulvey is suggesting here that more radical approaches to representation in film already have shifted the register by freeing "the look of the camera into its materiality in time and space" (13), and this is what enables our passionate detachment as viewers. In doing so, tactics of attraction—visibility and rupture—are employed to encourage criticality.

I spend time unpacking this dialogue here because it helps support my overarching argument that memes are an aesthetic medium, which draw heavily on disruptive formal tactics from previous eras of countercultural art. What makes memes such a significant force for advancing critical conversations within activist spaces on the internet is that they rupture dominant culture through irony, juxtaposition, and defamiliarization via a highly visual media form (or attractions). In doing so, gesture toward not only new languages of desire but also new kinds of visual pleasures. By situating memes within a trajectory of resistant media including film, I wish to ask: If classical narrative dominance tamed earlier cinemas of attractions, are memes an echo of those attractions returned in a differently mediated untamed form? And if so, especially in the context of feminist and queer meme cultures, how does this offer us new articulations of desire and visual pleasure? And if this is the case, how do they enact these new articulations? I would suggest that they do so through different kinds of gags and visual tricks available through platform affordances. The idea of gags or visual pranks feels especially significant for thinking through memes as a twenty-first-century outcome of the cinema of attractions, or perhaps a digital media of attraction. While there is an endless array of visual delights I could bring to illustrate this, I will focus my attention today on a duet and a stitch as two memes prominent in social media spaces at present that utilize montage, gags, and rupture.

I start with a revisiting of the stitch, which I explored in detail in the previous chapter. As noted there, this is a video-based social media gimmick where one piece of media is reposted on an account and then responded to in a side-by-side framing by the account's content creator. In a TikTok video posted by Hillbilly Gothic, the account of popular banjo musician Clover-Lynn (@hillbillygothicc), the performer places herself and her banjo in the left side of a split screen to respond to manosphere influencers on the right side of the screen (see fig. 4.3). At the start of one video, she leans forward in the frame as if listening intently to what the man on the second screen is saying. The man, who remains nameless in the duet, begins an information-sharing video with a caption that reads, "Why no masculine man wants an 'Alpha Female'" (Hillbilly Gothic, "Youd think"). We hear his audio reading out this caption, and on the left side, Clover-Lynn tilts her head backward, rolling her eyes and offering an internal groan with the gesture. While the man keeps speaking on the right side of the frame, the left image cuts to a wider shot of Clover-Lynn, from a low angle so she commands the frame. She sits on a bed playing a riff on her banjo, the audio drowning out what the man on the left says. As she plays, she looks down to the bottom of her frame as if watching him talk. Her expression is both annoyed and inquisitive as if she is figuring out how to respond via her melody. The effect is one of pure delight. It was reposted by the popular Still We Rise (SWR) account on Instagram (@still-werise) with the caption "YESSSSSSS TO THIS @hillbillygothicc ♂ 😶 😂 😌 i need the whole album #stillweriseloves." Comments on the original TikTok video include "the hero we love," "you're like Orpheus when he saves his crew by playing his lyre louder than the sirens trying to lure them to death," and

FIGURE 4.3. "Youd think theyd learn." Screenshot of still image
from a duet video by TikTok account @hillbillygothicc.

"I needed a banjo years ago," as if to suggest this is an excellent way to drown out forms of misogyny in public.

This is not Hillbilly Gothic's first "interruptive" duet; she has posted many to rupture the monologues of men on the internet speaking against LGBTQIA+ communities, witchcraft, women wearing "too much" makeup, some truly incel-level dating advice about consent, and the importance of women's submissiveness. She gets tagged in egregious manosphere content by followers with requests for duets, to which she often complies. Within this we see the gimmick of split-screen editing as well as audio overlay to interrupt and critique a very real issue on the internet—the profitable spread of misogynist disinformation that is linked to a rise in technology-facilitated gender-based violence (Demas).

Like the duet by Hillbilly Gothic suggests, video gimmicks are used extensively in activist media to clap back at social media content that peddles forms of disinformation and online hate, including, in the example I will discuss here, technology-facilitated gender-based violence. In a post from the popular TikTok account @thatdancermoses, there is a stitch that counters internet hate via upbeat dance routines. The account is run by Moses Williams, who runs accounts on multiple platforms, which include dance videos, dance instruction, tutorials, and increasingly, videos pushing back on misogynist and racist content from the manosphere. In a stitch from 2024 posted by No Holes Barred (@no_holes_barred_podcast) on Instagram, Williams starts with a clip of well-known misogynist influencer Myron Gaines sitting at a microphone recording his *Fresh and Fit* podcast. He is yelling into the microphone while jabbing his finger in the air, angrily making his point regarding women complaining they don't have a male romantic partner, that it is their fault (his words are much more abusive and do not merit repeating). To counter this violent screed, Williams abruptly cuts from the clip, with the man screaming midsentence, into a locked-off shot of Williams in his brightly lit apartment. He begins dancing to a version of "Boogie Woogie Bugle Boy" with added lyrics cheerfully repeating, "I just need you to shut the fuck up," over and over. Moses dances with a cane prop, doing a modified tap routine, while the text overlay reads, "Somebody call the wambulence / We've got another 'Alpha Male' whining about women . . . / Just a bunch of babies" (No Holes Barred). The dance is joyful, energizing, cathartic. Williams ends the choreography by giving the camera the middle finger. We can read this as a gesture toward the earlier part of the stitch and the misogyny it performs. The first shot is jarringly aggressive, laying clear how virulent and dangerous the rhetoric spilling out of the manosphere is and how easily it encourages forms of antiwoman radicalization. For social media users that purposefully avoid that area of the digital landscape, this is a stark reminder and an uncomfortable and dispiriting one. This is what makes the response by Williams so significant.

As outlined in the previous chapter, stitches can be used, as Williams uses them, for critical interventions into dominant culture. This stitch above participates in a form of rupture that uses the principles of montage to suture together two radically distinct video clips. The contrast between them produces significant dissonance and defamiliarization. The use of remix to add new lyrics to the big band song gives us a temporal defamiliarization. The use of dance helps elevate the joy of the catharsis as the moving body draws us into the scene. The choice of the content creator to perform the dance in the everyday space of his apartment also usefully pushes against the spectacle of "TikTok houses," or fashionable, ornate living spaces that offer a backdrop of luxury for influencer content. It thus destabilizes a fictional narrative that circulates in dominant social media content around capitalist success and the production of lifestyle envy. It is also a startling contrast to the very recognizable aesthetic of the manosphere shown in the original clip it is responding to. The image of an angry man screaming into the microphone in his darkened studio is an unfortunately common trope of contemporary digital landscape. The aesthetic replication of this is tied to a proliferation of misogyny and technology-facilitated gender-based hate and violence that is reaching alarming levels as of late and spilling into our real-life spaces at increasing rates. What the stitch does is productively free the look of the camera, the one that validates the angry man screed, into its materiality in time and space by jolting us out of the dark room and into the joyful rage of the sunny apartment where we can dance our anger out with the artist and the cursing lyrics. The montage edits between these two, effectively placing the audience into a dialectics of passionate detachment. What I aim to get at here is that memes in a variety of forms utilize tactics and ideas that are well known to us as scholars of cinema history and theory. I believe montage, spectacle, and visual pleasure are increasingly showing up in social media activist experimentation as ways of pushing back against the callous commodification of hate and divisiveness the internet likes to pedal for clicks.

I want to keep thinking through how these legacies are in significant and transformative dialogues with each other in the current moment of mashups, remakes, and remixes of meme culture. A Bakhtinian understanding of the carnivalesque is useful here. For Bakhtin, carnival is linked to spectacle, as it is based in the culture of the marketplace and thus becomes the nucleus of culture. Further, the carnival exists on the border between art and life, as it reveals a form of life in play and playful form (Bakhtin 217). In the carnival, there is no distinction between actors and spectators; it is a spectacle people live within, and as a demarcated space outside of life, it is a "celebrated temporary liberation from . . . the established order; it marked the suspension of all hierarchical rank, privileges, norms and prohibitions" (218). What this enables is the loss of social hierarchies at the time-space of the carnival, a suspension of everyday structures. Carnival experience is opposed to that which was "ready-made and completed," seeking instead a dynamic of "changing, playful, undefined forms" (219). It is a site of both change and renewal, logic of the "inside out" shifting binaries, becoming a parody of the noncarnival world. The carnivalesque in culture offers viewers forms of parody that sometimes reveal the grotesque and abject of the everyday. It also places an emphasis on bodily experience, thus making us aware of the material conditions of social relations and ensuring this as a key point of resistance (221). The stitch by Moses offers a Bakhtinian flipping of the everyday script of misogyny enabled by platforms that do little to regulate the spread of hate and a growing community of male influencers profiting off this lack of recourse. It suspends the everyday structures of an internet designed to be unwelcoming to women and queer, neurodivergent, disabled, and racialized communities and offers forms of parody that playfully liberate viewers from the established order of masculinist media.

The Pleasure Activism of Queer Meme Interventions

Returning to the Barbie meme conversation from chapter 2, I want to reflect on the pleasure activism of queer interventions into toxic masculinity that arose after the movie's release. Just after the *Barbie* movie was released, the popular Instagram account @abnormalize.being posted a curated video roundup, and the first four videos in the carousel showed a strong use of meme video stitches for addressing toxic masculinity in humorous ways. For instance, the first video in the roundup is a stitch from TikTok creator Nik Hagen (@nikhagen) that begins with a short clip of a young white male in a preppy white T-shirt and khaki shorts emphatically telling the camera that "if you are a man and you watched the *Barbie* movie you are 100% a beta." The rest of the stitch includes Hagen responding in a comedic monologue where he gleefully admits, as if speaking to the original poster (OP), that he saw the movie, and then willingly comes out as a beta. In the monologue, he asks the OP what happens next now that he identifies as beta and runs various scenarios like telling his doctor or declaring it on a census. The humor partly comes out of how campy and enthusiastic, as well as enthusiastically queer, Hagen's performance is, which breaks apart the entire argument being made in the OP around the rigidity of masculine gender roles.

As Karen Zaiontz and Kristen Cochrane argue, "Digital feminism . . . was never born free," and thus feminist activists and content producers "must claim autonomy over their craft (i.e., Memes, blogs, podcasts) by other means" (139). This chapter explores these other means, suggesting that feminist and queer activists employ joy and pleasure as part of their tactical resistance against toxic femininity and toxic masculinity. This work "embrace[s] paradox through comic contradiction" and forms of irony "which through viral image and text not only capture the constraints of heteronormativity but dismantle its discursive logic" (Zaiontz and Cochrane 152). As we know, "social media feminist humor and irony are used" rhetorically and "play a central role in increasing feminist audiences and mobilizing feminist connectivity (Papacharissi), collectivity, and solidarity" (Lawrence and Ringrose 212). To put it succinctly, feminist memes offer a "shared sensibility . . . cultivated through irony and wit to expose inequality" (Lawrence and Ringrose 214). In feminist digital content that parodies cultural fears of man-hating feminist rhetoric, the tenor of the memes veers "between humor and anger" (Lawrence and Ringrose 215). As I have collaboratively written about elsewhere, feminist digital media, especially that tied to the visual tactics of memes, challenges "traditional assumptions of what visual cultural protest looks like" and instead offers "a different kind of protest" through circulation of "feminist activist content" that "flips the script" on what we imagine protest to be (Wiens and MacDonald, "Dwelling" 42). What such accounts offer instead are "communal visioning for a better future" (Wiens and MacDonald, "Dwelling" 43), often tied to hope, joy, and emergent possibilities (a. brown, *Pleasure Activism*). Humor and rage make for an attractive combination that draws audiences to feminist memes because it both outlines the true stakes of living in a heterocapitalist, white supremacist, patriarchal culture, while giving us the tools to ease that burden with moments of laughter and joy. In other moments, the jokes are grim, but then again so are our possible futures. This grimmer sense of humor in feminist and queer memes gives us permission to release our tension while finding commonality among the assemblage of viewers also hailed by the meme's content.

The memes considered in this conclusion contain forms of critical politics to reimagine what can and should be. They do so by defamiliarizing what already is: the tired, played-out contortions of white supremacist, heteropatriarchal, capitalist world views. It does not represent these as fact but shows us different landscapes full of color, texture, unfamiliar pairings; like feminist uses of collage that predate these memes, they join disparate elements to provide viewers with a set of "emergent textualities" (Wiens and MacDonald, "Dwelling" 42) that are also a call to action for viewers to imagine a different way forward.

Pebbling and Dead-Birding

I share a lot of memes with friends and loved ones as a hazard of my research. It was such a moment of joy, then, when I was recently on Instagram and saw a reposted tweet that stated: "The act of sending friends & family little videos and tweets and memes you find online" is called pebbling and is named after the phenomena of penguins bringing pebbles to the ones they love (@nursekelsey). While the phenomenon among penguins is in fact scientifically proven (Potter), *penguin pebbling* is also a term used in neurodivergent communities to describe a form of communication used to express care (Stimpunks Foundation), including excerpts from media, small found objects, online content. Discussions around the term within neurodivergent communities include over 111 million posts on TikTok and a large array of Reddit threads. The tweet that I saw had taken the in-group identifier of penguin pebbling within neurodivergent community conversations and extended it to a more public audience. While this extension does risk extrapolating away from the specific ways the term helps build identity within these original communities, the tweet's intent appears to celebrate an aspect of digital platform sharing affordances that can be used to offer care to others in our networks.

In the original tweet, a variety of different responses followed in the comments, many of which were variants of people finding joy in discovering the term and noting they would share this info with their loved ones. One comment shared that they call this "dead-birding" to reflect how a cat brings their captured prey as a present to their owners. As is the reality of Twitter (now X), there were naysayers who shot down the term as being useless and superfluous to describing a very common thing. This curmudgeonly take was quickly ratioed with a meme of Michael Scott from *The Office* looking off-screen, with the text "You are the thief of joy." Whether superfluous or not, the term *pebbling* connotes more than just an act of sharing select digital content, for its ties to acts of love and care situate it in the realm of joy and pleasure. This is akin to the other forms of pleasure-based digital media tactics outlined in this conclusion, including joyscrolling and humorous stitch performances, which can both lead to content worth pebbling.

Pebbles are often single posts that announce identity markers, such as a frog hiding under a blanket with imposter syndrome, that one shares with someone and adds commentary to, such as "me right now." This pebble offers a performance of the sharer's identity and current mindset, to be affirmed by the person they are sharing it with, thus creating a loop of recognition and acknowledgment that signifies connection and care. As a broad-based media practice, pebbling is a way that platform users have found to select from our endless streams of content elements that we identify as meaningful in some way, which we then share with people in our network. It is a way of building intimate online communities that are shielded from public scrutiny. The sharing of content in the more closed-door spaces of message chats allows for the pebble to spark a conversation, or at the least an emoji, that validates the act of sharing. Pebbles operate differently from public curated posts like carousel decks and reels or stories. The latter are created in the interest of addressing large publics to deliver a message that, no matter how joyful or funny, has an intentional angle of sharing a perspective or critique.

Pebbles are more private: they are selected, or curated, and shared with a limited number of people through direct message groups for the intention of a personal dialogue among people in an already well-established relationship. A quick review of the pebble posts shared across my own group chats in each week will show commiseration content on the trials of parenting tweens, middle age woes, cheese appreciation posts, romantasy fandom in-jokes, and conspiratorial love letters to "office besties" for making it all bearable. This suggests that the content we share as a form of care to those we are in close relation to is, like all things, highly specific to the user. Sometimes pebbles announce a shared pleasure that demarcates an aspect of one's relationship to be celebrated or mutually recognized as something that makes it unique. Other times the shared post may name a certain displeasure the people in the group chat face either separately or together, and the distillation of the displeasure in this form offers an opportunity for either commiseration or acts of support and solidarity.

An often-shared type of pebble across different chat groups in my network are posts by poetryisnotaluxury (@poetryisnotaluxury), an Instagram account that curates select poems to respond to moments and events in global culture. The poems selected by the account have a way of signaling the kinds of heavy grief, fear, and sometimes hope we carry with us collectively. They make some small sense out of these emotions through the words of poets. The account remixes existing poetry texts into the meme format to gather users to collectively consider what the poems mean in our current contexts. Often when they arrive on my feed, they seem to be exactly what I need to help me face the struggles of current social-political life. And often because they offer that glimmer of insight or a moment of relief, I share them with those who I know are carrying the same fears, dread, and existential reckonings. This is a form of pebble gathering that offers thoughtful guidance via a content creator that I have no relationship to except for through their posts. However, the content helps me build communities of support and meaning making. It is a form of pleasure gathering, even if it is as a response to great displeasure and distress. This suggests that pebbling as an internet practice has a variety of uses. I have more than likely only named the select few that I engage in, leaving out an array of others that different communities of users have developed in their online encounters.

The meme content as pebble in these instances is highly relational and uses the affordances of direct message conversations for more private forms of connection and meaning making. This creates a space of pleasure, care, and joy that, through articulations of what hurts and defines us, good or bad, helps us toward better articulating our own and collective relationships to our personal everyday forms of activism, resistance, and justice. The metaphors of penguins offering pebbles and cats bringing dead birds to loved ones are apt as they show the ways in which, despite all the ugliness the internet now brings, there are ways we can employ it for more careful and sustainable ends.

Meme-ing for Survival in Real Time

"The best revenge is living well" is a phrase I joyfully encountered for the first time while attending a Dirty Bingo event hosted by Shirley the Drag Queen in the late 1990s. The phrase was posted on the coasters of the bar, The Living Well, where the queer bingo events took place. The sentiment encapsulated perfectly for me the tensions I was reconciling between the fulsomeness of queer joy and the oppressive and devastating effects of queerphobia, not only for me personally but within community and familial spaces. This felt acute just one short decade after the cruel indifference of institutions toward the AIDS crisis. None of this could be separated from the noticeable creep of neoliberalism and the breakdown of social and collective structures by corporate and state greed circulating around me. My relationship to aesthetics, activism, and community cannot be disentangled from that moment, which was perhaps a turning point for me. The tensions between (necro)capitalism and the revelry and rebelliousness of queer resistance were then, as they are now, in high relief.

This is perhaps what drew me to the forms of queer and feminist resistance I discovered online in the 2010s. For me there were echoes and resonances worth exploring that I felt were not yet captured by scholarly accounts of social media.

Part of our identity as activists is to interpret the images, gestures, slogans, and discourse from these earlier eras and translate them into our present actions. Think for instance of the popular phrase "We are the granddaughters of the witches you didn't burn" currently found on placards, buttons, and T-shirts (Janega; Halperin). In presenting this statement on our clothing, our protest signs, and our social media accounts, we are reperforming the image of a witch as a socially rebellious outsider and enemy of the patriarchy. In noting the temporal lineage of "granddaughter," the phrase reaches back to an imagined set of feminists as an anchor. It also acknowledges the deep misogyny and violence of the history of witch trials and suggests a present-day reckoning with patriarchal attempts to destroy and silence feminists or anyone refusing the path of heteronormative timelines (marriage, children, domestic care labor). This exemplifies a form of reenactment that we perform in our own communicative vernaculars both online and offline, and they are suffused with nostalgia, hauntings, and desire.

I returned recently to this merging of past political-aesthetic moments with present-day media practices in a series of meme carousel decks created in June 2024 by Feminist Think Tank (FTT), the research collective I codirect in Canada. FTT is a multidisciplinary, multigenerational group of feminist and queer scholars who work together to develop practice-based means of countering digital hate and online misogyny. We hang out a lot, talking and resource sharing, parsing feminist theory and world events, and making collaborative art, including memes. We have been running an Instagram account since 2019 that archives and amplifies instances of feminist and queer media and activism that resonate for the present. In our early years, we used to host a series during Pride Month that highlighted our queer icons or "queercons." In 2024 we returned to this and to our central mandate to explore how the personal is political in our visual cultural lives. To do so, we invited members to create "queer kaleidoscopes," or carousel decks of the visual and cultural ephemera that brought them to their queerness, a set of personalized queer kinships to share with our followers in the hopes that it would inspire them to reflect on and create similar kaleidoscopes in their own minds and content (see fig. 4.4).

For my kaleidoscope, this phrase "the best revenge is living well" sums up a certain ethos of what it meant to come to queerness in the late 1990s as a young art student in Toronto. There was a rebelliousness steeped in histories of resistance that were both mournful and full of angry energetic joy. It brings me right back to the scrappy DIY aesthetic of the work being made all around me during that time, evoking a predigital mashing-up of different media into sculptural canvases, superimposed photo prints, intricately step-printed and collaged on film strips, installations, performances, and of course, zines. Technology was to be appropriated, broken apart, played with, and reassembled. Nothing was sacred, and what was deemed sacred by dominant culture was open for disassembly and critique. My kaleidoscope post looks very different from one created by a Gen Z member of the FTT team. In mine, there are references to the pop-hued rebelliousness of Le Tigre alongside book covers for earlier queer literature by Jeanette Winterson. In my colleague's, there are references to more recent queer movies and music that reflect the landscape they emerged from and move within. There are overlaps that support our experiences in FTT around intergenerational connection as a form of

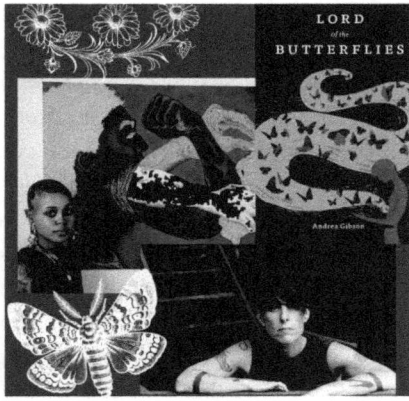

FIGURE 4.4. "This is our FTT queer kaleidoscope!" Used with permission from Feminist Think Tank (@aesthetic.resistance).

activism. Read together, they offer a mapping of queer affective histories via memes. In these posts and others generated by FTT members, attention is paid to the trajectories of feminist art that inform us. We understand that the work we do today trying to amplify feminist and queer activist discourse is part of a much longer history of media resistance.

Uncertain but Necessary Meme Utopias

I want to close this book with a final example from the Trans Bears collective. "An Ambiguous Utopia" is a postapocalyptic narrative told through memes that was created by the Trans Bears collective and published in the *Critical Meme Reader: Global Mutations of the Viral Image* from 2021 (Arkenbout et al.). In its published form, it looks somewhat like a short zine made up of image and text, with a prologue and epilogue to bookend the narrative it contains. The piece asks viewers to consider the "radical potential" for memes to foster an understanding "that change is always possible even with limited means" (Trans Bears 275). The piece is creative and theoretical, combining the best impulses of earlier forms of activist media and culture jams with an influential meme studies publication. The narrative details the experiences of the Meme Squad, as they "make mischief" through different periods of time, including "The Ruins," "The Collapse," "the Makeshift Times," and finally a place known as "Deep Adaptation" (275). Each point in the narrative includes descriptions of the period's environment accompanied by visual collages of memes to illustrate it. Starting their story at the time of The Ruins, the piece describes a temporal moment that sounds like the present:

> Our Meme Squad met at a time we now refer to as The Ruins. Human and natural systems were on the brink of collapse. Our societies and politics were the remnants of violent pasts, built on a logic of expansion, exploitation and extraction. Much of our work and leisure were organized around producing value for corporations. Financial wealth was the main indicator of success and determined our position in the social hierarchy.
>
> The circumstances left us exhausted, isolated and alienated—everyone on their own island. Few were imaginative enough to question the narrative we were fed: that it was easier to imagine the end of the world than the end of the systems that governed our lives. As apathy grew, irony and cynicism were normalized in online and offline culture. (277)

The white type is set in a black box that is layered on top of a generic nighttime cityscape. The point of view in the image looks at the skyscraper lit overhead by a pinkish, red-orange sky and purple-gray clouds that blend into the building's silhouette. The neon pink text at the top says, "The Ruins." At the bottom of the collage are two photos bordered by white edges and framed sequentially as if in a comic strip. The first image is a wide shot of two parked golf carts at the bottom left of the frame. The rest of the frame is filled with large green trees bordering the golf course and a forest fire raging just behind it. In the second image directly beside it, a man is putting a golf ball in the bottom of the frame, with the same forest fire in the background and a speech bubble captioned, "This is Fine" (277).

In this single page, there are a variety of visual and textual images collaged together to pictorially outline what The Ruins looks and feels like. It relies on recognition by viewers of the popular "This is Fine" meme, taking the meme out of its original context of a cartoon dog drinking a cup of coffee at a table in a burning room. In the Trans Bears collage, it is remixed into a noncartoon, photorealistic representation of our world. The shift is made from the everyday domestic space of the kitchen table in the original meme to a golf course on fire, and from a cartoon dog to a man who is seemingly finishing his golf game *at all costs* (Trans Bears 275). This remix indexes the anticapitalist critique advanced by the Trans Bears in the overall narrative. On the next page, the narrators note that not everyone was willingly ignoring the impending apocalypse and that there were people in the days of The Ruins looking for other ways of being who found each other largely through memes. This second page visually reenacts a social media group chat and includes memes that express digital cultural vernacular (276). The rest of the narrative's alleged pages follow the Meme Squad through the end of civilization, precipitated by a corporate takeover of the internet. This collapse forced resistors underground into the "dark forest," a nascent form of what would become the "Subaltern Web"; a place of outcast communities who interrogated power structures and laid the foundations for a different world to emerge (277). The Collapse era forced new ways of gathering offline. In the Makeshift era, the Subaltern Web became a distributed commons, and a shared purpose of care and mischief grew (280).

The tale ends in Deep Adaptation, which is a hopeful point in the narrative after years of despair. In it, a memetic symbiosis grows between the natural world and human society, where structures become organized by nature's rhythms, and the Web is powered by plugging into the mycelial network via adapted technology (Trans Bears 282). The narrators from Deep Adaptation declare the advancement of an important epistemological collapse between nature and culture, which allows for more careful and integrated forms of living interspecially (283). In the epilogue, the Trans Bears write: "All we're really saying is that 'nonsense' can be an effective counter to hegemonic 'common sense.' Don't let the bullies win. And most importantly: don't forget to lol together" (285).

The work encapsulates perfectly what I believe is the most promising ethos of memes, summed up in this quote: "Our reality may be grim, but our future doesn't have to be. Let us, for the love of memes, make it playful, euphoric, abundant. Let us dance upon the graves of nihilist media and worship our new gods: the memes" (Arkenbout and Scherz 16). It offers us a parable for a potential future of technology-facilitated social and ecological collapse and the means with which to get out of the dystopian outcome to a different but livable possible future. Like the concepts of pleasure and joy circulating through this chapter, Arkenbout and Scherz call us to be playful and euphoric in our use of memes to reject the media structures that seek to constrain, control, and silence us. Trans Bears think through what the result of this could look like, inviting us to preemptively imagine how we are to respond to such dystopic possibilities. They employ the space of academic publishing to disseminate a narrative that also resembles a zine, which is made up of meme vernaculars and aesthetics. In this way, it is a rich text that is emblematic of what culture jamming can look like in the digital era.

Collectively, the work of feminist and queer activist meme makers and their counterparts in art across the last century illustrate a historical trajectory of culture jamming. The role of collage within meme culture extends the earlier impulses of artists like Höch and others into resistant modes of digital remixing as a form of political critique. The remix of the "Horrors Persist" memes from the opening of the book, as well as the use of collage in the feminist starter pack memes discussed above, show an expanded use of memes as a type of culture jam that complicates our understanding of how to survive and make meaning in late-stage capitalism. The reenactments of Barbie and other iconic figures of femininity are distorted and undermined in feminist memes, like the way those same figures were upended by feminist performance artists decades earlier. The different uses of montage, and editing gimmicks found in carousel decks, parody videos, and stitches, also use formal tactics to intervene in dominant culture to critical ends. In all of these ways, memes are a key mode of culture jamming in the present.

Culture jamming emerged as a concept and practice in the 1980s "as a reaction to . . . [the] overwhelming flow of media imagery" that was creating what critics saw as a society of "passive consumers" and has resurfaced in the digital era (Jenkins, "What Do You Mean"). It clearly builds on a history of interventions from Dadaism, Guy Debord's critique of the society of spectacle, as well as critiques of mass culture brought forward by the Frankfurt School (Jenkins, "What Do You Mean"; Debord; Adorno). As Moritz Fink and Marilyn DeLaure, the authors of *Culture Jamming: Activism and the Art of Cultural Resistance,* argue, culture jamming in the digital era is broader than its previous presence as "parody ads and altered billboards" (qtd. in Jenkins, "What Do You Mean"). Presently, they continue, culture jamming tactically contests "not only . . . consumer culture, but also intervene[s] in politics and social movements" and, as such, is now, in the post-truth era of divisiveness and online hate, needed "now more than ever."

What Trans Bears does within this digital culture jamming context is mash up a variety of media formats (memes, zines, short stories, nostalgic punk and new wave style, dystopian fiction) to present a wholly unique text. The fact that the work is contained within a critical scholarly reader is also significant, as it brings the ethos of culture jamming to the pursuit of meme scholarship, demonstrating through its content one potential application of critical media theory when rendered through mimetic form. This demonstrates that collage and remix are as significant to expanding on the impulses of political move-ments today as they have been at different points in the last century. In the work of the Trans Bears meme zine, we see the use of well-recognized memes being resignified as artifacts of a strikingly recognizable yet dystopian time-line of a future societal collapse and regrowth. The memes are taken out of their everyday context of content located on our social media timeline and placed into an activist-academic art piece that maps out a potential future for viewers. It puts theory into practice and invites us to imagine what alternative structures of media could look like, even if bracketed in the framework of a speculative narrative.

Revisiting a quote cited in the introduction, "the artistic lineage of memes is spun out of some of 20th-century art's most revolutionary ideas" (Bucknell), I have endeavored in this book to make plain what I see as some of the most compelling links between memes and this history of rebellious art and art movements. For me the links are abundantly clear, and they offer me comfort. In the face of technology monopolies with outsized power to structure our lives, our social relations, our emotional states, and our access to information, it is hard to remain optimistic about our techno-futures. And yet, the fact that there are sections of digital culture where the active articulation of resistance is unfolding much like it did in different corners of the world throughout the twentieth century, often in relation to the dominant technologies and visual culture of the time, is instructive. What, I would ask, is more revolutionary than the collective force of activist memes intent on finding ways out of the white supremacist, heteropatriarchal, capitalist structures that constrain us?

What I hope readers get from a book on the aesthetics of memes is a more fulsome understanding of the activist tactics they can contain and why these tactics matter when speaking about the value of memes. The book offers a snapshot of meme practices and digital culture at a given moment in time. It is an archive of how we were using and thinking about memes at a turning point in techno-cultural history but also at a moment fraught with a seemingly unending list of geopolitical tragedies, environmental stressors, global health crises, and divisive, topsy-turvy cultural upheavals. In all this, I would agree with Knapp that memes "help us think about the group as a psychic object" (336) and perhaps also a political, discursive one. Memes in this final context, then, act as a medium of collective fantasy and the unconscious that provide "a more incisive appreciation of how our technological conjuncture reimagines and re-attires the pathologies of the group" insofar as they "un-contain fantasies as much as they contain them" (225). In doing so, they "index the pathological dimensions of everyday life" (335–36). Memes are, to be sure, silly, unlimited, accessible, and expendable forms of mass media. They are also vectors of hate and disinformation. They are all these things because of the formal elements that produce their rhetorical power and their technological ease as spreadable, remixable media. I also believe they are sites of survival for communities of thinkers, artists, and activists trying to find a way through the chaotic swirl of digital living in precarious and uncertain times. What they offer is a space for making meaning, making art, making jokes, making connections. They become an object of sharing, or pebbling, that indicates care, intimacy, friendship, and a showing of oneself in vulnerability to others, a vital element of media culture in the face of our loneliness pandemic. They also become artifacts that we can dwell with, forge affective understandings through, and use to curate our culture in ways that encapsulate the vital force of a moment in time. Finally, they offer us a means for unpacking these fraught moments with others in acts of teaching, learning, and assembling to produce greater coalitions of critical assemblages that join us together in meme-ing for the resistance.

ACKNOWLEDGMENTS

I have wanted to write a book for a very long time. The fact that it has finally been accomplished owes a great deal of recognition and thanks to many people. This includes first and foremost my editor, Rebecca Bostock, at The Ohio State University Press for being intrigued enough by a short article I wrote to reach out and then gamely listen to my pitch for this book. I am grateful for her interest and her patience as I navigated the process of writing this book and all the first-time jitters it brought out in me. I also want to acknowledge the extremely supportive and insightful comments of the reviewers for this book, as their engagement with it made the work much stronger. I want to acknowledge the Social Sciences and Humanities Research Council of Canada for the grant funding I held during the time of writing as well as support from the O'Donovan Chair in Communication Across the Curriculum, which both offered me dedicated spans of time for researching and completing the book. There were many people who worked in the service of supporting my research with this book. I want to thank members of my research team, including Sabrina Low, Nevetha Kugathas, Dena Huang, Jay Smith, Sid Heeg, Melanie Lim, Sakeenah Ashique, Tara Gallagher-Harris, and Amaya Kodituwakku, for their tireless work collecting and organizing memes and meme research. Thank you as well to peer reviewers of the book at various stages, including Brooke Barnes and Julia Polyck-O'Neill. I want to offer special thanks to the two researchers who were at the fore of making this book come to life:

Kate Bradley, who stood beside me as I built up these ideas and tirelessly supported me with quick and incisive literature reviews and meme archiving as well as stimulating and refreshing daily conversations around feminist and queer social media. I also wish to thank Thuvaraka Mahenthrian, who picked up where Kate left off and ushered this book into being with constant support and expert wrangling of all logistics. I am endlessly grateful to you both and lucky to have had this chance to work with you. I am eternally grateful for the tireless work of digital archivist Nick Ruest at York University, who has found innovative solutions to my unending research questions and collection quests and has made into a reality my vision for an open-access meme repository that both supports this project and far exceeds it.

This book came about because of a great many conversations within my scholarly community. This group of people brings joy to the everyday of academic labor. I want to thank my colleagues for engaging in generative and truly fascinating conversations around memes, social media, activism, protest, and misogyny. These include the entire Digital Feminist Network, as well as my international colleagues Suay Özkula, Patricia Prieto-Blanco, Jing Zheng, and Maria Brock, among others. I offer a special mention to the book's generous readers, Radhika Gajjala and Heather Suzanne Woods, two scholars I am always grateful to be in conversation with. I also want to thank my intellectual community, including but not limited to Jordana Cox (the midwife of this book), Alysia Kolenstis, Kelly Grindrod, Mina Momeni, Katy Fulfer, Michelle MacArthur, and Sarah Klein. The greatest appreciation goes to my closest collaborator, Brianna Wiens, who bravely faces this world of research with me daily and brings so much astute, ethical, and brilliant intellectual energy to every meme, hashtag, and viral media event we encounter together. I think collaborative connections like ours are rare, and I will never take for granted how enriched my scholarly world is for having you in it.

I want to thank my family for supporting and sustaining me through this long academic journey over the last two decades, especially to my mother, Terri MacDonald; my father, Ken MacDonald; and my mother-in-law, Julia Balaisis. This gratitude extends to my sister, Lauren, who I hold a deep bond with and who I can reliably share memes with at all hours of the day and night. My deepest thanks go to my partner and love, Nick Balaisis: for the many forms of nourishment and adventure you have brought to our life. You have held fast by my side through every phase of my intellectual journey and given me the love I needed to carry on and explore my path and purpose. I'm forever grateful to get to traipse through this life with you.

And finally, this book is dedicated to my children, whom I simply adore. May you always find joy, pleasure, and the tools for resistance in the aesthetic. I hope your delight in the beauty of the world continues to compel you to act in accordance with your soul's purpose.

WORKS CITED

AbsurdistMemer [@absurdistmemer]. "#hamlet . . . #memes #writtenword." *Instagram,* 30 Jan. 2019, https://www.instagram.com/p/BtRtQXXlKP-/?igsh=eTBpcjloem5vaXR4.

Ades, Dawn. "Dada and Surrealism." *Concepts of Modern Art: From Fauvism to Postmodernism,* edited by Nikos Stangos, 3rd ed., expanded and updated, Thames and Hudson, 1994, pp. 110–37.

Adorno, Theodor. *The Culture Industry: Selected Essays on Mass Culture.* Routledge, 2001.

Alhassen, Maytha, and Zaheer Ali. "By Any Memes Necessary: A Case for Critical Media Literacy." *Los Angeles Review of Books,* 19 May 2021, https://lareviewofbooks.org/article/history-making-and-remembering-a-case-for-critical-media-literacy/.

Alice in Wonderland. Directed by Clyde Geronimi et al., Disney, 1951.

Althusser, Louis. "Ideology and Ideological State Apparatuses: Notes towards an Investigation." *Lenin and Philosophy and Other Essays.* Monthly Review, 1972, pp. 85–126.

Anable, Audrey. "Platform Studies." *Feminist Media Histories,* vol. 4, no. 2, 2018, pp. 135–40.

Anger, Kenneth. *The Inauguration of the Pleasure Dome.* Mystic Fire Video, 1966.

Anger, Kenneth. *Rabbit's Moon.* Puck Film Productions, 1972.

Anger, Kenneth. *Scorpio Rising.* Puck Film Productions, 1963.

Apter, Emily. "'Women's Time' in Theory." *Differences,* vol. 21, no. 1, 2010, pp. 1–18, https://doi.org/10.1215/10407391-2009-013.

Araki, Gregg. *The Doom Generation.* Trimark Pictures, 1996.

Arkenbout, Cloë. "Political Meme Toolkit: Leftist Dutch Meme Makers Share Their Trade Secrets." *Critical Meme Reader II: Memetic Tacticality,* edited by Chloë Arkenbout and Laurence Scherz, Institute of Network Cultures, 2022, pp. 20–31.

Arkenbout, Chloë, and Laurence Scherz, editors. *Critical Meme Reader II: Memetic Tacticality.* Institute of Network Cultures, 2022.

Arkenbout, Chloë, et al. "Introduction: Global Mutations of the Viral Image." *Critical Meme Reader: Global Mutations of the Viral Image,* edited by Chloë Arkenbout et al., Institute of Network Cultures, 2021, pp. 8–17.

Arkenbout, Chloë, et al, editors. *Critical Meme Reader: Global Mutations of the Viral Image.* Institute of Network Cultures, 2021.

Ask, Kristine, and Crystal Abidin. "My Life Is a Mess: Self-Deprecating Relatability and Collective Identities in the Memification of Student Issues." *Information, Communication & Society,* vol. 21, no. 6, June 2018, pp. 834–50, https://doi.org/10.1080/1369118X.2018.1437204.

Atoe, Osa. *Shotgun Seamstress Anthology: The Complete Zine Collection.* Soft Skull Press, 2022.

Aumont, Jacques, and Lee Hildreth. "Montage Eisenstein I: Eisensteinian Concepts." *Discourse,* no. 5, spring 1983, pp. 41–99.

Austin, J. L. *How To Do Things with Words.* 2nd ed., Harvard UP, 1975.

Bakhtin, M. M. *Rabelais and His World.* Translated by Hélène Iswolsky, MIT Press, 1968.

"Barbara Kruger—Bio." *The Broad,* https://www.thebroad.org/art/barbara-kruger. Accessed 2 May 2024.

Barbie. Directed by Greta Gerwig, performances by Margot Robbie and Ryan Gosling, Warner Bros. Pictures, 2023.

Barbie [@barbiethemovie]. "Meet more Barbies and Kens, and Allan . . . #BarbieTheMovie." *Instagram,* 4 Apr. 2023, https://www.instagram.com/p/CqnXuSELtC8/?utm_source=ig_web_copy_link.

Barlow, Melinda. "Feminism 101: The New York Women's Video Festival, 1972–1980." *Camera Obscura: Feminism, Culture, and Media Studies,* vol. 18, no. 3 (54), Dec. 2003, pp. 3–38, https://doi.org/10.1215/02705346-18-3_54-3.

Barnett, Clive. "Neither Poison nor Cure: Space, Scale and Public Life in Media Theory." *Media Space: Place, Scale and Culture in a Media Age,* edited by Nick Couldry and Anna McCarthy, Routledge, 2004, pp. 58–74.

Barthes, Roland. *Mythologies.* Translated by Annette Lavers, Hill and Wang / Les Lettres nouvelles, 1972.

Bartky, Sandra Lee. "Foucault, Femininity, and the Modernization of Patriarchal Power." *Feminist Theory Reader,* edited by Carole McCann, Seung-kyung Kim, and Emek Ergun, Routledge, 2020, pp. 342–53.

Bates, Thomas R. "Gramsci and the Theory of Hegemony." *Journal of the History of Ideas,* vol. 36, no. 2, 1975, pp. 351–66, https://doi.org/10.2307/2708933.

The Beatles. "Happiness Is a Warm Gun." *The Beatles,* Apple Records, 1968.

Beizer, Janet. *Ventriloquized Bodies: Narratives of Hysteria in Nineteenth-Century France.* Cornell UP, 1994.

Benjamin, Ruha. *Race after Technology: Abolitionist Tools for the New Jim Code.* Polity Press, 2019.

Benjamin, Ruha. *Viral Justice: How We Grow the World We Want.* Princeton UP, 2022.

Berger, Maurice. *Minimal Politics: Performativity and Minimalism in Recent American Art.* Fine Arts Gallery, University of Maryland, 1997.

Berners-Lee, T. "WWW: Past, Present, and Future." *Computer,* vol. 29, no. 10, 1996, pp. 69–77, https://doi.org/10.1109/2.539724.

"Bernie Sanders Mitten Meme Raises Big Bucks for Charity." *Al Jazeera,* 27 Jan. 2021, https://www.aljazeera.com/news/2021/1/27/bernie-sanders-mitten-meme-grabs-big-bucks-for-charity.

Bernstein, Emma Bee. "Medium Specificity." *Chicago School of Media Theory,* https://lucian. uchicago.edu/blogs/mediatheory/keywords/medium-specificity/. Accessed 3 Mar. 2023.

Black Liturgies [@blackliturgies]. "Seeing an overwhelming amount of 'well let's get to work'. . . ." *Instagram,* 6 Nov. 2024, https://www.instagram.com/p/DCB9KLEuYzL/?img_index=6.

Blazwick, Iwona. "Foreword: The Beauties of Fortuity: Hannah Hoch (1889–1978)." *Hannah Höch,* edited by Dawn Ades and David F. Herrmann, Prestel, 2022, pp. 4–7.

Bolter, Jay David, and Richard Grusin. *Remediation: Understanding New Media.* MIT Press, 2000.

Bordo, Susan. *Unbearable Weight: Feminism, Western Culture.* 2nd ed., U of California P, 2003.

Bordwell, David. "The Idea of Montage in Soviet Art and Film." *Cinema Journal,* vol. 11, no. 2, spring 1972, pp. 9–17, 1972, https://doi.org/10.2307/1225046.

boyd, danah, and Kate Crawford. "Critical Questions for Big Data." *Information, Communication & Society,* vol. 15, no. 5, June 2012, pp. 662–79, https://doi.org/10.1080/1369118X.2012.678878.

Breslin, Susannah. "Meet Trophy Wife Barbie: She Smokes, Drinks, and Raises Hell." *Forbes,* 1 June 2016, https://www.forbes.com/sites/susannahbreslin/2016/06/01/trophy-wife-barbie/.

Bril, Marijn. "Memes in the Gallery: A Party inside an Image Ecology." *Critical Meme Reader II: Memetic Tacticality,* edited by Chloë Arkenbout and Laurence Scherz, Institute of Network Cultures, 2022, pp. 178–90.

brown, adrienne maree, editor. *Pleasure Activism: The Politics of Feeling Good.* Illustrated ed., AK Press, 2019.

Brown, Adrienne Maree [@adriennemareebrown]. "empires fall . . . i love you." *Instagram,* 6 Nov. 2024, https://www.instagram.com/p/DCCVcnkPOuz/?img_index=9.

Brown, Bill. "Re-Assemblage (Theory, Practice, Mode)." *Critical Inquiry,* vol. 46, no. 2, winter 2020, https://doi.org/10.1086/706678.

Bucher, Taina, and Anne Helmond. "The Affordances of Social Media." *The SAGE Handbook of Social Media,* edited by Jean Burgess, Alice Marwick, Thomas Poell, Taina Bucher and Anne Helmond, 2018, pp. 233–53, https://doi.org/10.4135/9781473984066.n14.

Bucknell, Alice. "What Memes Owe to Art History." *Artsy,* 30 May 2017, https://www.artsy.net/ article/artsy-editorial-memes-owe-art-history.

Budd, Robin, et al. *Beetlejuice.* ABC, 1989–91.

Bukatman, Scott. "Spectacle, Attractions and Visual Pleasure." *The Cinema of Attractions Reloaded,* edited by Wanda Strauven, Amsterdam UP, 2006, pp. 71–82, https://www.jstor.org/ stable/j.ctt46n09s.

Burton, Anthony Glyn. "Wojak's Lament: Excess and Voyeurism under Platform Capitalism." *Critical Meme Reader: Global Mutations of the Viral Image,* edited by Chloë Arkenbout et al., Institute of Network Cultures, 2021, pp. 18–26.

Butler, Judith. *Bodies That Matter.* Routledge, 1999.

Butler, Judith. *Gender Trouble: Feminism and the Subversion of Identity.* Routledge, 1990.

Butler, Judith. "Merely Cultural." *New Left Review,* vol. 1, no. 227, 1998, pp. 33–44.

Butler, Judith. *Notes towards a Performative Theory of Assembly.* Harvard UP, 2018.

Carpenter, Hope. [@hopehealingarts]. "A love letter to all the moods and feelings moving through me . . . Hope." *Instagram,* 23 Nov. 2023, https://www.instagram.com/p/Cz_ wHmMuEs5/?img_index=1.

Carroll, Noël. "The Specificity of Media in the Arts." *Journal of Aesthetic Education,* vol. 19, no. 4, 1985, pp. 5–20, https://doi.org/10.2307/3332295.

Chadwick, Whitney. *Women, Art, and Society*. 5th ed., Thames & Hudson, 2012.

Chander, Anupam, and Madhavi Sunder. "Dancing on the Grave of Copyright? The Past and Future of the Internet: A Symposium for John Perry Barlow." *Duke Law & Technology Review*, vol. 18, 2019, pp. 143–61.

Chávez, Aída [@aidachavez]. "ladies what's your makeup routine . . . we riot at midnight." *Twitter*, 27 Sep. 2018, 5:21 p.m., https://x.com/aidachavez/status/1045468565787332608.

Chen, Nick. "Gregg Araki: 'It's disconcerting how topical The Doom Generation is.'" *Dazed Digital*, 21 June 2023, https://www.dazeddigital.com/film-tv/article/60157/1/gregg-araki-the-doom-generation-50-shades-grey-queer-interview.

Chun, Wendy Hui Kyong. *Discriminating Data Correlation, Neighborhoods, and the New Politics of Recognition*. MIT Press, 2021.

Chun, Wendy Hui Kyong, et al. *New Media, Old Media: A History and Theory Reader*. 2nd ed., Routledge, 2016.

Cleaning For The Sitter [@cleaningforthesitter]. "In fact get out . . . #Karen." *Instagram* (reposted from *Twitter*), 25 Nov. 2020, https://www.instagram.com/cleaningforthesitter/p/CICTohclryX/.

Clusterduck. "Chat Archive." *Meme Manifesto*, https://mememanifesto.space/#!archive-top.

Clusterduck. "Detective Wall." *Meme Manifesto*, https://mememanifesto.space/detective-wall.

Clusterduck. "The Iceberg." *Meme Manifesto*, https://mememanifesto.space/#!iceberg-top.

Clusterduck. "Meme Manifesto." *Meme Manifesto*, https://mememanifesto.space/#!about-top.

Conley, Tara L. "A Sign of the Times: Hashtag Feminism as a Conceptual Framework." *Networked Feminisms: Activist Assemblies and Digital Practices*, edited by Shana MacDonald et al., Lexington Press, 2021, pp. 21–47.

Copland, Simon. "Reddit Quarantined: Can Changing Platform Affordances Reduce Hateful Material Online?" *Internet Policy Review*, vol. 9, no. 4, 2020, pp. 2–26.

Craven, Wes. *Scream*. Dimension Films, 1996.

Cyclista Zine [@cyclista_zine]. "These last few days . . . propagandist machines." *Instagram*, 27 Feb. 2022, https://www.instagram.com/p/CafTmK_uImu/.

D'Angelo, Frank J. "The Rhetoric of Intertextuality." *Rhetoric Review*, vol. 29, no. 1, 2010, pp. 31–47, https://doi.org/10.1080/07350190903415172.

Dango, Michael. "Meme Formalism." *Los Angeles Review of Books*, 18 Dec. 2019, https://lareviewofbooks.org/article/meme-formalism/.

Darms, Lisa, editor. *The Riot Grrrl Collection*. Feminist Press, 2013.

Debord, Guy. *Society of the Spectacle*. Black and Red Publisher, 2002.

de Certeau, Michel. *The Practice of Everyday Life*. Translated by Steven Rendall, U of California P, 1984.

de Certeau, Michel, et al. *Living and Cooking*. Edited by Luce Giard, U of Minnesota P, 1998. Vol. 2 of *Practice of Everyday Life*, http://www.jstor.org/stable/10.5749/j.ctt5vkbhw.

Demas, Jerusalem. "Are Young Men Really Becoming More Sexist?" *The Atlantic*, 25 June 2024, https://www.theatlantic.com/podcasts/archive/2024/06/young-men-sexist-feminism-gender/678764/.

Denisova, Anastasia. "How to Define 'Viral' for Media Studies?" *Westminster Papers in Communication and Culture*, vol. 15, no. 1, Mar. 2020, pp. 1–4, https://doi.org/10.16997/wpcc.375.

Deutsche, Rosalyn. "Not-Forgetting: Mary Kelly's Love Songs." *Grey Room (2006)*, no. 24, July 2006, pp. 26–37, https://doi.org/10.1162/grey.2006.1.24.26.

Deuze, Mark. "Participation, Remediation, Bricolage: Considering Principal Components of a Digital Culture." *Information Society,* vol. 22, no. 2, Apr. 2006, pp. 63–75, https://doi.org/10.1080/01972240600567170.

Diamond, Elin. "Brechtian Theory / Feminist Theory: Toward a Gestic Feminist Criticism." *TDR (1988–),* vol. 32, no. 1, spring 1988, pp. 82–94, https://doi.org/10.2307/1145871.

Diamond, Elin. *Unmaking Mimesis: Essays on Feminism and Theatre.* Routledge, 1997.

Didi-Huberman, Georges. *Invention of Hysteria: Charcot and the Photographic Iconography of the Salpêtrière.* MIT Press, 2004.

D'Ignazio, Catherine, and Lauren F. Klein. *Data Feminism.* MIT Press, 2020.

Di Placido, Dani. "'Bill Hader Dancing' Meme, Explained." *Forbes,* 4 July 2023, https://www.forbes.com/sites/danidiplacido/2023/07/04/bill-hader-dancing-meme-explained/.

Disssgrace [@disssgrace]. "I dream of learning who I am outside of capitalism." *Instagram,* 26 Apr. 2023, https://www.instagram.com/p/CrgCol8Om93/?img_index=1.

Disssgrace [@disssgrace]. "'When is enough going to be enough? When will the sanctity of American lives . . .' @mayorbmscott." *Instagram,* 26 Apr. 2023, https://www.instagram.com/p/Crn1q_rOZTn/?img_index=1.

Disssgrace [@disssgrace]. "yearning for a world where queer futures can flower." *Instagram,* 29 Apr. 2023, https://www.instagram.com/p/Crn1q_rOZTn/?img_index=1.

Doane, Mary Ann. *Femmes Fatales: Feminism, Film Theory and Psychoanalysis.* Routledge, 1991.

Dominick, Nora. "The 'Barbie' Movie Tagline 'She's Everything. He's Just Ken.' Has Created a Great New Twitter Meme, So Here Are 35 of the Best." *BuzzFeed,* 5 Apr. 2023, https://www.buzzfeed.com/noradominick/barbie-movie-shes-everything-hes-ken-tweet-roundup.

Donovan, Joan, et al. *Meme Wars: The Untold Story of the Online Battles Upending Democracy in America.* Bloomsbury Publishing, 2022.

Dos Santos, Marcelo Alves, et al. "The Virtuous Cycle of News Sharing on Facebook: Effects of Platform Affordances and Journalistic Routines on News Sharing." *New Media & Society,* vol. 21, no. 2, 2018, pp. 398–418, https://doi.org/10.1177/1461444818797610.

Duncombe, Stephen. *Notes from Underground: Zines and the Politics of Alternative Culture.* 3rd ed., Microcosm Publishing, 2017.

Durham, Meenaskshi, and Douglas M. Kellner. *Media and Cultural Studies: Keyworks.* Wiley-Blackwell, 2001.

Eco, Umberto. *Travels in Hyperreality: Essays.* Translated by William Weaver, Harcourt, 1986.

Eichhorn, Kate. "Feminism's There: On Post-Ness and Nostalgia." *Feminist Theory,* vol. 16, no. 3, 2015, pp. 251–64, https://doi.org/10.1177/1464700115604127.

Eimear [@flotsamm]. "Some 🎉 memes 🎉 . . . 💚 💚." *Instagram,* 23 Jan. 2022, https://www.instagram.com/p/CZFTu3ns3pL/?img_index=1.

Eisenstein, Sergei. *Film Form: Essays in Film Theory.* Harcourt, 1969.

Eklund, Douglas. "The Pictures Generation." *Heilbrunn Timeline of Art History.* Metropolitan Museum of Art, 2004, http://www.metmuseum.org/toah/hd/pcgn/hd_pcgn.htm.

Erlich, Victor. "Russian Formalism." *Journal of the History of Ideas,* vol. 34, no. 4, 1973, pp. 627–38, https://doi.org/10.2307/2708893.

Expanding Brain Meme Generator. *imgflip,* https://imgflip.com/memegenerator/Expanding-Brain.

Fahrenthold, David A. "Trump Recorded Having Extremely Lewd Conversation about Women in 2005." *Washington Post,* 12 Apr. 2023, https://www.washingtonpost.com/politics/trump-recorded-having-extremely-lewd-conversation-about-women-in-2005/2016/10/07/3b9ce776-8cb4-11e6-bf8a-3d26847eeed4_story.html.

Felski, Rita. "Telling Time in Feminist Theory." *Tulsa Studies in Women's Literature,* vol. 21, no. 1, spring 2002, pp. 21–28.

Feminist Think Tank [@aesthetic.resistance]. "This is our FTT queer kaleidoscope! . . . Happy Pride!—Moon Mod 🌙." *Instagram,* 28 June 2024, https://www.instagram.com/p/C8xZRbdys7W/?utm_source=ig_web_copy_link.

Ferrari, Fabian, and Mark Graham. "Fissures in Algorithmic Power: Platforms, Code, and Contestation." *Cultural Studies,* vol. 35, no. 4–5, Sept. 2021, pp. 814–32, https://doi.org/10.1080/09502386.2021.1895250.

Finkel, Lena. "Exclusive: The Genius behind Trophy Wife Barbie Talks Feminism, Period Stigma, and Melted Boobs." *Femestella,* 28 May 2018, https://www.femestella.com/tag/trophy-wife-barbie/.

Fleming, Andrew. *The Craft.* Columbia Pictures, 1996.

For The Wild [@for.the.wild]. "The moods today are transformation, revolution, and care 💚." *Instagram,* 19 Mar. 2023, https://www.instagram.com/p/Cp_gC6NrbpS/?img_index=1.

Foucault, Michel. *Fearless Speech.* Semiotext(e), 2001.

Foucault, Michel. "Of Other Spaces." Translated by Jay Miskowiec, *Diacritics,* vol. 16, no. 1, 1986, pp. 22–27, https://doi.org/10.2307/464648.

Freeman, Elizabeth. "Introduction." *Queer Temporalities,* special issue of *GLQ,* vol. 13, no. 2–3, 2007, pp. 159–76.

Freeman, Elizabeth. *Time Binds: Queer Temporalities, Queer Histories.* Duke UP, 2010.

Fried, Michael. *Art and Objecthood: Essays and Reviews.* U of Chicago P, 1998.

Gajjala, Radhika, et al. "Get the Hammer Out! Breaking Computational Tools for Feminist, Intersectional 'Small Data' Research." *Journal of Digital Social Research,* vol. 6, no. 2, 2024, pp. 9–26.

"Galaxy Brain." *Know Your Meme,* 2017, https://knowyourmeme.com/memes/galaxy-brain.

Gallup, Idil. "The 'Grotesque' in Instagram Memes." *Critical Meme Reader: Global Mutations of the Viral Image,* edited by Chloë Arkenbout et al., Institute of Network Cultures, 2021, pp. 27–39.

Gerecke, Alana, and Laura Levin. "Moving Together in an Era of Assembly." *Canadian Theatre Review,* vol. 176, fall 2018, pp. 5–10, https://doi.org/10.3138/ctr.176.001.

Gibbings, Sheri Lynn, et al. "New Frontiers in the Platform Economy: Place, Sociality, and the Embeddedness of Platform Mobilities." *Mobilities,* vol. 17, no. 5, Sept. 2022, pp. 633–44, https://doi.org/10.1080/17450101.2022.2128691.

Glitsos, Laura, and James Hall. "The Pepe the Frog Meme: An Examination of Social, Political, and Cultural Implications through the Tradition of the Darwinian Absurd." *Journal for Cultural Research,* vol. 23, no. 4, 2020, pp. 381–95, https://doi.org/10.1080/14797585.2019.1713443.

Goldberg, Roselee. *Performance: Live Art 1909 to the Present.* Thames and Hudson, 1979.

Gordon, Len. "Sara Shakeel: From Dental Drills to Crystal Brilliance, Meet the Queen of Crystals." *Art Plugged,* 11 Sept 2024, https://artplugged.co.uk/sara-shakeel-from-dental-drills-to-crystal-brilliance-meet-the-queen-of-crystals/.

griefmother [@griefmother]. "green green green." *Instagram,* 12 May 2024, https://www.instagram.com/p/C64BTdPsZom/?img_index=1.

griefmother [@griefmother]. "love changes you." *Instagram,* 11 Apr. 2024, https://www.instagram.com/p/C5oDU6sMCdJ/?utm_source=ig_web_copy_link.

griefmother [@griefmother]. "my end of year exhibition piece! ♥ ○ ▲ ■." *Instagram,* 20 May 2024, https://www.instagram.com/p/C7M1kbusjBN/?img_index=2.

Griffin, Hollis. "Living Through It: Anger, Laughter, and Internet Memes in Dark Times." *International Journal of Cultural Studies,* vol. 24, no. 3, May 2021, pp. 381–97, https://doi.org/10.1177/1367877920965990.

Groeneveld, Elizabeth. *Making Feminist Media: Third-Wave Magazines on the Cusp of the Digital Age.* Wilfrid Laurier UP, 2016.

Guadagno, Rosanna E., et al. "What Makes a Video Go Viral? An Analysis of Emotional Contagion and Internet Memes." *Computers in Human Behavior,* vol. 29, no. 6, Nov. 2013, pp. 2312–19, https://doi.org/10.1016/j.chb.2013.04.016.

Gunn, Daniel P. "Making Art Strange: A Commentary on Defamiliarization." *Georgia Review,* vol. 38, no. 1, 1984, pp. 25–33, https://www.jstor.org/stable/41398624.

Gunning, Tom. "The Cinema of Attraction(s): Early Film, Its Spectator and the Avant-Garde." *The Cinema of Attractions Reloaded,* edited by Wanda Strauven, Amsterdam UP, 2006, pp. 381–88.

Gunning, Tom. "Attractions: How They Came into the World." *The Cinema of Attractions Reloaded,* edited by Wanda Strauven, Amsterdam UP, 2006, pp. 31–40.

Haddow, Douglas. "Meme Warfare: How the Power of Mass Replication Has Poisoned the US Election." *The Guardian,* 4 Nov. 2016, https://www.theguardian.com/us-news/2016/nov/04/political-memes-2016-election-hillary-clinton-donald-trump.

Hagen, Nik. [@nikhagen]. "#stitch with Jack Flood truly curious. Any info is appreciated! #beta #man #barbie #pink #fyp." *TikTok,* 25 July 2023, https://www.tiktok.com/@nikhagen/video/7259837447998131499.

Halberstam, Jack. *The Queer Art of Failure.* Duke UP, 2011.

Hale, Adrian. "There Is an After-Life (for Jokes, Anyway): The Potential for, and Appeal of, 'Immortality' in Humor." *HUMOR,* vol. 31, no. 3, Aug. 2018, pp. 507–38, https://doi.org/10.1515/humor-2017-0105.

Hall, Alex. [@lezzie_borden]. "Initiating the first day of autumn with queerpocalypse blessings . . . ." *Instagram,* 23 Sep. 2023, https://www.instagram.com/p/CxilSeXMdnx/?img_index=1.

Halperin, Anna K. Danziger. "Witches Are Having a Moment in 2022." *Washington Post,* 31 Oct. 2022, https://www.washingtonpost.com/made-by-history/2022/10/31/witches-patriarchy-halloween/.

Hamilton, Philip. "The Horrors Persist But So Do I." *Know Your Meme,* https://knowyourmeme.com/memes/the-horrors-persist-but-so-do-i.

Hannah, Kathleen. *Rebel Girl: My Life as a Feminist Punk.* Harper Collins, 2024.

Hanßen, Martin. "'The Disturbingly Humanoid Face of the Lamb of God Has Shocked Many': Visual Strategies in Internet Memes on the Restoration of the Ghent Altarpiece." *Critical Meme Reader: Global Mutations of the Viral Image,* edited by Chloë Arkenbout et al., Institute of Network Cultures, 2021, pp. 118–29.

Harding, James M. *Cutting Performances: Collage Events, Feminist Artists, and the American Avant-Garde.* U of Michigan P, 2012.

Harrison, Charles, and Paul Wood. *Art in Theory, 1900–2000: An Anthology of Changing Ideas.* Wiley-Blackwell, 2003, pp. 259–60.

Harry Potter and the Sorcerer's Stone. Directed by Chris Columbus, performances by Daniel Radcliffe, Rupert Grint, and Emma Watson, Warner Bros. Studio, 2001.

Hartley, John. *Communication, Cultural and Media Studies: The Key Concepts.* 3rd ed., Routledge, 2002.

Hebdige, Dick. *Subculture: The Meaning of Style.* Methuen, 1979.

Hencz, Adam. "How Art Memes Have Become the Art World's Newest Form of Criticism." *Artland Magazine,* https://magazine.artland.com/how-art-memes-have-become-the-art-worlds-newest-form-of-criticism/.

Herrmann, Daniel F. "The Rebellious Collages of Hannah Hoch." *Antologia/Anthology,* by Dawn Ades and David F. Herrmann, Grupo Editorial Tomo, 2008, pp. 8–15.

Higgins, Dick. "Dick Higgins 1938–1998: Intermedia." *Inter,* no. 73, 1999, pp. 32–52.

Highfield, Tim, and Tama Leaver. "Instagrammatics and Digital Methods: Studying Visual Social Media, from Selfies and GIFs to Memes and Emoji." *Communication Research and Practice,* vol. 2, no. 1, Jan. 2016, pp. 47–62, https://doi.org/10.1080/22041451.2016.1155332.

Hillbilly Gothic [@hillbillygothicc]. "Hey yall." *Instagram* [Story], 8 Nov. 2024.

Hillbilly Gothic [@hillbillygothicc]. "Youd think theyd learn." *TikTok,* 16 Aug. 2022, https://www.tiktok.com/@hillbillygothic/video/7132540687668481323?lang=en.

Höch, Hannah. "On Collage." *Hannah Höch,* edited by Dawn Ades and David Herrmann, Prestel, 2022, p. 16.

Hockin-Boyers, Hester, et al. "Complicating Gender through Memes." *Meme Studies Research Network,* 19 July 2021, https://memestudiesrn.wordpress.com/2021/07/19/complicating-gender-through-memes/.

Hofmeyr, Annelies [@trophywifebarbie]. "Heavy Period Feels 😩 ✂️ Prints available 🌀 Link in bio #TrophyWifeBarbie #shitjustgotreal." *Instagram,* 24 Sep. 2017, https://www.instagram.com/p/BZenfgZFnIx/.

Hofmeyr, Annelies [@trophywifebarbie]. "When people tell me to smile 🔪😖🔪#TrophyWifeBarbie #shitjustgotreal." *Instagram,* 7 May 2018, https://www.instagram.com/p/BifZhUKhrdA/.

Hofmeyr, Annelies [@trophywifebarbie]. "Yay! My divorce went through today! #TrophyWifeBarbie." *Instagram,* 20 Nov. 2015, https://www.instagram.com/p/-UpgdSvwfQ/.

hooks, bell. *Racism: Naming What Hurts.* Routledge, 2012.

House, Rachael. [@rachaellhouse]. "This zine, protesting violence against women, is available to download for a donation to Housing for Women, link in my bio." *Instagram,* 22 June 2021, https://www.instagram.com/p/CP-QkiRl3sN/.

The Hunger Games. Directed by Gary Ross, performances by Jennifer Lawrence, Josh Hutcherson, and Liam Hemsworth, Lionsgate Films, 2012.

Huntington, Heidi E. "Pepper Spray Cop and the American Dream: Using Synecdoche and Metaphor to Unlock Internet Memes' Visual Political Rhetoric." *Communication Studies,* vol. 67, no. 1, Nov. 2015, pp. 77–93. https://doi.org/10.1080/10510974.2015.1087414.

Huntington, Heidi E. "Subversive Memes: Internet Memes as a Form of Visual Rhetoric." *AoIR Selected Papers of Internet Research,* Oct. 2013, https://spir.aoir.org/ojs/index.php/spir/article/view/8886.

ihatekatebush [@ihatekatebush]. "what's in my bag." *Instagram,* 21 Jan. 2024, https://www.instagram.com/p/C2YTk2AyxdL/.

Iles, Chrissie. *Into the Light: The Projected Image in American Art, 1964–1977.* Whitney Museum of American Art / H. N. Abrams, 2001.

Intelligent Mischief [@intelligentmischief]. "What if we governed with wisdom . . . #thefutureisnow." *Instagram,* 6 Mar. 2024, https://www.instagram.com/p/C4LShfVs4HS/.

Intelligent Mischief [@intelligentmischief]. "What if we were rooted in our own trajectory . . . #thefutureisnow." *Instagram,* 25 Feb. 2024, https://www.instagram.com/p/C3xtEkxrEhD/.

Intelligent Mischief [@intelligentmischief]. "What if we treated our art and culture as ceremonial . . . #thefutureisnow." *Instagram*, 1 Apr. 2024, https://www.instagram.com/p/C5OIUz1Mn2D/.

Jacobs, Ben, et al. "'You Can Do Anything': Trump Brags on Tape about Using Fame to Get Women." *The Guardian*, 8 Oct. 2016, https://www.theguardian.com/us-news/2016/oct/07/donald-trump-leaked-recording-women.

Janega, Eleanor. "Once Again, the History of Witch Trials Has Inspired the World's Most Annoying Merch." *Slate*, 29 Oct. 2023, https://slate.com/news-and-politics/2023/10/witch-tshirt-burning-granddaughters-history.html.

Jax, Kristel [@dyingbutfine]. "Fall vs. Delta." *Instagram*, 22 Sep. 2023, https://www.instagram.com/p/CxfuCUSAbVo/?img_index=1.

Jenkins, Henry. *Convergence Culture: Where Old and New Media Collide*. New York UP, 2006.

Jenkins, Henry. "What Do You Mean by "Culture Jamming"?": An Interview with Moritz Fink and Marilyn DeLaure (Part One)." *Henry Jenkins*, 30 Oct. 2017, https://henryjenkins.org/blog/2017/9/7/an-interview-with-moritz-fink-and-marilyn-delaurie-part-one.

Jenkins, Henry, and Nico Carpentier. "Theorizing Participatory Intensities: A Conversation about Participation and Politics." *Convergence: The International Journal of Research into New Media Technologies*, vol. 19, no. 3, Aug. 2013, pp. 265–86, https://doi.org/10.1177/1354856513482090.

Jenkins, Henry, and Mark Deuze. "Editorial: Convergence Culture." *Convergence: The International Journal of Research into New Media Technologies*, vol. 14, no. 1, Feb. 2008, pp. 5–12, https://doi.org/10.1177/1354856507084415.

Jenkins, Henry, Mizuko Ito, and danah boyd. *Participatory Culture in a Networked Era: A Conversation on Youth, Learning, Commerce, and Politics*. Polity, 2015.

Johnson, Mo. "By Any Memes Necessary: This Art Exhibit Takes Feminist Internet Culture from URL to IRL." *Bust*, 7 Feb. 2017, https://bust.com/meme-art-exhibit/.

Jones, Amelia. *Body Art / Performing the Subject*. U of Minnesota P, 1998.

Kanai, Akane. *Gender and Relatability in Digital Culture: Managing Affect, Intimacy and Value*. Palgrave Macmillan, 2019.

Kaprow, Allan. *Essays on the Blurring of Art and Life*. U of California P, 2003.

Kern, Stephen. *The Culture of Time and Space, 1880–1918*. With a new preface, Harvard UP, 2003.

Kiesewetter, Katie. "Feminist Art Punks (Syllabus)." *kaatiekisewetter.com*, Dec. 2021, https://www.katiekiesewetter.com/zines#/feminist-art-punks-syllabus/.

King, Katie. *Networked Reenactments: Stories Transdisciplinary Knowledges Tell*. Duke UP, 2011, https://doi.org/10.2307/j.ctv1198wfj.

King, Nia. *Queer and Trans Artists of Color: Stories of Some of Our Lives*. Edited by Jessica Glennon-Zukoff and Terra Mikalson, CreateSpace, 2014.

Kleivset, Birgitte [@smeigedag]. "#WeirdBarbie." *Instagram*, 31 July 2023, https://www.instagram.com/p/CvX2XjGIfBR/.

Knapp, Ivan. "Genes, Memes, Dreams." *Critical Meme Reader: Global Mutations of the Viral Image*, edited by Chloë Arkenbout et al., Institute of Network Cultures, 2021, pp. 330–37.

Knox, Arin [@arinsquirrel98]. "Soup anyone? . . ." *TikTok*, 23 Sept. 2021, https://www.tiktok.com/@arinsquirrel98/video/7011171897329061125?lang=en.

Kristeva, Julia. *The Kristeva Reader*. Edited by Toril Moi, Columbia UP, 1986.

Kristeva, Julia. *Powers of Horror: An Essay on Abjection*. Columbia UP, 1982.

Kuo, Rachel. "Animating Feminist Anger: Economies of Race and Gender in Reaction GIFs." *Gender Hate Online: Understanding the New Anti-Feminism,* by Debbie Ging and Eugenia Siapera, Springer International Publishing AG, 2019, pp. 173–93, http://ebookcentral. proquest.com/lib/waterloo/detail.action?docID=5825093.

Lawrence, Emilie, and Jessica Ringrose. "@Notofeminism, #Feministsareugly, and Misandry Memes." *Emergent Feminisms,* edited by Jessalynn Keller and Maureen E. Ryan, Routledge, 2018, pp. 211–32, https://doi.org/10.4324/9781351175463-13.

Legally Blonde. Directed by Robert Luketic, performances by Reese Witherspoon, Luke Wilson, and Selma Blair, Metro-Goldwyn-Mayer, 2001.

Lessig, Lawrence. *Remix: Making Art and Commerce Thrive in the Hybrid Economy.* Penguin Press, 2008.

Lévi-Strauss, Claude. *The Savage Mind* [*La pensée sauvage*]. Weidenfeld and Nicolson, 1962.

Lievrouw, Leah A. *Alternative and Activist New Media.* Polity, 2011.

Lingel, Jessa. *Digital Countercultures and the Struggle for Community.* MIT Press, 2017, https:// doi.org/10.7551/mitpress/9780262036214.001.0001.

Lippard, Lucy. *The Pink Glass Swan: Selected Feminist Essays on Art.* New Press, 1995.

Little Women. Directed by Greta Gerwig, performances by Saoirse Ronan, Emma Watson, and Florence Pugh, Sony Pictures Releasing, 2019.

Lorde, Audre. *Sister Outsider.* Crossing Press, 1984.

MacDonald, Shana. "The City (as) Place: Performative Re-Mappings of Urban Space through Artistic Research." *Performance as Research: Knowledge, Methods, Impact,* edited by Annette Arlander et al., Routledge, 2018, pp. 275–96.

MacDonald, Shana, and Brianna I. Wiens. "Back to the Future of Postfeminist Film: Hallmark, Netflix, and the 'New' Woman's Holiday Film." *Critical Perspectives on the Hallmark Hallmark Channel,* edited by Calren Lavigne, Routledge, 2024, pp. 42–51.

MacDonald, Shana, and Brianna I. Wiens. "Feminist Memes: Digital Communities, Identity Performance, and Resistance from the Shadows." *Materializing Digital Futures: Touch, Movement, Sound and Vision,* edited by Cinque Toija and Jordan Beth Vincent, Bloomsbury, 2022, pp. 123–40.

MacDonald, Shana, and Brianna I. Wiens. "Mobilizing the 'Multimangle': Why New Materialist Research Methods in Public Participatory Art Matter." *Leisure Sciences,* vol. 41, no. 5, Sept. 2019, pp. 366–84, https://doi.org/10.1080/01490400.2019.1627960.

MacDonald, Shana, et al. *Networked Feminisms: Activist Assemblies and Digital Practices.* Lexington Books, 2021.

Makholm, Kristin. "Strange Beauty: Hannah Höch and the Photomontage." *MoMA,* no. 24, 1997, pp. 19–23, https://www.jstor.org/stable/4381346.

Manovich, Lev. *The Language of New Media.* MIT Press, 2003.

Markham, Annette N. "Bricolage." *Keywords in Remix Studies,* edited by Eduardo Navas et al., Routledge, 2018, pp. 43–55, https://doi.org/10.4324/9781315516417-5.

McCluskey, Magan. "People Have Turned Bernie Sanders' Inauguration Fashion into So Much More than Your Standard Meme." *Time.com,* 21 Jan. 2021, https://time.com/5932101/ bernie-memes-mittens/.

McEvilley, Thomas. "Barbara Kruger." *Artforum,* 9 June 1986, https://www.artforum.com/events/ barbara-kruger-14-225086/.

McKinney, Cait. *Information Activism: A Queer History of Lesbian Media Technologies.* Annotated ed., Duke UP, 2020.

McMillan, Uri. *Embodied Avatars: Genealogies of Black Feminist Art and Performance.* New York UP, 2015.

Meagher, Michelle. "Improvisation within a Scene of Constraint: Cindy Sherman's Serial Self-Portraiture." *Body & Society,* vol. 13, no. 4, 2007, pp. 1–19, https://doi.org/10.1177/1357034X07085536.

Merjian, Ara H., and Mike Rugnetta. *From Dada to Memes.* 2 Dec. 2020, https://www.artnews.com/art-in-america/interviews/memes-dada-political-collage-1234577740/.

Mielczarek, Natalia, and W. Wat Hopkins. "Copyright, Transformativeness, and Protection for Internet Memes." *Journalism & Mass Communication Quarterly,* vol. 98, no. 1, Mar. 2021, pp. 37–58, https://doi.org/10.1177/1077699020950492.

Millais, John E. *Ophelia.* 1851, Tate Britain, London. Painting.

Miller, Lucy J. "Feelings Trump Facts: Affect and the Rhetoric of Donald Trump." *Affect, Emotion, and Rhetorical Persuasion in Mass Communication,* edited by Lei Zhang and Carlton Clark, Routledge, 2019, pp. 195–204.

Milner, Ryan M. "Hacking the Social: Internet Memes, Identity Antagonism, and the Logic of Lulz." *Fibreculture Journal,* no. 22, 2013, pp. 62–92.

Milner, Ryan M. "Pop Polyvocality: Internet Memes, Public Participation, and the Occupy Wall Street Movement." *International Journal of Communication,* vol. 7, 2013, pp. 2357–90.

Milner, Ryan M. *The World Made Meme: Public Conversations and Participatory Media.* MIT Press, 2016.

Miltner, Kate. "'There's No Place for Lulz on LOLCats': The Role of Genre, Gender, and Group Identity in the Interpretation and Enjoyment of an Internet Meme." *First Monday,* vol. 19, Aug. 2014, https://doi.org/10.5210/fm.v19i8.5391.

Mina, An Xiao. *Memes to Movements: How the World's Most Viral Media Is Changing Social Protest and Power.* Beacon Press, 2019.

Miyazaki Hayao, dir. *Spirited Away.* Studio Ghibli, 2001.

MoMA. *The Photomontages of Hannah Hoch.* 1997. Exhibition catalogue. www.moma.org/calendar/exhibitions/241.

Monteil, Abby. "Barbie Pissed Ben Shapiro Off So Bad He Made a 40-Minute Video about It." *Them,* 25 July 2023, https://www.them.us/story/barbie-movie-ben-shapiro.

Moody-Ramirez, Mia, and Andrew B. Church. "Analysis of Facebook Meme Groups Used during the 2016 US Presidential Election." *Social Media + Society,* vol. 5, no. 1, Jan. 2019, https://doi.org/10.1177/2056305118808799.

Mortensen, Mette, and Christina Neumayer. "The Playful Politics of Memes." *Information, Communication & Society,* vol. 24, no. 16, Dec. 2021, pp. 2367–77, https://doi.org/10.1080/1369118X.2021.1979622.

Mulvey, Laura. "Visual Pleasure and Narrative Cinema." *Screen,* vol. 16, no. 3, Oct. 1975, pp. 6–18, https://doi.org/10.1093/screen/16.3.6.

Murthy, Vivek H. *Confronting Health Misinformation: The U.S. Surgeon General's Advisory on Building a Healthy Information Environment.* US Department of Health and Human Services, 2021, https://www.hhs.gov/sites/default/files/surgeon-general-misinformation-advisory.pdf.

Musgrave, Tyler, et al. "Experiences of Harm, Healing, and Joy among Black Women and Femmes on Social Media." *CHI '22: Proceedings of the 2022 CHI Conference on Human Factors in Computing Systems,* Apr. 2022, pp. 1–17, https://doi.org/10.1145/3491102.3517608.

Nagle, Angela. *Kill All Normies: Online Culture Wars from 4Chan and Tumblr to Trump and the Alt-Right.* Tantor, 2017.

Nakamura, Lisa. *Digitizing Race: Visual Cultures of the Internet.* U of Minnesota P, 2007.

Neghabat, Anahita. "Ibiza Austrian Memes: Reflections on Reclaiming Political Discourse through Memes." *Critical Meme Reader: Global Mutations of the Viral Image,* edited by Chloë Arkenbout et al., Institute of Network Cultures, 2021, pp. 130–41.

Nelson, Libby. "'Grab 'em by the Pussy': How Trump Talked about Women in Private Is Horrifying." *Vox,* 7 Oct. 2016, https://www.vox.com/2016/10/7/13205842/trump-secret-recording-women.

Nesvig, Kara. "Barbie Movie Memes: All the Best 'She's Everything He's Just Ken' Jokes to Make You Laugh." *Teen Vogue,* 6 Apr. 2023, https://www.teenvogue.com/story/barbie-movie-memes-shes-everything-hes-just-ken-jokes.

Nevetha [@nevetha188]. "CHAOS, DESTRUCTION, MAYHEM . . . my work here is done." *Instagram,* 27 Nov. 2024, https://vm.tiktok.com/ZMhTCPJTy/.

Ngai, Sianne. *Theory of the Gimmick: Aesthetic Judgement and Capitalist Form.* Harvard UP, 2022.

Ngai, Sianne. "Theory of the Gimmick." *Critical Inquiry,* vol. 43, no. 2, 2017, pp. 466–505.

Noble, Safiya Umoja. *Algorithms of Oppression: How Search Engines Reinforce Racism.* New York UP, 2018.

No Holes Barred [@no_holes_barred_podcast]. "Wait for it. . . . That's a catchy tune." *Instagram,* 13 July 2023, https://www.instagram.com/p/Cuon3kYtfw-/.

notthirsttraps [@notthirsttraps]. "don't bother me i'm studying!!!" *Instagram,* 6 Feb. 2024, https://www.instagram.com/p/C3BYSXtSNdf/?img_index=5.

notthirsttraps [@notthirsttraps]. "i love entertaining the masses" slide deck. *Instagram,* 22 Sep. 2023, https://www.instagram.com/p/CxgLGdcxE7N/?img_index=1.

notthirsttraps [@notthirsttraps]. "this is just a list of my favorite movies" slide deck. *Instagram,* 23 Jan. 2024, https://www.instagram.com/p/C2eARJbLT-j/?img_index=1.

notthirsttraps [@notthirsttraps]. "to be perceived / is to be misunderstood" slide deck. *Instagram,* 31 Oct. 2023, https://www.instagram.com/p/CzFOyC2Pk-M/?img_index=1.

nursekelsey [@nursekelsey]. "Recently I learned that the act of sending your friends & family little videos and tweets and memes you find online it's called pebbling, like how penguins bring pebbles back to their little penguin loved ones . . . ." *Twitter/X,* 21 May 2024, 5:06 p.m., https://x.com/nursekelsey/status/1793025484596359208.

O'Brien, Elizabeth. "Zines: A Personal History." *New England Review,* vol. 33, no. 2, 2012, pp. 89–99, https://doi.org/10.1353/ner.2012.0037.

Oxford, Kelly [@kellyoxford]. "These 10th grade photos were taken two weeks apart when I was fourteen years old. A moment in which I confirmed my suspicions that everything is bullshit." *Instagram,* 5 Oct. 2023, https://www.instagram.com/p/CyCX6WvP1PU/?img_index=4.

Papacharissi, Zizi. *Affective Publics: Sentiment, Technology, and Politics.* Oxford UP, 2014, https://doi.org/10.1093/acprof:oso/9780199999736.001.0001.

Parry, Kyle. *A Theory of Assembly: From Museums to Memes.* U of Minnesota P, 2023.

Pena, Mary. "Black Public Art: On the Socially Engaged Work of Black Women Artist-Activists." *Open Cultural Studies,* vol. 3, no. 1, 2019, pp. 604–14, https://doi.org/10.1515/culture-2019-0053.

Phillips, Whitney. *This Is Why We Can't Have Nice Things: Mapping the Relationship between Online Trolling and Mainstream Culture.* MIT Press, 2015.

Phillips, Whitney, and Ryan M. Milner. *You Are Here: A Field Guide for Navigating Polarized Speech, Conspiracy Theories, and Our Polluted Media Landscape.* MIT Press, 2021.

Piepmeier, Alison. "Why Zines Matter: Materiality and the Creation of Embodied Community." *American Periodicals*, vol. 18, no. 2, 2008, pp. 213–38, https://www.jstor.org/stable/41219799.

Pollard, Tom. "Alt-Right Transgressions in the Age of Trump." *Perspectives on Global Development & Technology*, vol. 17, no. 1–2, Jan. 2018, pp. 76–88, https://doi.org/10.1163/15691497-12341467.

Pollock, Griselda. "Moments and Temporalities of the Avant-Garde 'in, of, and from the feminine.'" *New Literary History*, vol. 41, 2010, pp. 795–820.

Potolsky, Matthew. *Mimesis*. Routledge, 2006.

Potter, Alex. "The Gift to Win a Penguin's Heart." *BBC Earth*, https://www.bbcearth.com/news/the-gift-to-win-a-penguins-heart.

The Powerpuff Girls. Directed by Craig McCracken et al., Cartoon Network, 1998.

Queer Death Stories [@queer_death_stories_]. "Me," image 1 of "Heyyy 🫰 💜 🖤Here is another #moodboard in honor of one of my all time faves Kenneth Anger" slide deck. *Instagram*, 28 May 2023, https://www.instagram.com/p/CszKoCvOE-l/?img_index=1.

Raaberg, Gwen. "Beyond Fragmentation: Collage as Feminist Strategy in the Arts." *THE INTERARTS PROJECT: Part Three: Representing Women*, special issue of *Mosaic: An Interdisciplinary Critical Journal*, vol. 31, no. 3, Sept. 1998, pp. 153–71, https://www.jstor.org/stable/44029815.

Radin, Sara. "Are You a Doomscroller or Joyscroller? And What Does That Say about You?" *Stylist*, 2020, https://www.stylist.co.uk/life/what-is-doomscrolling/458703.

Radway, Janice. "Zines, Half-Lives, and Afterlives: On the Temporalities of Social and Political Change." *PMLA*, vol. 126, no. 1, Jan. 2011, pp. 140–50, https://www.jstor.org/stable/41414086.

Rambukkana, Nathan, and Keer Wang. *Digital Intimacies*. Oxford Bibliographies, 2020. https://doi.org/10.1093/OBO/9780199756841-0250.

Ramdarshan Bold, Melanie. "Why Diverse Zines Matter: A Case Study of the People of Color Zines Project." *Pub Res Q*, vol. 33, 2017, pp. 215–28, https://doi.org/10.1007/s12109-017-9533-4.

Rathke, Lisa. "Bernie Sanders' Mittens, Memes Help Raise $1.8M for Charity." *Associated Press*, 27 Jan. 2021, https://apnews.com/article/bernie-sanders-mittens-memes-charity-3f8afd8e8a5a0b8b9709dd6d4d30ec13.

Reckitt, Helena, and Peggy Phelan. *Art and Feminism*. Phaidon Press, 2001.

Reductress [@reductress]. "Nation Rejects Far-Left Position of 'Woman.'" *Instagram*, 6 Nov. 2024, https://www.instagram.com/p/DCCBmo9sjTL/?utm_source=ig_web_copy_link&igsh=MzRlODBiNWFlZA==.

Rentschler, Carrie A. "Rape Culture and the Feminist Politics of Social Media." *Girlhood Studies*, vol. 7, no. 1, 2014, pp. 65–82, https://doi.org/10.3167/ghs.2014.070106.

Rentschler, Carrie A., and Samantha C. Thrift. "Doing Feminism in the Network: Networked Laughter and the 'Binders Full of Women' Meme." *Feminist Theory*, vol. 16, no. 3, Dec. 2015, pp. 329–59, https://doi.org/10.1177/1464700115604136.

"Resist Heteronormativity." *Queer Anarchy Now!* 19 Oct. 2020, https://queeranarchynow.wordpress.com/2020/10/19/resist-heteronormativity/.

Ricci, Benedetta. "Portraits of America: Cindy Sherman's Untitled Film Stills." *Artland*, https://magazine.artland.com/portraits-of-america-cindy-shermans-untitled-film-stills/.

Richardson, Randi. "'She's Everything. He's Just Ken.' New 'Barbie' Poster Leads to Memorable Memes." *Today*, 7 Apr. 2023, https://www.today.com/popculture/movies/shes-everything-hes-just-ken-barbie-memes-rcna78661.

Ringrose, Jessica, and Emilie Lawrence. "Remixing Misandry, Manspreading, and Dick Pics: Networked Feminist Humour on Tumblr." *Feminist Media Studies,* vol. 18, no. 4, July 2018, pp. 686–704, https://doi.org/10.1080/14680777.2018.1450351.

Riot [@riotaddams]. "Roses are red, violets are blue, Nick Fuentes the witches are coming for you." *Twitter,* 12 Nov. 2024, https://www.threads.net/@riotaddams/post/DCQqONARuwZ/roses-are-red-violets-are-blue-nick-fuentes-the-witches-are-coming-for-you.

Robinson, Hilary. *Visibly Female: Feminism and Art: An Anthology.* Edited and introduced by Hilary Robinson, Camden, 1987.

Rogers, Matt. "Contextualizing Theories and Practices of Bricolage Research." *Qualitative Report,* Jan. 2015. https://doi.org/10.46743/2160-3715/2012.1704.

Rogoff, Irit. "Studying Visual Culture." *The Visual Culture Reader,* edited by Nicholas Mirzoeff, 2nd ed, Routledge, 2002, pp. 24–36.

Roxi Horror [@roxiqt] "ME, 10: I want to marry a prince. . . ." *Instagram,* 10 Aug. 2020, https://www.instagram.com/p/CDtf4fsnv7H/?hl=en.

Russell, Legacy. *Glitch Feminism: A Manifesto.* Verso, 2020.

S Wild [@ruminationsofthewild]. "The horrors persist, But so do I, And so do we collectively 💚 💚 🐦 Love Always, S." *Instagram,* 7 July 2024, https://www.instagram.com/ruminationsofthewild/p/C9IlKRuJfxn/.

Schmidt, Leonie, and Jeroen Kloet. "Bricolage: Role of Media." *The International Encyclopedia of Media Effects,* edited by Patrick Rössler et al., Wiley, 2017, pp. 1–9, https://doi.org/10.1002/9781118783764.wbieme0116.

Schneider, Rebecca. *The Explicit Body in Performance.* Routledge, 1997.

Schneider, Rebecca. *Performing Remains: Art and War in Times of Theatrical Reenactment.* Routledge, 2011.

Sederholm, Helena, et al. "Meme Layers in the Times of Pandemic." *International Journal of Education through Art,* vol. 18, no. 2, June 2022, pp. 161–79, https://doi.org/10.1386/eta_00092_1.

Shakeel, Sara [@sarashakeel]. "It's a Fantasy 🐱 x 🎟 . . . SaraShakeel x Ai." *Instagram,* 23 Jan. 2024, https://www.instagram.com/p/C2cSHHZoKra/?utm_source=ig_web_copy_link.

Shakeel, Sara [@sarashakeel]. "Remind me, what is it that you are looking for?" *Instagram,* 29 Apr. 2024, https://www.instagram.com/p/C6W1i79ilq9/?utm_source=ig_web_copy_link.

Shapiro, Ben. "The Left Freaks Out Because I Hated the 'Barbie' Movie. Here's the Real Reason Why." *Daily Wire,* https://www.dailywire.com/news/the-left-freaks-out-because-i-hated-the-barbie-movie-heres-the-real-reason-why. Accessed 12 Dec. 2024.

Sharf, Zack. "'Barbie' Posters Unveil Every Barbie and Ken Actor in Margot Robbie's Film: Dua Lipa, Simu Liu and More." *Variety,* April 4, 2023, https://variety.com/gallery/barbie-movie-posters-cast/fs3ogt1auaezul3/.

Sharma, Sarah. "A Feminist Medium Is the Message." *Re-Understanding Media,* by Marshall McLuhan, 2022, pp. 1–19. *ResearchGate,* https://doi.org/10.1215/9781478022497-001.

Shearing, Lois. "Women Are Using the 'Barbie Test' on Their Boyfriends." *Cosmopolitan,* 27 July 2023, https://www.cosmopolitan.com/uk/love-sex/relationships/a44661142/boyfriend-barbie-test/.

Shifman, Limor. *Memes in Digital Culture.* MIT Press, 2014.

Shin, Yuna. "The Radical Elegance of Memes for Hard-to-Describe Feelings." *Medium,* 2 Oct. 2021, https://uxdesign.cc/explaining-the-radical-elegance-of-memes-for-hard-to-describe-feelings-b2a49d565ad3.

Shiva, Vandana. "On Becoming Untameable." *Practical Wisdom for Times of Renewal Zine,* For the Wild, Apr. 2024, https://forthewild.world/shop/times-of-renewal-zine.

Sick Sad Girlz Club [@sicksadgirlz]. "The girlz are enduring . . . ." *Instagram*, 7 June 2024, https://www.instagram.com/p/C76xDsFMFLN/?img_index=2.

Simmons, Laurie. "Purple Woman / Kitchen / Second View." *The Met Collection*, https://www.metmuseum.org/art/collection/search/285415.

Siobhán Gordon [@siobhaneen_queen_of_dreams]. "Fixed it." *Instagram*, 8 Nov. 2024, https://www.threads.net/@siobhaneen_queen_of_dreams/post/DCHCxrORyFd?xmt=AQGzjXXFX cpDRJgmoigrzXosPtWgx4qonVj8tSeutkzAIQ.

Skågeby, Jörgen, and Lina Rahm. "What Is Feminist Media Archaeology?" *Communication + 1*, vol. 7, no. 1, Oct. 2018, https://doi.org/10.7275/fthf-h650.

Skelly, Kaitlyn [@paperstackedonpaper]. "It's Scary," image 1 of "spooky season might be over . . . 😌 🐻 " slide deck. *Instagram*, 19 Nov. 2023, https://www.instagram.com/p/Cz2DUN3RoJi/?img_index=1.

A Soft Wrongness [@asoftwrongness]. "It's not just you . . ." slide deck. *Instagram*, 27 Mar. 2023, https://www.instagram.com/p/CqTNflFOraO/.

Solnit, Rebecca [Rebecca Solnit]. "They want you to feel. . . ." *Facebook*, 6 November 2024, https://www.facebook.com/share/p/1A4Bx64p81/.

Sparby, Erika M. *Memetic Rhetorics: Toward a Toolkit for Ethical Meming.* U of Michigan P, 2023. *ACLS Humanities EBook*, https://doi.org/10.3998/mpub.12207107.

Srnicek, Nick. *Platform Capitalism*. Polity, 2016.

Still We Rise [@_stillwerise]. "SWR Weekly: PRIDE EDITION . . . ." *Instagram*, 11 June 2024, https://www.instagram.com/p/C8F5TLEyDvL/?img_index=1.

Still We Rise [@_stillwerise]. "YESSSSSSS TO THIS @hillbillygothicc ♂ 😄 😆 😊 i need the whole album #stillweriseloves." *Instagram*, 8 Feb. 2024, https://www.instagram.com/p/C3HIssiLfj2/?img_index=1.

Stimpunks Foundation. "Mutual Aid and Human-Centered Learning for Neurodivergent and Disabled People." *Stimpunks.org*, https://stimpunks.org/glossary/penguin-pebbling/.

Sugg, Deborah. "Hannah: Höch's Practise of Photomontage." *Women Artists Slide Library Journal*, no. 29, June 1989, pp. 31–32, https://go-gale-com.proxy.lib.uwaterloo.ca/ps/i.do?p=AON E&sw=w&issn=09510230&v=2.1&it=r&id=GALE%7CA264012479&sid=googleScholar&lin kaccess=abs.

Take-Off. Directed by Gunvor Nelson, performances by Ellion Ness, studio, 1972.

Thompson, Chrissy, and Mark A. Wood. "A Media Archaeology of the Creepshot." *Feminist Media Studies*, vol. 18, no. 4, July 2018, pp. 560–74, https://doi.org/10.1080/14680777.2018.14 47429.

Trans Bears. "An Ambiguous Utopia." *Critical Meme Reader: Global Mutations of the Viral Image*, edited by Chloë Arkenbout et al., Institute of Network Cultures, 2021, pp. 269–88.

Tuters, Marc. "LARPing & Liberal Tears: Irony, Belief and Idiocy in the Deep Vernacular Web." *Post-Digital Cultures of the Far Right: Online Actions and Offline Consequences in Europe and the US*, edited by Maik Fielitz and Nick Thurston, Transcript Verlag, 2019, pp. 37–48, https://doi.org/10.14361/9783839446706.

Umberto, Eco. "'Casablanca': Cult Movies and Intertextual Collage." *In Search of Eco's Roses*, special issue of *SubStance*, vol. 14, no. 2 (47), 1985, pp. 3–12, https://doi.org/10.2307/3685047.

Vail, Tobi, and Melissa Klein. "Jigsaw, Number 3." *Dig DC*, DC Punk Archive, Melissa Klein Collection, 1 Jan. 1991, http://hdl.handle.net/1961/dcplislandora:38099.

"Vermont Folklife Archive Unveils Bernie Sanders Mitten Memes Collection." *American Folklore Society*, 26 Jan. 2023, https://americanfolkloresociety.org/vermont-folklife-archive-unveils-bernie-sanders-mitten-memes-collection/.

Wark, Scott. "A Postdigital Angel of History? On 'Meme Theory.'" *Critical Meme Reader: Global Mutations of the Viral Image,* edited by Chloë Arkenbout et al., Institute of Network Cultures, 2021, pp. 165–75.

Weick, Karl E. *Making Sense of the Organization.* Wiley-Blackwell, 2000.

Weiss, Joanna. "What 'Barbie' Says about the Gender Wars." *Politico Magazine,* 21 July 2023, https://www.politico.com/news/magazine/2023/07/21/barbie-has-something-to-say-about-the-post-patriarchy-00107319.

Welkos, Robert W. "Treasures of Paris (Hilton) Offered for $20 Million." *Los Angeles Times,* 3 Feb. 2006, https://www.latimes.com/archives/la-xpm-2006-feb-03-me-paris3-story.html.

Wiens, Brianna I. "How To Use Creative and Embodied Digital Methods." In *SAGE Research Methods: Doing Research Online,* edited by Karen Gregory, Sage Publications, 2022, https://dx.doi.org/10.4135/9781529608359.

Wiens, Brianna I. "Virtual Dwelling: Feminist Orientations to Digital Communities." *Networked Feminisms: Activist Assemblies and Digital Practices,* edited by Shana MacDonald, Brianna I. Wiens, Michelle MacArthur, and Milena Radzikowska, Lexington Books, 2021, pp. 85–108.

Wiens, Brianna I., and Shana MacDonald. "Dwelling as Method: Lingering in/with Feminist Curated Data-Sets on Instagram." Special Issue of *JDSR: Methodological Developments in Visual Politics & Protest,* edited by Suay Ozkula, Tom Divon, Hadas Schlussel, and Danka Ninkovic, vol. 6, no. 2, 2024, pp. 27–45, https://doi.org/10.33621/jdsr.v6i2.211.

Wiens, Brianna I., et al. *Stories of Feminist Protest and Resistance: Digital Performative Assemblies.* Lexington Books, 2023, https://rowman.com/ISBN/9781666913521/Stories-of-Feminist-Protest-and-Resistance-Digital-Performative-Assemblies.

Wiggins, Bradley E. *The Discursive Power of Memes in Digital Culture: Ideology, Semiotics, and Intertextuality.* Routledge, 2019.

Wiley, Dorothy, and Gunvor Nelson. *Schmeerguntz.* Canyon Cinema, 1995. Film.

Williams, Raymond. *Keywords: A Vocabulary of Culture and Society.* Croom Helm, 1976.

Wisnoski, Alexandra K [@chaosgirlclub]. "Ur in his DMs." *Instagram,* 17 May 2023, https://www.instagram.com/p/CsXCmPNOuqb/?img_index=1.

The Wizard of Oz. Directed by Victor Fleming, Loew's, 1939.

Wolfe, Shira. "Art Movement: Pictures Generation." *Artland Magazine,* https://magazine.artland.com/art-movement-pictures-generation/. Accessed 23 Dec. 2024.

Wood, David Murakami. "Platform Capitalism, Empire and Authoritarianism: Is There a Way Out?" *Centre for International Governance Innovation,* 15 Mar. 2021, https://www.cigionline.org/articles/platform-capitalism-empire-and-authoritarianism-there-way-out/.

Woods, Heather Suzanne, and Leslie Ann Hahner. *Make America Meme Again: The Rhetoric of the Alt-Right.* Peter Lang, 2019.

Zaiontz, Karen, and Kristen Cochrane. "Meme Feminisms: Tactical Irony on Social Media." *Stories of Feminist Protest and Resistance: Digital Performative Assemblies,* edited by Brianna I. Wiens, et al., Lexington Press, 2023, pp. 145–56.

Zhang, Ruichen, and Bo Kang. "From Propaganda to Memes: Resignification of Political Discourse through Memes on the Chinese Internet." *International Journal of Human–Computer Interaction,* vol. 40, no. 11, 28 Dec. 2022, pp. 3030–49, https://doi.org/10.1080/10447318.2022.2158260.

Zuckerberg, Donna. *Not All Dead White Men: Classics and Misogyny in the Digital Age.* Harvard UP, 2018.

INDEX

DIGITAL MEDIA, FEMINIST RESISTANCE

SHANA MACDONALD AND BRIANNA I. WIENS, SERIES EDITORS

This new series seeks to bring together scholarship on feminist media practices that, at their core, understand feminism as necessarily intersectional, coalitional, and resistant. The forms of media we seek to explore include film, television, print media, performance, visual art, digital media, social media, and material media as tied to resistance movements including zines, protest posters, slogans, and more.

The Art of Memes in Feminist Digital Culture
SHANA MACDONALD

www.ingramcontent.com/pod-product-compliance
Lightning Source LLC
Chambersburg PA
CBHW030649270326
41929CB00007B/283